Birth and
After Birth

and Other Plays
A Marriage Cycle

Birth and After Birth

and Other Plays

A Marriage Cycle

Tina Howe

THEATRE COMMUNICATIONS GROUP
NEW YORK
2010

Birth and After Birth and Other Plays: A Marriage Cycle is published by Theatre Communications Group, Inc., 520 Eighth Avenue, 24th Floor, New York, NY 10018-4156

Birth and After Birth, Approaching Zanzibar and *One Shoe Off* were previously published in *Approaching Zanzibar and Other Plays* by Theatre Communications Group in 1995.

This publication is made possible in part with public funds from the New York State Council on the Arts, a State Agency.

TCG books are exclusively distributed to the book trade by Consortium Book Sales and Distribution.

LIBRARY OF CONGRESS CATALOGING-IN-PUBLICATION DATA
Howe, Tina.
Birth and after birth and other plays : a marriage cycle / Tina Howe.—1st ed.
p. cm.
ISBN 978-1-55936-321-1
I. Title.
PS3558.O894B58   2009
812'.54—dc22   2009041300

Cover design by Phoebe Flynn Rich
Cover photo by Russell Underwood/CORBIS
Text design and composition by Lisa Govan

First Edition, March 2010

To Norman

My beloved husband of almost fifty years
whose first words upon waking up in our cozy bedroom
on November 8, 2003, were:
"It got very windy this morning, my dollop,
did it blow away our tent?"

Contents

A Marriage Cycle

An Introduction

THESE ARE MY MARRIAGE PLAYS, the plays that got me in trouble. It took twenty-three years before *Birth and After Birth* saw the light of day, *Approaching Zanzibar* left half the critics mystified, and both *One Shoe Off* and *Rembrandt's Gift* received universally hostile reviews. Every playwright has lovingly bound scripts of such plays tucked away in their Drawer of Laughing and Forgetting, along with Edith Wharton's autograph, a first edition of *A Room of One's Own* and fading ticket stubs from Ionesco's *La Cantatrice Chauve* performed at the Théâtre de La Huchette in 1960.

So the question arises, why did they cause such distress?

Because the author is a frisky woman, because they take on the dailiness of married life and, most threatening of all, because they're written in a surreal, operatic style. When a hyper four year old makes his entrance in *Birth and After Birth*, he's played by a large hairy man. When a menopausal wife gets a hot flash in *Approaching Zanzibar*, she rips off her blouse and pours champagne all over herself. When a salad is tossed at a dinner party in *One Shoe Off*, the hostess flings it over the guests as well. And when a couple prays for divine intervention so they won't be evicted from their loft in *Rembrandt's Gift*, the great man himself shows up, in full seventeenth-century regalia.

One rarely witnesses such things onstage. And forget about the dinner party scene in my first play *The Nest*, when the heroine rips off all her clothes and dives into a gigantic wedding cake to be licked clean by one of the guests! The critic of the *New York Times* wrote that of the ten worst plays he'd ever seen in his life, this went right to the top. Needless to say, we closed within twenty-four hours.

Mercifully, times have changed since those dark days, and we're seeing more and more plays written by frisky women, but I came of age during the heyday of Absurdism when it was the fellas who were shaking up perceptions of what was stage worthy—Pirandello, Genet, Ionesco, Beckett and Albee. Their artistry and daring were thrilling as they scrambled logic and language, but where were their female counterparts, shaking up what was stageworthy for *us*? Since I was a hopelessly unevolved feminist with no ax to grind, who better to take on the challenge than me? As they say, fools rush in where angels fear to tread.

When the Women's Movement blasted onto the scene in the 1970s, I was thrown out of the one discussion group I tried to join. After all the other ladies had choked back tears, reliving their anxieties about marriage and childbearing, and it was my turn to share, I told them about my agony, trying to nail the ending of a new play. One by one, their eyes started to narrow. "Ohhhhh, we get it," they hissed. "You're a *writer*! You're here to spy on us! To steal our stories! You're not one of us! Out! Out! GET OUT!"

Of course I was more interested in talking about my art than my life, I came from a family of writers, after all. My grandfather, Mark A. De Wolfe Howe, published more than fifty books in his lifetime, won a Pulitzer for biography in 1924, and completed his last book of poetry at the age of ninety-six. His children were writers and their children were writers and poets as well. My issues with my gender were further complicated by the fact that my mother was an intimidating role model. She towered over my father, wearing her preposterous hats both indoors and out. She wasn't just physically larger, but her emotional outbursts and flights of fancy were of epic proportions as well. Since I was her physical double in height, every time she looked at me, she shook her head, sighing, "Poor Tina, what are we going to do about your appearance?"

I was teased mercilessly in the all-girl schools I attended on the Upper East Side of Manhattan. Not only was I a head taller than them, but I also had a lisp, since my front baby teeth had been knocked out by a swing in Central Park. Say "scissors" my diminutive classmates would taunt.

"Thithers."

"Again, again!" they'd scream, as tears of laughter rolled down their faces.

This period finally came to an end when my permanent teeth came in (to be quickly sheathed in braces, of course), but I kept growing taller and more freakish looking. My best friend at Chapin was the fattest girl in class, so the two of us clung to each other, looking like the trylon and perisphere from the 1939 New York World's Fair. I would hardly grow into a male-bashing feminist, it was all I could do to make it through the day with my own gender!

What I've learned over the years is, it's one thing when male playwrights write about women, but when we do it, the structure and rhythms are different. Ambiguity floods in and therein lies the threat. We tend to see conflicting aspects of a situation at the same time, blending the tragic with the comic, and the noble with the absurd. Female poets and novelists have been doing it for years. Women who write for the theater have to walk a finer line, because our musings come to life. The audience actually *sees* us in flagrante delicto. We can poke gentle fun at our foibles, but the minute our heroines start to challenge the system, be it within the family or society at large, the critics tend to get nervous. Those of us who know the ropes adopt distancing strategies to mute or dress up these challenges, making them more palatable. I've been doing it for years, but not in these plays. These are the ones where I rip off my white gloves.

So, why keep writing plays like this, you ask? Can't you see the freight train bearing down on you? Alas, there's a pesky Calvinist gene embedded in us New Englanders—the weight of original sin that dogs our every move. What difference does it make if we write plays that shock or close in at night? We're doomed anyway. It's part of the equation. As Ecclesiastes tells us:

Vanity of vanities, saith the Preacher, vanity of vanities; all is vanity. What profit hath a man of all his labor which he taketh under the sun? One generation passeth away and another generation cometh: but the earth abidith for ever.

The careful reader will notice that this collection is a cycle that essentially follows the same beleaguered couple as they maneuver through the milestones of marriage—legitimizing their roles as parents in *Birth and After Birth*, embracing these roles in a family road trip in *Approaching Zanzibar*, struggling as empty nesters in *One Shoe Off* and, finally, hanging on for dear life in their sunset years in *Rembrandt's Gift*. No wonder these plays are written in an operatic scale, look what this pair has endured—raising a toddler who weighs two hundred and fifty pounds; driving all the way across the country to reach a dying relative before it's too late; struggling to keep their footing in a house that's sinking into the ground; and, finally, facing eviction because their loft has become a fire hazard, having become so cluttered with old theater costumes.

So why should an audience root for this pair? Things just keep going from bad to worse! And they stay *together*! Through thin and thinner! Most plays about marriage end in desertion or adultery. What am I saying? That fidelity is more exciting?

It depends on your point of view. Temptation flashes its jeweled tail in all these plays—and always at the wife, by the way. Succumbing would certainly be fun to watch, but resisting is much tougher, and this is where the husband comes in. He's the one that invariably slays the beast and cuts off its tail. Not the lover. And rarely the wife.

So what if it's been years since Walter, a former actor, picks up a sword in *Rembrandt's Gift*? If some lecherous Dutch artist is going to make eyes at his wife, he'll challenge him to a duel. Why *not* show an old man fighting for his wife with dazzling swordplay? In my plays the husband always saves the day. It's the *man* who brings solace and hope. The *man* who doffs his feathered hat.

And this from a *woman* who writes plays! How subversive is *that*?

Tina Howe
New York City
February 2010

Birth and
After Birth

Production History

Birth and After Birth received its world premiere in September 1995 by the Wilma Theater in Philadelphia. It was directed by Paul Berman. The set design was by Jerry Rojo, costume design was by Maxine Hartswick, lighting design was by Paul. M. Fine and sound design was by Eileen Tague. The cast was as follows:

SANDY APPLE	Kate Skinner
BILL APPLE	David Ingram
NICKY APPLE	Rob Leo Roy
MIA FREED	Jessica Sager
JEFFREY FREED	Greg Wood

Birth and After Birth was produced in March 1996 by the Woolly Mammoth Theatre Company in Washington, D.C. It was directed by Howard Shalwitz. The set design was by Lewis Folden, costume design was by Jan Schloss Phelan, lighting design was by Marianne Meadows and sound design was by Daniel Schrader. The stage manager was Cheryl L. Repeta. The cast was as follows:

SANDY APPLE	Lee Mikeska Gardner
BILL APPLE	Mitchell Hérbert
NICKY APPLE	Hugh Nees
MIA FREED	Hanna Klein
JEFFREY FREED	Buzz Mauro

A revised version of *Birth and After Birth* was produced in October 2006 by the Atlantic Theater Company in New York City. It was directed by Christian Parker. The set design was by Takeshi Kata, costume design was by Bobby Frederick Tilley II, lighting design was by Josh Bradford and sound design was by Obadiah Eaves. The production stage manager was Matthew Silver. The cast was as follows:

SANDY APPLE	Maggie Kiley
BILL APPLE	Jeff Binder
NICKY APPLE	Jordan Gelber
MIA FREED	Kate Blumberg
JEFFREY FREED	Peter Benson

Characters

SANDY APPLE, the mommy, thirties

BILL APPLE, the daddy, a businessman, thirties

NICKY APPLE, their four-year-old son, played by an adult

MIA FREED, an anthropologist, thirties

JEFFREY FREED, her husband, also an anthropologist, forties

Act One

The Apples' living room, a surreal but spare blend of suburbia and something wilder. There's the usual sofa, dining area and armoire, but trees are looming in the distance as if one day the house could be swallowed up by a jungle. Today is Nicky's fourth birthday, so the place is decorated with crepe paper streamers and balloons. An oversized HAPPY BIRTHDAY *banner crisscrosses the ceiling. But none of this is quite visible since it's four-thirty in the morning and still dark. Sandy and Bill are in their bathrobes, racing to get everything ready before Nicky gets up. Bill shakes a tambourine.*

BILL: God I love tambourines!

SANDY: Sssssssssssshhhhhhhhh!

BILL: They kill me!

SANDY: Not so loud.

BILL: What is it about tambourines?

SANDY: Bill . . .

BILL *(Shaking it with rising enthusiasm)*: They bring out the gypsy in me!

SANDY: You'll wake him up. How often does your only child turn four?

BILL *(Singing the tune from* Carmen*)*: "Toreador-a, don't spit on the floor-a . . . Use the cuspidor-a, that's what it's for-a . . ."

SANDY: At least you got some sleep last night.

BILL: If I had my life to live over, I'd be a tambourine virtuoso.

SANDY: I haven't even started wrapping the masks yet.

BILL: Imagine being the greatest tambourine virtuoso in the world.

SANDY: To say nothing about all his new musical instruments . . . drums and kazoos . . .

BILL *(Starting to dance)*: Concerts on every continent.

SANDY: Horns and harmonicas . . .

BILL: Europe, Australia, South America . . .

SANDY: Zithers and triangles . . .

BILL: Africa, Greenland, Pago-Pago . . . THEY'D GO CRAZY FOR ME IN PAGO-PAGO! Rip off all my clothes and worship me!

SANDY: Not so fast! What about me?

BILL: What *about* you?

SANDY: What am *I* supposed to do while you're being worshipped in Pago-Pago? *(Long pause)* I'm waiting . . .

BILL *(Reaching for her)*: Why, you'll be dancing *with* me, silly girl.

SANDY *(Pulling away)*: Whoa . . . Just a minute, buster! What if I want to dance *alone*? *(Lowering her voice)* In . . . *Salamanca*! *(Launching into a lively flamenco number with a rose between her teeth)*

BILL *(Astonished)*: Honey?!

SANDY *(Grabbing some unwrapped castanets)*: What if I want to turn a few heads on my *own*?

BILL: What's come over you?

SANDY *(More and more into it, in a Spanish accent)*: Exhaustion, Don José de la Madre Mia . . . I am so tired I am not myself, but a wild thing!

BILL *(Grabbing her)*: DANCE WITH ME, CARMELITA! The night is young and the moon . . . she is high!

(They dance, stomping and yelping. Then Nicky bursts in.)

NICKY *(Tearing around the room in his pajamas)*: PRESENTS, PRESENTS, WHERE'S MY PRESENTS?

SANDY *(Jumping out of Bill's arms)*: Oh Nicky, you scared me! We were just . . .

NICKY: Presents, presents, where's my presents?

SANDY: Mommy and Daddy have been up all night getting everything ready for Nicky's party. Does Nicky want to see what they've done? Does he? One, two, three . . .

(Sandy flips on the lights, revealing the birthday banner and balloons. Nicky's stopped in his tracks.)

NICKY: Wow!

BILL: Don't make a move until Daddy gets his video camera!

SANDY: Just look at you, Mommy's great big four year old!

BILL *(Turning his camera on)*: I'll bet you never expected anything like this, old buddy, did you? You never dreamed it would be like this!

NICKY *(Racing around the room)*: Presents, presents! Where's my presents?

BILL: Daddy's present to Nicky is a whole video of Nicky's birthday.

SANDY: Such a big boy . . . it seems like only yesterday I was bringing him home from the hospital.

NICKY: There they are! *(Finding his presents and diving in headfirst)* Presents! Presents! Ooooooooooh, look at all my presents!

BILL: Keep it up, Nick, you're doing great, just beautiful . . . beautiful.

SANDY: Nicky, you're not supposed to open presents now. Presents after cards, you know that's the way we do it!

(Sandy starts picking up the shredded wrapping. Nicky tears open his presents, a series of toy instruments which he plays with rising abandon—drums, guitars, triangles, plastic horns, harmonicas, zithers, etc.)

BILL *(Filming)*: Atta boy, Nick, show 'em how good you can play.

SANDY: Nicky, I asked you to wait. We do cards first, that way we avoid all this mess at the beginning.

BILL: Over this way . . . look at Daddy. Oh, Nicholas, are we making a hell of a video!

NICKY: A red wagon!

(Nicky pulls the wagon around the room in raptures.)

BILL: Towards Daddy, honey, come towards Daddy. Oh, Christ, I don't believe this kid.

SANDY: Nicky, how is Mommy going to clean all this up? Do you want to have your party inside a great big mess?

BILL: Stop everything, Nick! Daddy just got an idea! Let's get some footage of Nicky pulling Mommy in his new red wagon! *(Carrying Sandy and setting her in the wagon)* Come on, Mommy, Nicky's going to give you a ride.

SANDY: Hey, what are you doing? It's five-thirty in the morning. I haven't even brushed my teeth yet.

NICKY: Nicky's going to pull his great big Mommy present.

BILL *(Filming)*: Too much . . . Oh, Jesus . . . Jesus . . . Too much!

SANDY: Please, Bill, I'm a mess.

NICKY: Look at Nicky, Daddy. Nicky's pulling his big mommy present!

SANDY: I've got to clean up.

BILL: Will you look at that kid go! Don't tell me my son isn't football material!

(Nicky pulls Sandy around the room making hairpin turns. He suddenly sees an unopened present and runs off to it.)

Hey, where are you going? You were doing great!

NICKY: More presents, more, more, more!

SANDY: My breath smells.

BILL: Hey, Nick, what the hell? You were pulling Mommy and doing great. Now come back here and pick up that handle!

SANDY: You don't care!

BILL: I've got an idea. Let's put some of these presents in with Mommy!

(Bill starts piling presents on top of her.)

SANDY: I haven't even had a chance to pee.

NICKY *(Throwing his last opened present across the room)*: Nicky's presents are all gone!

BILL: Daddy asked you to pick up that wagon handle and pull!

NICKY: I wanted a bunny . . . and a puppy . . . and a pony! You said I could have a pony for my birthday. Where's my pony?

SANDY: I stay up all night decorating the room, wrapping the presents, blowing up the balloons, making a really nice party, and what does he do? Just tears into everything. Rips it all up! Ruins the whole thing!

(She gets out of the wagon.)

BILL: All the presents are in the wagon, so get over here, Nicholas and pull!
NICKY: You promised me a pony. You promised!
SANDY: And not one thank you. I never heard one thank you for anything.
BILL: I'm waiting!
SANDY: Do you know what my mother would have done if I had trashed all my birthday presents and never said thank you?
BILL *(Slamming down his camera)*: Thanks a lot, Nicky. Thanks for ruining a great video!
SANDY: She'd have flushed them down the toilet, that's what she would have done!

(Nicky gets in the wagon, lies down and sucks his thumb.)

BILL: Jesus Christ, Nicky.

(Silence.)

SANDY: He shouldn't be up this early.
BILL: He got up too early.
SANDY: I have a good mind to take you back to your room!
BILL: If you ask me, he should be sent up to his room!
SANDY: Do you want Daddy to take you back to your room?
BILL: You'd better watch it, young man, or it's up to your room.
SANDY: How would you like to be sent back to your room on your birthday?
NICKY: My room?

(Silence.)

BILL: He got up too early.
SANDY: Come on, Bill, take him on up.

(Silence.)

BILL: The kid gets away with murder.

(Sandy sighs.)

Absolute murder . . .

(Sandy sighs. Silence.)

(Imitating Nicky's sucking sound) He sounds like some . . .
sea animal . . . some squid or something. *(Imitating the sound
again)*

SANDY: All children suck their thumb when they're upset.

BILL: You'll get warts on your tongue if you keep that up!

SANDY: I used to suck mine.

BILL: To say nothing about wrecking your bite.

SANDY *(Popping her thumb into her mouth)*: This one.

BILL: Do you know how much fixing that boy's teeth is going to
cost? About fifteen thousand dollars, that's all!

SANDY: I sucked my thumb until I was twenty-two.

BILL: You'll have warts on your tongue and fifteen-thousand-
dollar braces on your teeth!

SANDY: I used to suck it during lunch hour when I worked at the
insurance company. I'd go into the ladies' room, lock the
door, sit on the toilet, pop it in my mouth and just . . . suck
away. *(Laughing)* It sounds ridiculous, a grown woman
sucking her thumb in the ladies' room. Come to think of it,
I didn't stop sucking it until Nicky was born. I was still going
at it when my water broke. It's funny how that sucking
instinct gets passed on from the mother to her child.

(Silence.)

BILL: Four years old . . . Wow!

SANDY *(Scratching her head)*: Ever since I got up this morning
I've had this itching.

BILL *(Flopping down beside Nicky)*: Daddy's made videos of all
your birthdays, Nick, and number four is going to be the
best. The best!

SANDY: It's strange, because I've never had dandruff. When I looked in the mirror this morning, I saw an old woman. Not old, old, just used up. *(She scratches her head, a shower of sand falls out)* It's the weirdest thing, it doesn't look like dandruff or eczema, but more like . . . I don't know . . . my brains are drying up and leaking. I'm like some punctured sandbag . . .

BILL: If Daddy didn't make videos on your birthday, then none of us would remember what you looked like when you were little. Hell, me and my camera were there when you popped out of Mommy with your fist in the air! *(Picking up his camera, shooting Nicky at close range)* Time passes in the blink of an eye, Nick. Take it from your old man, before you know it you'll be crumpled up in a nursing home wondering where your life went. Why do you think I take all these videos? To give you proof you were here so you can see just how incredible you were. I mean, *are!*

SANDY *(Shaking out more sand)*: Look at me! And now my hair is falling out. Poor Mommy's going bald. *(Scratching and leaking more sand)* When she looked in the mirror this morning, she saw an old woman.

BILL: You won't be one of those lonely old men, but will have videos to entertain you and all your pals at the nursing home—birthdays, Christmases, trips to the zoo . . . Shit, you'll be the most popular guy in the place! "Have you seen Nick Apple's video of his fourth birthday party?" the little old ladies will say, crowding into your room with their wheelchairs. All for that backwards glance at the radiance of youth.

SANDY: Poor old leaking Mommy . . . Bald as an egg.

BILL: Some day you'll thank me for this.

(Silence.)

Come on, give Daddy a big smile now. I tell you, when the Freeds see this video tonight, they'll eat their hearts out.

SANDY: Jeffrey and Mia are coming over to celebrate with us. Jeffrey and I are first cousins, so we have the same grandpa.

BILL: Jeffrey may take good slides, but I promise you he's never seen anything like this!

SANDY: They're bringing you a special present and everything.

NICKY: Presents!

BILL: When it comes to videos, I'm the best.

SANDY: And you know what great presents Jeffrey and Mia give. Remember the Chinese imperial warrior doll they gave you last year?

NICKY: Presents, presents!

BILL: King of the heap, leader of the pack!

NICKY: I want to make my birthday wish.

SANDY: I feel so sorry for them. I wish there was something we could do.

BILL: It's none of our business.

SANDY: But not to have children . . .

NICKY: I want to blow out my candles and make my wish!

BILL: You can't run other people's lives.

SANDY: Neither of them wants children!

BILL: Their careers are very important to them.

SANDY: But they're missing so much.

BILL *(Handing Nicky a wild animal mask)*: Hey, Nicky, how about putting on this mask. Come on, give us a roar.

SANDY: Put on the mask for Daddy!

BILL: Come on Nick, run around the room and pop out from behind the chairs.

NICKY: I don't have to if I don't want to.

BILL: I said pop out from behind the chairs!

SANDY *(Putting the mask on Nicky)*: Look at Nicky!

NICKY: I want raisins.

BILL: Move!

NICKY *(Collapsing on the floor)*: Raisins!

BILL: Will you please get him to run around the room and pop out from behind the chairs!

SANDY: Come on, Nicky.

NICKY: Raisins!

BILL: I SAID: MOVE!

(Nicky pops out from behind the chairs, knocking them over as he goes.)

Easy, easy.

SANDY: Not so wild.

BILL: I didn't tell you to knock them over.

SANDY: Do something, Bill.

(Nicky flops down in his wagon.)

BILL *(Slamming his camera down)*: Thanks a lot, Nicholas, I'll remember this.

(Silence.)

SANDY *(Starts cleaning up)*: Just look at this mess!

(Silence. Bill opens his briefcase and pulls out a letter.)

BILL: I wish you'd look at this letter sometime. It came through the office mail last month. I told you about it the other day, remember? It's from Continental Allied. *(Reading)* "Dear Mr. Apple: It has come to the attention of the accounting department that certain papers in the Fiedler file are either missing or incomplete."

NICKY: Hey, Mommy, let's play Babies!

SANDY: Not now, honey, Mommy has to clean up.

BILL: "You assured us last month that the Fiedler account had been settled, but now it appears there have been certain . . . irregularities . . . Mr. Brill has brought to our attention the outstanding work you did on the Yaddler account."

NICKY *(Putting on his baby mask)*: Babies, Babies! I want to play Babies!

BILL: "Rest assured, everyone here at Continental Allied knows what a delicate procedure that was . . ." "Delicate"? They don't know the half of it! I was smiling out of one side of my mouth and going crazy out the other!

(Nicky crawls onto the sofa, cooing and gurgling.)

SANDY *(Joining him on the sofa)*: All right, all right . . .

(Nicky hands her a mommy-type mask.)

(Putting it on) Sweet baby . . .

BILL: These guys I do business with are killers. *Killers!* I've been thinking about assuming a new identity so I can give them a taste of their own medicine. You know, become one of those happy-go-lucky types that stabs you in the back while shaking your hand. I'd cultivate a whole new "casual" look with distressed jeans and designer shoes . . .

SANDY *(Rocking Nicky)*: Do you know what baby Nicky looked like when he was born, hmmm? A shiny blue fish! Mommy's little trout!

NICKY: I was blue?

SANDY: Of course you were blue! All babies are blue when they're inside their mommies' tummies. That's because there's no air in the plastic bag they live in.

NICKY: I want to be blue again, I want to be blue again!

BILL: I'd change my name to . . . Forest . . . No, Jon without the *H*! . . . No . . . Charles!

SANDY: Once a baby pops out of the plastic bag, he breathes air for the first time. And do you know what happens then?

BILL: Charles E. Zinn . . .

SANDY: He turns bright pink! As pink as a seashell!

BILL: I like that!

SANDY: Actually, you were a little jaundiced at birth, so your skin was more gold than pink. Mommy's precious goldfish!

NICKY: I was gold?

SANDY: Fourteen-karat!

NICKY: Son of a bitch!

SANDY *(Shocked)*: Nicky!

BILL: They'd call me Charley E.Z., for short. Good old Charley E.Z., who could sell a blind man a jigsaw puzzle!

SANDY: And your little arms were so skinny, they waved every which way. Do you know what baby Nicky's arms looked like?

NICKY: Nicky was such a good baby, all blue and gold inside his plastic bag.

SANDY: French-fried potatoes, that's what they looked like!

(Sandy and Nicky erupt into gales of laughter.)

BILL: How would you like to be married to Charley E.Z.—man-about-town and salesman of the year? I'll tell you one thing, it would put an end of all these letters about "professional inconsistency." *(Waiting for a response)* You're not even listening to me! You don't give a good shit if I'm fired! All you care about is playing your moronic baby games with Nicky! I don't get it! I just don't get it!

(Bill storms out of the room. Long silence. Sandy takes off her mask.)

NICKY: Daddy's mad.
SANDY: Daddy's mad.

(Silence.)

Just look at this mess! *(She starts cleaning up)*
NICKY: I don't like it when Daddy's mad.
SANDY: God, Nicky, you have to destroy everything you touch!
NICKY: I want grape juice.
SANDY: I don't understand you. One minute you're the sweet baby Mommy brought home from the hospital and the next, you're a savage!
NICKY *(Tearing off his mask)*: I said I want grape juice!
SANDY: You don't care if Jeffrey and Mia walk into a shit-house!
NICKY: I'm going to die if I don't have grape juice and then you'll be sorry!
SANDY: Well, you can't have grape juice. You'll spoil your appetite for tonight.
NICKY: I want grape juice, I want grape juice, I want grape juice!
SANDY: Mommy said no grape juice.
NICKY *(Hurtling into the middle of her cleaning)*: Grape juice!
SANDY *(Shaking him with each word)*: Mommy. Said. No!

(Silence. Nicky makes a strangled sound.)

Oh God!

(Nicky faints flat on the floor.)

Oh God, oh God, oh God!

(Silence.)

Billlllll! Nicky's fainted!

BILL *(Flying over to Nicky)*: What happened?

SANDY: Oh, Bill, help him.

BILL: Quick, the ice!

SANDY *(Rushing out of the room to get it)*: It's all right, Nicky, Mommy's getting some ice, Mommy will make you all better.

(She returns and tosses the ice over Nicky.)

BILL: Come on, Nicker, move those legs of yours. Let's see a little action here! Get some water, Sandy!

(She rushes out of the room and returns with a glass of water, which she hurls in Nicky's face.)

Keep that circulation going! Keep those veins and arteries open! Come on, Sandy, this calls for artificial respiration.

SANDY *(Flopping down next to him)*: Artificial respiration? I haven't done that in years. *(She starts breathing into Nicky's mouth)*

BILL *(Pumping Nicky's arms back and forth)*: One, two and one two . . . One, two and one two . . .

SANDY: Isn't that what you do to a drowning victim?

BILL: Faster, faster, he isn't breathing.

SANDY: We should be doing the *Heimlich maneuver*!

BILL: The Heimlich maneuver?

SANDY *(Squeezing Nicky around the stomach)*: Ugh, ugh!

BILL *(Still attempting artificial respiration)*: That's for choking victims!

SANDY *(Stopping cold)*: You're right, you're right. I mean that other thing . . . PDQ . . . SOS . . . CRP . . .

BILL: CPR! CPR!

(They both start pounding on Nicky's chest.)

Harder, harder! Use some muscle!

SANDY: I'm trying.

BILL *(Establishing a rhythm)*: One, two, three, push! One, two, three, push!

SANDY: I'm so out of shape!

BILL: One, two, three, push!

BILL AND SANDY: One, two, three, push! *(Etc.)*

(Nicky finally opens his eyes. Sandy and Bill sigh with relief. Silence.)

NICKY *(Weakly)*: Sing to me.

SANDY *(Cradling him in her arms, singing)*:
     Hush little baby, don't say a word,
     Momma's gonna buy you a mockingbird.
     And if that mockingbird don't sing,
     Momma's gonna buy you a diamond ring.

NICKY: More, more . . .

(Silence.)

SANDY: We got it in time.

BILL: Jesus.

SANDY: What would I do if this ever happened when you weren't here?

BILL: Well, luckily, it only seems to happen when *I am* here.

SANDY: I don't know what I'd do without you.

BILL: Nick Apple is four years old today!

NICKY: It hurts being born.

SANDY: I know, honey, I know.

NICKY: It hurts Nicky's head and stomach.

BILL: So tell me, Nick, how does it feel being four? Do you feel any different?

SANDY: "Four" sounds so old.

NICKY: I feel . . . sweeter.

SANDY *(Hugging him)*: Oh, Nicky . . .

BILL: And what else?

NICKY: Softer.

BILL: You nut.

NICKY: And cuter.

SANDY: Oh, Nickyyyyy.

NICKY: And furrier!

BILL: Furrier?

NICKY *(Sticking out his hands)*: When I woke up this morning, I saw fur on my hands, white fur.

BILL: The kid's got fur on his hands!

SANDY: My baby!

BILL: And it's growing up his arms!

NICKY: Nicky's turning into a furry rabbit.

SANDY: Oh, Nicky!

NICKY: I like being a furry rabbit!

SANDY: My baby! What will we do?

NICKY *(Sticking it out)*: Look, there's fur on my tongue, too!

BILL: Well, son of a gun!

NICKY: And on my teeth.

BILL: We'll have to get carrots and lettuce.

SANDY *(Lowering her voice)*: What will the neighbors say?

BILL *(Likewise)*: They'll never know. We'll keep it a secret.

SANDY: Bill, I'm scared.

NICKY *(Whispering)*: I'll only leave the house at night. During the day I'll hide under my bed eating carrots. Mommy will plant a special vegetable garden out back with nothing but carrots—huge juicy carrots the size of baseball bats.

BILL *(Grabbing his video camera and filming)*: Great, great! Does that kid have an imagination or what?

NICKY *(Not moving)*: I'll drop down on all fours. I'll develop X-ray vision and supersonic hearing. I'll see sunken treasure under the ocean and black holes beyond the sun. I'll be known as . . . Rabbit Boy!

SANDY AND BILL: Rabbit Boy!

BILL: Do you believe this kid? He could direct movies!

NICKY *(Seeing it all in his mind's eye)*: I'll predict earthquakes and avalanches, heat waves and sandstorms. I'll leap over fences and streams, build vast underground tunnels linking the great cities of the world. Cairo, Istanbul, Addis Ababa . . . I'll feed the hungry and clothe the poor, erase injustice and bring world peace. And when the going really gets rough, I'll put on my cloak and do Rabbit Magic . . . *(He rises, puts on his special cloak and prepares to do one of his magic tricks)* Watch closely, my hands will never leave my arms.

SANDY: Oh, Nicky and his magic tricks!

BILL: My son . . . Mine!

NICKY *(Grabbing a rigged frying pan and lighting a fire in it; he sings)*: "They asked me how I knew, my true love was true. So I smile and say, what a lovely day. Smoke gets in your eyes . . ."

(He pulls a toy rabbit out of the flames.)

SANDY AND BILL *(Clapping)*: Hooray Nicky! Yay! Bravo! Bravo!
NICKY: Let's play Rabbit Says.
SANDY: Oh, Nicky, not now.
NICKY: Rabbit says, "Raise your hands!"
BILL: Later, Nick.
SANDY: Please, honey.
NICKY: Rabbit says, "Raise your hands!"
BILL: We have the whole rest of the day.
NICKY: Rabbit says, "Raise your hands!"

(They raise their hands.)

Rabbit says, "Scratch your nose."

(They scratch their noses.)

Rabbit says, "Lift your right leg."

(They do. Then Sandy and Bill do everything he says.)

Rabbit says, "Lift your left leg." Rabbit says, "Stick out your tongue." Reach for the sky! *(Nicky laughs, clapping his hands)* I tricked you, I tricked you! Rabbit says, "Rub your belly." Rabbit says, "Hop on two feet." Hop on one foot!

(They blindly obey.)

You did it! You did it! *(Going faster and faster)* Rabbit says, "Lie on the floor." Rabbit says, "Get up." Rabbit says, "Fart."

(Bill makes a farting noise.)

SANDY: Not this again!
NICKY: Rabbit says, "Fart again."

(Bill does.)

SANDY: I'm not playing, it's disgusting.
NICKY: Rabbit says, "Fart three times in a row."

(Bill does.)

SANDY: It isn't funny, Nicholas!

NICKY: Rabbit says, "Run after Nicky and play Fart Tag."

(Bill chases Nicky around the room, making a farting sound every time he tags him.)

SANDY: If this is the only way you can celebrate Nicky's birthday, it's just pathetic!

(Sandy stares into space as Bill and Nicky start playing in slow motion.)

My front teeth feel loose . . . *(Leaning over, shaking a shower of sand out of her hair)* It's the strangest thing, I've been smelling the sea all morning. We're hundreds of miles away from it, but that bitter salty smell of low tide is unmistakable. I noticed it the moment the sun came up. *(She inhales, shaking more sand out of her hair)* Nicky, I'd like you to come back to the table and open your cards.

BILL *(Pulling Nicky into his lap)*: Nicky's four!

NICKY: I love you, Daddy.

BILL: I love you, too.

NICKY *(Hugging Bill)*: This much!

BILL: My *boy.* My son.

NICKY *(Squeezing him tighter)*: No, *this* much! Uuuugh!

BILL: All mine!

NICKY *(Squeezing with all his might)*: This much! UUUUUUHHH!

BILL *(Gasping for air)*: Easy, Nick, easy . . .

(Their hugging disintegrates into a wrestling match. Bill starts tickling Nicky.)

Tickle, tickle . . .

NICKY *(Laughing)*: Don't . . .

SANDY *(Opening a card, reads)*:
    This little pony comes galloping by,
    With a smile on his face and a gleam in his eye.

Seems it's somebody's birthday, "Neigh, neigh, neigh,"
Somebody special who's four today!

From Walter and Amy, and look, they sent twenty-five dollars.
BILL *(Still tickling Nicky)*: Is Nicky ticklish?
NICKY *(Screaming with pleasure)*: Stop . . . Stop!
BILL: I tell you, Nick, we're going to have a great party tonight!
SANDY *(Beside herself)*: WILL YOU LOOK AT THIS! Nicky got a card from Mrs. Tanner, his nursery school teacher, and they have a strict policy of not sending individual cards on the children's birthdays! And . . . *(In a singsong, hiding it behind her back)* . . . a metronome from your music teacher, Miss Prudenskaja!

(Nicky takes it and turns it on.)

It's important for a child to form attachments outside the home.
BILL: Children need guidelines!
SANDY: Spare the rod and spoil the child.
BILL: If they're not given boundaries, they may be emotionally crippled for life!
SANDY: I believe in discipline!
BILL: Children learn from observation!
SANDY: Tolerance comes from awareness.
BILL: Self-respect is built on sharing!
SANDY: Reading readiness precedes cognition!
BILL: The child is father to the man.
SANDY: Great oaks from little acorns grow.
NICKY *(Gravely)*: "Let us sit upon the ground, And tell sad stories of the death of kings."

(Sandy and Bill look at him, amazed.)

SANDY: Nice!
BILL: Very nice.

(Silence.)

SANDY: Jeffrey and Mia are missing so much. I feel sorry for them.
BILL: It's their choice.

SANDY: But *never* to have children . . .

BILL: Their careers are very important to them.

NICKY: I love birthdays! What I love most is blowing out the candles and making my wish.

SANDY: What if they changed their minds tonight? With us!

NICKY: Because Mr. Boo told me birthday wishes come true.

BILL: Jeffrey and Mia have been married for twelve years. I don't think they're suddenly going to change their minds at Nicky's party.

SANDY: But what if they did?

NICKY: I know just the wish I'm going to make! And it's going to come true because Mr. Boo said so.

SANDY: Because of what a great family we are.

BILL: What's going to happen tonight is we're going to have one hell of a party and I'm going to show one hell of a video!

SANDY: I don't know, I have a feeling . . .

NICKY: When can I blow out the candles and make my wish?

SANDY: Imagine being a woman and not wanting to experience childbirth.

BILL: People have different needs.

SANDY: But never to have your own baby.

NICKY: When can I blow out the candles and make my wish?

SANDY: It would be so good for them.

BILL: As anthropologists studying children of primitive cultures, they see a lot of suffering.

NICKY: I want to make my wish.

BILL: Once you've seen babies dying of starvation, I'm sure you think twice before bringing more children into the world.

SANDY: But their baby wouldn't starve.

NICKY: I want to make my birthday wish!

SANDY: They'd have a beautiful baby.

BILL: They're not interested in having a beautiful baby, they're interested in studying primitive children!

NICKY: Mommy, can I make my birthday wish now?

SANDY *(Angry)*: No, you cannot make you wish now. Mommy's talking to Daddy and it's very important. *(Pause)* But how can they understand primitive children if they don't have children of their own?

BILL: Just because I can articulate their reasons for not having children doesn't mean I agree with them!

NICKY: Daddy, can I make my birthday wish now?

SANDY: Well, you don't have to be so pompous about it. People do change!

BILL: It's very unlikely.

SANDY: But it could happen.

BILL: Well, anything *could* happen, but that doesn't mean . . .

NICKY *(Whining)*: Please, Daddy, can I make my . . .

SANDY: Shit, Nicky, can't you let Mommy and Daddy have a conversation?!

BILL: Mommy and Daddy are talking now.

NICKY *(Starting to cry)*: No fair, no fair.

SANDY: He's impossible!

BILL *(To Nicky)*: You'll have to wait!

(Nicky cries louder.)

SANDY: Keep this up, Nicky, and there won't *be* any birthday party!

NICKY: Go on, yell at me and be mean. I don't care because I haven't made my birthday wish and when I do, it will come true because Mr. Boo said so!

(He runs out of the room. Long silence.)

BILL: Kids!

SANDY: Kids . . .

(Silence.)

BILL: Remember the parties we used to have? One I'll never forget was my eleventh.

SANDY: My eighth was the best. I invited the entire class. It was on a Saturday afternoon and we strung white streamers from one end of the dining room to the other.

BILL: My mother let me invite the whole class. Thirty-three kids came!

SANDY: The girls got pincushions for favors and the boys got yo-yos that glowed in the dark, but instead of having cake and ice cream, my mother made this incredible baked alaska.

BILL: We decorated the whole place in red—red streamers, red balloons, red tablecloth . . .

SANDY: When she brought it to the table, everyone gasped. It was three feet high and covered with peaks of egg white.

BILL: Shit, everything was red! My mother even put red food coloring in the cake.

SANDY: I can still remember the taste, like sweetened snow.

BILL: That was the birthday I got my red bike. And when we finished eating the red cake and red raspberry ice cream, we played games.

SANDY: I don't know where we got the room, but we actually set up twenty-seven chairs for musical chairs.

BILL: Darts, ducking for apples . . .

SANDY: We played it once, then twice.

BILL: Then we set up chairs and played musical chairs.

SANDY: By the fifth round we decided to alter the rules a little.

BILL: But after a while we changed the rules.

SANDY: When you sat down in a chair, you grabbed someone of the opposite sex, and they sat in your lap.

BILL: It was getting boring with the same old rules.

SANDY: And then you had to . . . had to . . .

BILL: So you grabbed a girl and both sat on the chair together.

SANDY: You had to, had to . . .

BILL: And you kissed the girl for as long as you could without coming up for air, and whoever kissed the longest played in the next round.

SANDY: We played musical chairs.

BILL: After the kissing part, we began unbuttoning the girls' blouses and putting our hands inside.

(Bill pulls Sandy onto his lap.)

SANDY: We played it once, twice, three times.

BILL *(Nuzzling her)*: And feeling what there was to feel. Oh, it was nice, it was very nice.

SANDY: By the fifth round we decided to alter the rules a little.

BILL *(Deftly slipping his hands in her robe)*: And each time the music stopped you grabbed another girl and reached down into another blouse . . .

SANDY: When you sat down in a chair, you grabbed someone of the opposite sex and he sat in your lap.

BILL *(Starting to get amorous)*: After a while we forgot about the musical part of the game, and everyone was just lying all over the chairs, kissing and feeling up.

SANDY: I don't know why the grown-ups didn't . . .

BILL: Some of us even got our pants off.

SANDY *(Resisting)*: Bill . . .

BILL *(And more amorous)*: We locked the door and pulled down the shades.

SANDY: Not now!

BILL: Tommy Hartland and I got five girls under the table.

SANDY *(Still resisting)*: We can't . . .

BILL *(And even more amorous)*: But by the time we got our jockeys off, the girls panicked and were back in the game with someone else, and there were Tommy Hartland and I, horny as hell, surrounded by all these goddamned red streamers and strawberry gumdrops.

SANDY: I remember, my mother made this baked alaska. It was covered with egg whites.

BILL: Come on, give us a kiss.

SANDY: Bill! . . .

BILL: Let's be spontaneous for once.

SANDY: What do you think you're doing?

BILL: Live dangerously!

SANDY: But what if Nicky comes in?

BILL: Screw Nicky!

SANDY: I said, no!

BILL *(Starting a fresh assault)*: "A bird in the hand is worth two in the bush!"

SANDY: Okay, but make it quick.

(As Bill moves in for the kill, Nicky bursts into the room, draped in Sandy's underwear—bras adorn his head and shoulders, a pair of panty hose is wrapped around his neck and a slip trails from his waist. He's stricken with jealousy.)

NICKY: Mommy?! Daddy?!

(Sandy and Bill scream and fly off the sofa, hastily putting themselves back together.)

SANDY: Nicky?!

BILL: You little prick!

NICKY: What are you doing?

BILL: Thanks a lot!

SANDY: That's a seventy-five-dollar bra you've got wrapped around your ears!

BILL: You owe me, big time. *Big time!*

NICKY: I want grape juice!

BILL: I never even *dreamed* of going through my mother's underwear drawer!

NICKY: I want grape juice! I want grape juice!

SANDY: That's it! The child's got to be punished.

NICKY: And I. Want. Ice. In. My. Grape. Juice!

BILL: Well, you can't have ice in your grape juice, you little—

SANDY *(Shoving a glass of grape juice at him)*: Here's your damned grape juice. Without ice. Nice and *warm!*

NICKY *(Hurling the glass to the floor, breaking it)*: Then I won't drink it!

SANDY *(Rushing for a Dust Buster)*: Look out, broken glass, broken glass!

BILL: Did you see what he did? He deliberately threw his glass on the floor!

NICKY *(Lunging toward the broken glass)*: I want to make my birthday wish! I want to make my birthday wish!

BILL *(Pulling him back)*: Mommy said look out!

NICKY *(Starting to cry)*: Daddy hurt me, Daddy hurt me.

SANDY *(Frantically vacuuming)*: It's all over the floor. Don't anybody go near there until I clean it up!

BILL: I didn't hurt him, for Christ's sake, I was just pulling him away from the glass!

NICKY: You did so hurt me, you stupid idiot!

(Nicky kicks Bill in the shins.)

BILL *(Shaking Nicky with each word)*: Don't. You. Ever. Hit. Your. Father!

(Nicky wails as Sandy keeps vacuuming.)

Did you see that? Your son just kicked me in the shin.

SANDY: If you ever deliberately break a glass like that again, I'll . . .

BILL *(Examining his wound)*: He broke the skin.

SANDY: That's it! Take him up to his room, there'll be no party!

BILL: My own son drew blood.

SANDY: I'll phone Jeffrey and Mia and tell them to forget the whole thing.

BILL: You'd better get the peroxide to sterilize it with.

(Nicky lies down in his wagon and makes his strangled sound.)

SANDY: Come on, Bill, take him up to his room. We're calling the party off.

NICKY: But what about my cake?

SANDY: No birthday party for Nicky this year.

NICKY: And the candles?

BILL: You can spend the rest of the day up in your room.

NICKY: What about my wish?

SANDY: The child has to be punished.

BILL: It's your own fault.

SANDY: We warned you.

NICKY: You mean, I won't have any party at all?

BILL: We tried.

SANDY: We gave you every chance.

BILL: Maybe next time you'll listen.

SANDY: It hurts us more than it hurts you.

BILL: Maybe next year you'll be a better boy.

SANDY: I asked you to open your presents after the cards!

NICKY: No party? No wish?

BILL: We certainly don't enjoy doing this, Nicky.

SANDY: No party, and that's that.

(Nicky runs out of the room crying. Silence.)

God almighty!

BILL: Jesus Christ!

SANDY: What's happening?

BILL: We had a real chance there.

SANDY: Where's my little boy?

BILL: I was cooking with gas!

SANDY: He's getting so big.

BILL: *Son of a bitch!*

SANDY: Or maybe we're starting to shrink . . .

BILL: He has to ruin everything.

SANDY: I don't understand . . .

BILL: It happens every time. Every fucking time! *(Pause)* So, what do you say we go back to bed and pick up where we left off?

SANDY *(A million miles away)*: Hmmmmm?

BILL: I said . . . how about heading back upstairs?

SANDY: May I ask you something?

BILL: Can't it wait?

SANDY: It's important.

BILL: Okay, okay, but it better be good.

SANDY: Promise you won't laugh.

BILL *(Depressed)*: Whatever you say.

SANDY: Do you hear waves breaking?

BILL: Honey, we're thousands of miles from the ocean.

SANDY: I know, I know . . . but . . . *(Shutting her eyes)* Shhh! Listen!

(She gently nods her head in time with the breaking waves. Bill strains to hear them, too. Silence.)

(Depressed) Oh dear, I was afraid of that. *(She leans over and shakes a shower of sand out of her hair)*

BILL *(Sighs)*: Hey, we all have our moments . . .

(Silence.)

SANDY: Look at me . . .

BILL: So, what do you say we head back up to bed?

SANDY: I'm a ruin.

BILL *(Feeling amorous again)*: You look so beautiful in this early morning light.

SANDY: This is starting to get scary.

BILL: Your hair, your hands, your skin . . .

SANDY: I'm like some rotting carcass that's been washed up on the beach . . . some squid or octopus that's missing half its suckers, or whatever you call those creepy suction thingies . . . *(She makes weird sucking sounds and jerking movements)*

BILL: Honey . . . ?

SANDY: Wow . . . Remember when I used to talk?

BILL: "Used to talk"?

SANDY: I mean really say something.

BILL: You just did.

SANDY: It's getting scary.

BILL: You're talking now.

SANDY: Hold on. I'm going to try and talk.

BILL: Be my guest.

SANDY: Okay, here goes. I'm a mommy.

BILL: Very good.

(Silence.)

SANDY *(Suddenly wistful)*: Remember the week before Nicky was born?

BILL: Atta girl, keep going . . .

SANDY: Remember how he kicked? And how I had this fantasy that he was a trapeze artist doing loop-the-loops, swinging from one end of my womb to the other . . . doing double, triple, quadruple somersaults in midair . . . I mean, he was going *insane* in there! You saw how my stomach danced! It was as if he was trying to get up enough momentum to swing out into the world. And remember how I'd cheer him on . . . "Go Nicky . . . you can do it . . . Grab that trapeze! I'm right here, ready to catch you! Come to Mommy!" *(Near tears)* And then he did it! With my last push out he flew, with glitter and roses in his hair . . . And he was born! *(Long pause)* I'm so tired all of a sudden. Aren't you tired?

BILL: Wiped out.

(More and more exhausted.)

SANDY: There's nothing left.

BILL: I give up.

SANDY: Look at me . . .

BILL: It's hopeless.

SANDY: I can't move.

Act Two

Around six-thirty that evening. Sandy, Bill and Nicky sit around the birthday table dressed in party clothes. They wear party hats and are making barnyard sounds. Sandy clucks like a chicken, Bill howls like a coyote and Nicky oinks like a pig.

BILL: One, two, three—change.

> *(Sandy meows, Bill grunts like a gorilla and Nicky barks.)*
>
> One, two, three—change!
>
> *(Sandy whinnies, Bill whistles like a thrush and Nicky bleats like a goat.)*
>
> One, two, three—change!
>
> *(Sandy clucks like a chicken, Bill croaks like a frog and Nicky hoots like an owl.)*
>
> Stop! Mommy's out of the game! She already clucked before! *(Faster)* One, two, three—change!
>
> *(Bill hisses like a snake and Nicky gobbles like a turkey.)*
>
> One, two, three—change!

(Bill grunts like a gorilla and Nicky squeaks like a mouse.)

Stop the game! Daddy already made gorilla grunts before. Nicky wins!

SANDY AND BILL *(Applauding and whistling)*: Yay, Nicky, yay, Nicky!

NICKY: Let's play again.

SANDY: You're too good for us.

NICKY: Let's play again!

SANDY: They should be here any time now.

BILL: Is everybody ready for one hell of a party?

SANDY: Oh, Nicky, I can hardly wait!

BILL: They'll eat their hearts out when they see this video!

SANDY: The whole day would be perfect if only Jeffrey and Mia would change their minds about having children. Tonight, with us.

BILL: Sure, Jeffrey takes pictures on his travels, but he doesn't use a video camera.

(Nicky leaves the table and quietly plays with one of his toys.)

SANDY: And it's going to happen, you'll see.

BILL: He's more interested in isolated shots than capturing the sweep of it all . . . the story!

SANDY: They may have exciting careers now, but what about when they're retired and all alone in the world. If she waits much longer, it will be too late. Remember Diane Oak? Diane Oak waited until she was forty-five before she had Jonathan. Her cervix had shriveled up to the size of a lima bean and wouldn't even open for the birth.

NICKY: What's a cervix?

SANDY: She passed the ninth month, tenth, eleventh, twelfth . . . nothing happened. They finally had to induce her in the fifteenth.

NICKY: What's a cervix?

SANDY: When that poor baby was finally pulled out by cesarean section, he weighed thirty-six pounds and had a full set of teeth.

NICKY: *What's a cervix?*

BILL: It's a part of a lady.

NICKY: What part?

SANDY: The part the baby comes out of, sweetheart.

BILL *(Whispering)*: The hole.

NICKY: The poopie hole?

BILL: Not the poopie hole! The baby hole!

NICKY: Where's the baby hole?

(Bill indicates where it is on himself.)

SANDY: I certainly wouldn't want Mia to go through what Diane Oak did. All her female plumbing was ripped to shreds by that child.

BILL: Babies come out of the baby hole and poopie comes out of the poopie hole.

SANDY: Of course they could always adopt, but it just isn't the same.

NICKY: Where's the poopie hole?

(Bill indicates where it is on himself.)

SANDY: How she and Jeffrey can call themselves authorities on children when they've never had one of their own . . .

NICKY: Does Mia have a baby hole?

SANDY: She's never felt life moving inside her. It's so sad.

BILL: Of course Mia has a baby hole. All women have baby holes.

NICKY: Then why doesn't a baby come out of it?

SANDY: We don't get to travel like they do, we don't have their kind of freedom . . .

NICKY: Why doesn't a baby come out of Mia's baby hole?

SANDY: And Mia looks younger than me . . .

BILL: Maybe there is one in there, but it's stuck.

NICKY *(Laughing)*: Stuck in with the poopie.

SANDY: But she's missing the most basic experience a woman can have, and when you come right down to it, all she's left with are memories of other people's children.

NICKY: How does a lady tell whether she's going to have a baby or a poopie?

SANDY: Tape recordings and photographs of strangers.

BILL: Because if it's a baby inside her, her tummy swells up, and if it's a poopie inside her . . .

SANDY: Slides of foreign urchins eating raw elephant meat. I feel sorry for her.

BILL: We all have different needs.

SANDY *(Getting louder and louder)*: It's pathetic. Trying to have her own family through other people's children, and not even American children, but poor, starving . . .

(The doorbell rings.)

SANDY AND BILL *(Panicked)*: *They're here!*

SANDY *(Whispering)*: Oh, God, they heard us!

BILL *(Whispering)*: Don't be silly, they couldn't possibly have heard us.

SANDY: They heard us.

NICKY: Heard what?

BILL *(Going to the door)*: They didn't hear us.

NICKY: Heard *what*?

SANDY: Shhhhhhhhh!

(Bill opens the door. Mia and Jeffrey enter, out of breath. Jeffrey is professorial. Mia is a fragile beauty. Jeffrey, Mia, Sandy and Bill speak the following simultaneously:)

JEFFREY	MIA	SANDY:	BILL *(Slap-*
(Shaking hands with Bill): I'm sorry we're so late. Mia was delivering a paper at an anthropology convention and got tied up with a lot of questions at the end. *(Kissing Sandy)* Sandy, I'm sorry. Here, let me set this down . . . *(Putting down a slide projector and several boxes of slides)*	*(Kissing Sandy)*: Sandy, forgive us. I was giving a paper at the university and some visiting professors from Manila had all these questions about nutrition and life expectancy. I thought I'd never get away!	Mia, it's so good to see you! We were just saying what a wonderful couple you and Jeffrey are.	*ping Jeffrey on the back)*: We were beginning to worry about you, old man. I was afraid a group of cannibals had cooked you up for lunch. Jeffrey and Mia Flambé with a little hot sauce on the side . . .

(Bill laughs. Silence. Then Nicky, Bill, Mia, Sandy and Jeffrey speak the following simultaneously:)

NICKY:	BILL	MIA	SANDY:	JEFFREY
I'm four today. Four years old.	*(Kissing Mia):* Mia, you look beautiful. As always. A vision, an apparition, not of this world . . .	*(Kissing Nicky):* Nicky . . . Look at you! Four years old! I don't believe it!	Come in, come in, make yourselves at home.	*(Shaking hands with Nicky):* Happy birthday, Nicholas. Well, you're quite the grown-up now!

(Silence. Then Bill, Sandy and Mia speak the following simultaneously:)

BILL *(Leading them into the room)*: Come on in.	SANDY: We were beginning to worry . . .	MIA: Oh, Sandy, look at what you've done!

(Silence. Then Bill, Mia, Jeffrey and Sandy speak the following simultaneously:)

BILL: Well, folks, is everybody ready for a great party?	MIA: Jeffrey, look! . . .	JEFFREY *(Looking around)*: Nice, nice. Very nice!	SANDY: Nicky's been so excited . . .

(They laugh. Silence. Then Sandy and Bill speak the following simultaneously:)

SANDY: It just wouldn't have been a party without you!	BILL: And wait till you see the video we made . . . There's nothing like a kid's fourth birthday!

(Silence.)

NICKY: I got a wagon and masks.

JEFFREY: When the Tunisian hill child turns four, he's blindfolded and led into a swamp to bring back the body of a mud turtle for a tribal feast.

SANDY: No!

MIA: If he fails, he's expelled from the tribe.

JEFFREY: And left on the plains to be picked apart by giant caw-caws.

SANDY: How horrifying!

(Silence.)

MIA: In the Tabu culture, four is believed to be a magical age. I once saw a four-year-old Tabu girl skin a sixteen-hundred-pound zebra and then eat the pelt!

BILL: Son of a bitch!

NICKY: I can write my name.

MIA: Good for you!

JEFFREY: I saw that same child nurse a dead goat back to life.

BILL: Jesus!

JEFFREY: With her own milk!

NICKY: I pulled Mommy in my wagon.

MIA: Very nice!

BILL: And you should see his magic tricks . . .

SANDY: Unbelievable! *(Gesturing toward some chairs)* Sit down, sit down . . .

MIA: Sandy, everything's beautiful, just . . . beautiful!

JEFFREY: It's amazing what you can do with a little imagination and some helium.

NICKY: Mia, do you have a baby hole?

SANDY: *Nicky?!*

BILL: Nicky and I made this great video this morning, didn't we, Nick?

NICKY: Daddy and I made a video.

MIA: What fun!

SANDY: Bill and Nicky are very close. Ever since Nicky was born they were close.

NICKY *(To Mia)*: Do you have a baby hole?

SANDY: It's unusual to find a father and son as close as Bill and Nicky.

BILL: I wasn't at all close to my father.

SANDY: I was very close to my father.

MIA: I was close to my mother.

SANDY: I hated my mother.

BILL: I don't remember my mother.

JEFFREY: My mother and father were very close.

SANDY: That's interesting, because my mother and father weren't close at all.

(Silence.)

MIA: Sandy, this room is a work of art! I've never seen anything like it!

SANDY: Well, how often does your favorite son turn four?

NICKY: I got lots of presents.

MIA: You must have been up all night.

NICKY: I got a wagon.

MIA: I'll bet you did!

SANDY: And birthday cards . . . Nicky got twenty-seven birthday cards this year, including one from Mrs. Tanner, his nursery school teacher. And they have a strict policy of not sending individual cards on the children's birthdays. You know, they might forget somebody. So naturally Nicky was thrilled to be singled out like that.

(Sandy hands Mia the card.)

MIA *(Reading)*: "Happy birthday, Nicky. Sincerely, Mrs. Tanner."

SANDY *(To Nicky)*: Mrs. Tanner sent that specially to you, breaking all the school rules.

MIA: That's funny, this looks like *your* handwriting.

SANDY: So cousins, how long will you be with us before you disappear over the horizon on the back of some camel?

BILL: I can see you now—two tiny specks inching across the Sahara desert.

MIA: Her Ys and Ns are exactly like yours!

SANDY *(Entering Bill's fantasy)*: Water, water . . .

BILL *(Joining Sandy)*: Water, water . . .

MIA: And look at this *N*. No one makes *N*s like these, except you.

SANDY *(Snatching the card away)*: People will start thinking you don't like American children, the way you're always running off to interview toddlers in Iceland and Nigeria.

NICKY: I pulled Mommy in my wagon.

BILL: He's very strong for his age.

JEFFREY: One of the fascinating things about the Berbers is that parents regard spiritual strength more highly than physical strength.

NICKY: I pulled Mommy and all my presents too!

BILL: He also pulled a rabbit out of a flaming pan!

MIA: Almost any Berber child can converse with desert vegetation.

SANDY: No!

JEFFREY: To my mind, there are no children the equal of Berber children!

NICKY: I got instruments for my birthday.

SANDY *(Lowering her voice)*: Miss Prudenskaja, his music teacher, says he's a prodigy!

NICKY: Daddy made a video of me.

SANDY: Bill and Nicky are very close.

NICKY: I got masks for my birthday.

SANDY: Nicky and his masks . . .

BILL: Give that kid a mask, any kind of mask, and he's in heaven.

MIA: We've always been fascinated by masks and the whole phenomenon of taking on another identity.

(Nicky puts on a series of presidential masks—Lincoln, Roosevelt, Kennedy, Nixon, Reagan and Clinton—and speaks accordingly.)

JEFFREY: Remember those crocodile masks we were given in New Guinea?

NICKY *(As Lincoln)*: "Fourscore and seven years ago, our fathers brought forth on this continent, a new nation, conceived in liberty, and dedicated to the proposition that all men are created equal . . ."

BILL: And he's off!

SANDY: He gets so excited on his birthday, he's been up since six this morning.

MIA: Jeffrey and I were given crocodile masks in New Guinea that were made from a paste of dried insects.

JEFFREY: You had the feeling that if you left one on too long, you'd slowly turn into a crocodile as well.

NICKY *(As Kennedy)*: "And so, my fellow Americans, ask not what your country can do for you; ask what you can do for your country."

BILL: You think this is good, you ought to hear his Shakespeare.

MIA *(Depressed)*: I can imagine!

BILL: The kid's got a photographic memory!

SANDY: You know what time he got up this morning? Four-fifteen! It was still dark outside.

NICKY *(As Nixon)*: "I have never been a quitter. To leave office before my term is completed is abhorrent to every instinct in my body."

JEFFREY: He isn't going to go through every American president, is he?

SANDY: All right, Nicky, that's enough.

JEFFREY: We'll be here all night!

NICKY *(As Reagan)*: "General Secretary Gorbachev, if you seek peace, if you seek prosperity for the Soviet Union and Eastern Europe, if you seek liberalization: Come here to this gate! Mr. Gorbachev, open this gate! Mr. Gorbachev, tear down this wall."

BILL: Okay, Nick, let's take off the mask and calm down.

SANDY: The poor thing's exhausted, he's been up all night.

NICKY *(As Clinton)*: "My fellow citizens, today we celebrate the mystery of American renewal. This ceremony is held in the depth of winter, but by the words we speak and the faces we show the world, we force the spring . . ."

BILL: MOMMY SAID: CAN IT! *(Removing his mask)*

NICKY: Give it back, give it back!

SANDY: That's better. Now we can see your sweet face.

NICKY: I want my mask, I want my mask!

SANDY: Oh, let him keep it, it's his birthday.

BILL *(Giving it back)*: Okay, but no more monopolizing the conversation, understand?

(Nicky sucks his thumb through the mask. Silence.)

Take your thumb out of your mask.

(Nicky doesn't.)

SANDY: It's the strangest thing, but ever since I got up this morning, I've been smelling the sea. Its scent is all around me. *(She inhales deeply)* It's as if I set sail in a little dinghy and am becalmed in the middle of the ocean, bobbing up and down in my housedress. Maybe I'll catch a fish, and maybe I won't . . .

BILL: Honey?

SANDY *(Calling)*: Here, fishy, fishy, fishy . . . Here, fishy, fishy . . .

BILL: Sweetheart?

(Sandy runs her hands through her hair, and a shower of sand falls out. Silence.)

Tell us again, just how many languages can the two of you speak?

JEFFREY: Seventeen.   MIA: Thirteen.

SANDY: Jeffrey and Mia can speak fifteen languages, Nicky.

BILL: My maternal grandmother was Canadian and always spoke French around the house.

SANDY: My maternal grandmother was Dutch.

BILL: But us kids never learned it.

JEFFREY: Canadian French isn't considered a pure language, it's a dilution.

SANDY: I'm part Dutch on one side and Swedish on the other.

JEFFREY: Swedish, of course, is an offshoot of German.

BILL: I'm pure Canadian and a little Irish.

MIA: Gaelic! I love Gaelic! It's like talking with your mouth full of stones.

NICKY: What am I, what am I?

JEFFREY: Gaelic is one of the most ancient languages on earth. It came from the Celts, you know.

BILL: No wait, I forgot, I have some Greek blood in me, too.

SANDY: Oh, Mia, say a few words in a funny language.

NICKY: *What am I? What am I?*

BILL *(Angry)*: Canadian, Dutch, Swedish and a little Greek, okay?!

(Silence.)

MIA (*Adding clicking sounds and strange inhalations whenever she speaks the made-up language*): Talla zoo zoo feeple zip.

NICKY: What did you say?

SANDY (*Laughing*): Isn't it a riot?

BILL (*Laughing*): Jesus Christ!

NICKY: What did you say?

MIA: Happy birthday!

NICKY: Say something else.

SANDY: More, more, say more!

MIA: Dun herp zala zala cree droop soy nitch.

SANDY (*Roaring with laughter*): Stop, stop!

NICKY: Say it again, say it again!

BILL: Too much!

MIA: Dun herp zala zala cree droop soy nitch.

BILL: And what does that mean?

MIA: Merry Christmas.

(*Sandy, Bill and Nicky howl with laughter.*)

SANDY: That was Merry Christmas?

NICKY: Say "Nicky is four years old today."

MIA: Ooola oola zim dam zilco reet tree comp graaaaa, Nicky!

(*Sandy, Bill and Nicky laugh harder.*)

SANDY, BILL AND NICKY: Again, again!

MIA AND JEFFREY (*The clicking sounds and inhalations reaching their height*): Ooola oola zim dam zilco reet tree comp graaaaa, Nicky!

(*Sandy, Bill and Nicky laugh harder.*)

BILL (*To Nicky*): How would you like to be able to speak like that?

NICKY (*Gravely, with the same strange clicking and inhalations*): Lim biddle ree yok slow iffle snee buddle twee rat ith twank.

JEFFREY (*Translating it*): Two autumns. You left. I stayed.

JEFFREY AND MIA: Nice, nice . . .

SANDY AND BILL (*Stunned*): Very nice . . .

(*Long silence.*)

SANDY: We always have such a good time when you come over.

MIA: We wouldn't miss Nicky's birthday for the world.

SANDY: Who else has cousins that speak fifteen languages?

BILL: Hey, I haven't told Jeffrey and Mia about Charley E.Z., this crazy guy that works in our office.

SANDY *(Trying to stop him)*: Bill . . .

BILL: There's a shakedown going on and a couple of the top-level people are being let go. The things they do to try and hang on. Unbelievable. I guess something comes over a guy when he feels his job is threatened.

SANDY: Not now . . .

BILL: There's this fellow at work, Charles E. Zinn . . . Charley E.Z. we call him. He recently lost an important account, so word came down that Charley E.Z. was going to get axed.

JEFFREY: I don't think I've ever heard you mention a Charley E.Z. before.

SANDY *(In a singsong)*: Honeyyyyyyy . . .

BILL: He'd been getting these letters accusing him of "professional inconsistency"—whatever *that* means—so word came down that Charley E.Z. was going to get fired.

MIA: How awful!

JEFFREY: Poor guy.

(Sandy pulls an imaginary knife across her throat with a sound effect.)

BILL: So Charley E.Z. took action. And where did he take action? At the office retreat up at Devil Mountain State Park.

JEFFREY: Devil Mountain State Park?

MIA: I've never heard of it.

SANDY: Well, you know Bill and his crazy stories.

BILL: Every year Continental Allied foots the bill for a weekend of hiking, kayaking and stargazing in the wilderness. And this wasn't just sales, but the entire organization—accounting, payroll, personnel—everyone from office managers down to the bottom-feeders in the mailroom. We're talking over a hundred employees, zooming up the highway in a convoy of chartered buses singing old camp songs . . . *(Singing in a faraway voice)* "On top of old Smokey, all covered with snow, I lost my true lover for courting too slow . . ."

SANDY: And he's off . . .

MIA: Oh, I used to love that song.

MIA, JEFFREY AND BILL *(Singing together)*: "For courting's a pleasure, but parting is grief, and a false-hearted lover is worse than a thief . . ."

SANDY: Good old Bill, always the life of the party.

MIA, JEFFREY, BILL AND NICKY *(All swaying)*: "For a thief he will rob you and take what you have, but a false-hearted lover will lead you to your grave. The grave will decay you and turn you to dust . . ."

SANDY *(Overlapping)*: All right Nicky, that's enough!

JEFFREY: "One girl in a thousand a poor girl can trust."

(Silence.)

MIA: Well, what do you say we give Nicky our present now?

BILL: Where was I? Oh yes! Charley E.Z. up in wild and woolly Devil Mountain! *Fasten your seatbelts!*

(Nicky mimes fastening one.)

SANDY: We're in for a bumpy ride!

BILL: So we finally reach the campground, head off to our assigned spots and pitch our tents. Then this guy from the mailroom hauls out a harmonica and starts playing sad tunes . . .

(Nicky accompanies him on his harmonica throughout, playing very well.)

A campfire was lit and this . . . circle of flames leapt into the sky . . . What with our close proximity to each other and all that free booze that's not all that was leaping into the sky, let me tell you! Whoeeee!

SANDY: Honey, there's a child in the room!

BILL: Poor old Charley didn't know what was coming over him. I mean, the guy's married with a wife and a kid! They're very close.

(Sandy groans.)

The wife's a real looker and his son's a prince. A handful, but still a prince.

(Sandy groans again.)

And he suddenly finds himself in the *wilderness*, jammed up against all his coworkers who are feeling exactly the same way.

(Sandy's groans turn into little mewing sounds.)

So he decides it's time to restore his credibility on all fronts . . . He sets up his own personal tent away from the others, puts down a welcome mat and hangs up a little sign that says, "Yodeley-oh-ho-ho."
JEFFREY AND MIA: Yodeley-oh-ho-ho?

(Nicky quickly scribbles "Yodeley-oh-ho-ho" on a piece of paper, hangs it on the door of the armoire and plunges inside, slamming the door behind him.)

BILL *(Lowering his voice)*: As the loons, frogs and crickets are making whoopee by the lake, Charley unpacks his duffle bag and pulls out a secret stash of masks and wigs.

JEFFREY: No!   MIA: I love it, I love it!

BILL: He's been to these retreats before. He comes prepared!
SANDY *(Laughing)*: Just so you know, our storyteller here hasn't slept in over twenty-four hours!
BILL: There's a knock at the door . . .

(Nicky knocks inside the armoire.)

Or I should say "flap," since tents don't have doors.

(Nicky makes a rustling sound effect.)

And there stands Marianne from payroll. Beautiful Marianne Dingle with the blond ringlets and killer body . . .

MIA: And . . . ? And . . . ?

BILL: Charley greets her with a sexy, "Yodeley-oh-ho-ho," and she answers, *(In her voice)* "Yodeley-oh-ho-ho." The loons, frogs and crickets are going so crazy by now, they can't hear themselves talk, so he shows her his assortment of masks, she points to the zebra head and he puts it on . . . They rip off their clothes, drop down to the ground, and they're off! *Yodeley-oh-ho-ho!*

NICKY *(From inside the armoire)*: Yodeley-oh-ho-ho . . .

BILL: Soon, there's a line outside Charley's tent—all sexes and ages—office managers, temps, you name it. And he has a different mask for each one—mammal, reptile, monster and mythic. And this goes on for three nights in a row! THREE!

NICKY *(Opening and shutting his door wearing a variety of masks)*: Yodeley-oh-ho-ho . . . yodeley-oh-ho-ho . . . yodeley-oh-ho-ho . . .

SANDY: Easy, Nicky, easy . . .

JEFFREY: He's pulling our leg.

SANDY: That's my Bill.

BILL: Hey, I was there. I saw it all.

(Sandy storms off to an opposite corner of the room.)

MIA: I had no idea office workers could be so . . . frisky.

BILL: So . . . Charley's hoping his woodland performance will stem the tide of letters about professional inconsistency, but everything comes with a price. The poor guy's racked with guilt on the home front what with the wife and kid . . . I mean, Charley's an A1 husband and dad. True blue . . . So he's a total wreck! Well, you know what they say . . . Sometimes you have to cut off your nose to spite your face. *(Pause)* Hey, don't look so tragic! I make it up! This is a party! We're supposed to kick up our heels.

(Dead silence.)

MIA: Don't you think it's time we gave Nicky his present?

NICKY *(Opening and shutting the armoire door, putting on different masks)*: Yodeley-oh-ho-ho . . . Yodeley-oh-ho-ho . . .

SANDY: Jeffrey and Mia want to give you your present now, honey . . .

JEFFREY *(Puttering with his projector)*: Nicholas, you've never gotten a present like this!

SANDY: Presents!

MIA: I just hope he likes it, you never know with children.

JEFFREY: I was an only child like Nicky and something of a loner. What kept me going was my stamp collection. I imagined that each one was designed for me personally by someone very special. A man with sad eyes, a woman with six fingers, a boy who heard voices.

MIA: Don't get him started on his stamp collection.

NICKY *(Opening the armoire door)*: Yodeley-oh-ho-ho!

SANDY: Nicky, please, you're embarrassing us.

JEFFREY: My favorite was a two-cent stamp issued in 1901 showing a daredevil crossing Niagara Falls on a tightrope, but the printers screwed up and he had this . . . faint shadow . . . A dealer recently offered me $250,000 for that baby, but I wouldn't sell it. No way. I used to go up to the attic and pretend I was that shadow. *(Miming it)* The two of us would be inching along our wire, when he'd suddenly get an attack of vertigo and start to slip . . . I'd grab him in the nick of time, but that would throw me off. So there we'd be . . . five thousand feet above the rushing falls, clinging to each other for dear life, the crowd gasping, flashbulbs popping . . . but I'd always save the day. Soon it became part of our act. He'd fake losing his balance so I could take over. It's weird . . . You'd think *I* would have played the daredevil, but I didn't want that kind of attention. I preferred being invisible. *Shadow Man! (Long pause)* Strange . . .

(Silence.)

SANDY: It's the oddest thing, but one of my front teeth is loose. People don't lose their front teeth, do they?

MIA: The Qua tribe starts out with all their permanent teeth and then at the age of sixteen, every one falls out to be replaced by an entire set of baby teeth. It's a complete mystery to dental science.

SANDY: Ugh!

JEFFREY: Okay, folks, we're ready to go. Get Nicky, his present is all set.

SANDY: He's always so thrilled to see you.

BILL *(Knocking on the armoire)*: Come out, come out, wherever you are!

(Nothing happens. Silence.)

SANDY: Family means so much to him.

JEFFREY *(Dimming the lights)*: The show is about to begin.

SANDY: Oooooh, Nicky, I wonder what it is.

BILL *(Lowering his voice)*: Nicholas, will you get the hell out of there!

SANDY: You're being very rude, Nicky! *Mommy isn't going to forget this!*

BILL *(Dragging Nicky out)*: Now get over here and sit down!

(Bill sits Nicky down. The chairs have been rearranged to face the slide show, which flickers out over the audience. Silence.)

JEFFREY *(Waving his hand over the projector and box of slides)*: Happy birthday, Nicky.

MIA: Happy birthday.

NICKY: What is it?

JEFFREY: Your own screen and projector, with slides of children from all over the world.

(Jeffrey starts showing slides of children in native dress doing all kinds of remarkable things.)

SANDY: Ooooooooooh, Nicky . . .

BILL: What a present!

SANDY: Look, look . . .

MIA: Jeffrey took them all.

SANDY: They're just beautiful.

BILL: Son of a bitch!

JEFFREY: We figured this would be something he could work himself.

MIA: And learn from.

JEFFREY: It's a whole new world, Nicky. Make it yours!

BILL: Wow! What kind of film were you using?

SANDY: And Jeffrey and Mia said you could keep them!

NICKY: Isn't there anything else?

BILL: Shit, that's color!

NICKY: Something to unwrap?

JEFFREY: All you do is load the projector and then push this button when you want to see a new slide. Your mommy and daddy can help you with it.

NICKY: This is it?!

MIA: These are some of the children we worked with last year.

SANDY: Jeffrey and Mia lead very special lives, honey, they travel all over the world studying poor children.

JEFFREY: Oh, look! The Ios. They decorate their faces with an iridescent paint made out of powdered giraffe hooves.

MIA: It's very bad for their skin, actually.

SANDY: I can imagine.

MIA: They're extraordinary children. It's said they can fly. Jeffrey and I never saw them airborne, but our guide showed us pictures of them flying in formation over the Himalayas.

NICKY: I wish I could meet them.

MIA: Well, maybe some day.

NICKY: I don't have anybody to play with.

SANDY: That isn't true. You have Daddy and me to play with, you go to nursery school three mornings a week and don't forget your music lessons with Miss Prudenskaja.

NICKY: I hate Miss Prudenskaja. She's mean and she smells like toe jam.

JEFFREY: Actually, these slides don't represent the most amazing part of our trip last year.

NICKY: I don't have any friends.

JEFFREY: Our penetration into the bush.

SANDY: I didn't know you were allowed!

NICKY: I wish those children could come to my house.

JEFFREY: We penetrated the bush and saw things no human being has ever seen.

SANDY: Tell us everything, everything!

NICKY: I'm lonely.

JEFFREY: We encountered a civilization untouched by the Industrial Revolution. People living in the Stone Age.

(The lighting gets darker and eerie. As the scene progresses the jungle seems to move into the room with distant sound effects of chattering monkeys and parrots.)

SANDY: *Oooooooh, cavemen!*

JEFFREY: There are a bush people called the Whan See who are still arboreal.

(Sandy gasps.)

BILL: Jeeeez.

NICKY: I wish I could play with them.

BILL: Ssssshhhh.

JEFFREY: They live in trees and never come down to the ground.

MIA: What was so remarkable was that they were obviously *Homo sapiens* and not simian, yet they had this one extra-ordinary feature . . .

BILL: Christ, I hope you had a video camera with you.

MIA: A freakish biological throwback.

JEFFREY: Each and every one of them had a tail!

(Sandy, Bill and Nicky gasp.)

MIA: We couldn't believe our eyes the first time we saw them. We'd been cutting our way through deep brush when we suddenly heard this chattering above us. It sounded like children giggling. We looked up . . . and there were these . . . people . . . swinging through the branches by their tails.

JEFFREY: Small-boned with delicate features . . .

MIA: And covered with this silvery down that glittered so brightly we had to shade our eyes.

(Sandy, Bill and Nicky gasp.)

BILL: Did you get any footage?

MIA: And they had the most musical way of speaking . . . a kind of sighing almost.

(Nicky picks up a cello that was concealed somewhere in the living room and starts playing the first movement of Bach's unaccompanied Cello Suite no. 1 in G Major.)

JEFFREY: We were afraid they'd run away when they saw us, but they didn't. They just became very still and stared down at us.

(A sudden silence as everyone becomes aware of Nicky's playing.)

MIA: I had no idea Nicky could play the cello so well!
SANDY *(In a stage whisper)*: He's Miss Prudenskaja's star pupil!
MIA: He's really remarkable!
JEFFREY: Check out his *bowing* . . .
BILL: Go, Nick!
SANDY: That's my boy!

(They listen for several moments in amazement. He keeps playing, but lowers the volume.)

JEFFREY: Where was I?
MIA: When we first met the Whan See.
JEFFREY: Right, right . . . Because they exuded such docility, I reached up my hand to one and said, "We're American anthropologists, we come in peace."
SANDY: What a perfect thing to say!
BILL: Beautiful . . . beautiful.
JEFFREY: They became very excited and all started talking at once.
BILL: At least you had a tape recorder on you.
MIA: I've never seen such eyes . . . a kind of creamy pink . . . like looking into a strawberry parfait.
SANDY: Weren't you scared?
JEFFREY: You see, we, without tails and wearing clothes, were just as strange to their eyes.
MIA: After Jeffrey spoke, I said a few words, and then our guide gave them some chewing gum. Then as a body, they furled and unfurled their long silvery tails and chanted, "Whan See." So we chanted it back.
JEFFREY AND MIA *(Chanting)*: Whan See, Whan See, Whan See . . .
JEFFREY: Then one of them motioned us to join them. So we climbed a nearby tree and they gingerly approached us, touching our hair and skin.
SANDY: I would have died.

MIA: They were an exceedingly gentle people who had no words in their vocabulary for hate, anger or war.

JEFFREY: We spent an entire week with them.

MIA: It's amazing how fast you can adjust to living in a tree.

JEFFREY: And not once in all that time did we ever see one of them drop down to the ground, even though they could stand erect, run and even dance on their hind legs.

MIA: You should have seen them dance! They'd wrap their tails around a branch and start rocking back and forth, swaying higher and higher and then suddenly let go, catapulting through the trees like meteors.

JEFFREY: While the older members of the tribe banged on drums made of hollow tree stumps.

MIA: Our last day there they asked us to join them. The leader gripped me around the waist with his tail and started whirling me through the air. Everything was spinning and pulsing . . . There was this very strong smell about him . . . Cinnamon, cinnamon dust sprinkled through his fur . . . He spun me higher and higher and then let go . . . We went flying through the air . . . the speed . . . the height . . . those sparkling pink eyes . . . I could feel his heart and taste his fur . . . it was just . . . I can't even . . . I thought I'd . . . it was so . . .

(Silence, except for Nicky's playing. When he finishes he curls up on the floor with one of his toys and goes to sleep.)

BILL: Jesus!

SANDY: Oh, Mia . . .

JEFFREY: Other tribes in the bush have repeatedly tried to capture the Whan See because of their beauty and grace, but once a Whan See touches ground, it dies. Something happens to their center of gravity, their balance goes haywire.

SANDY: Oh, no . . .

BILL: I just hope you had a film crew with you!

JEFFREY: In spite of their ignorance of science and technology, they displayed incredible artistic sophistication. They did these bark carvings with their teeth that were absolutely stunning!

MIA: It was a form of relaxation. They'd sit in the shade, tearing out the most intricate designs.

JEFFREY: Their virtuosity was astonishing. On the one hand, they did representational carvings depicting familiar bush objects, but then they also did these highly abstract designs that resembled some sort of ancient calligraphy.

MIA: And of course that constant gnawing on tree bark provided them with excellent dental hygiene.

SANDY: I've never heard anything like this.

JEFFREY: They also did exquisite lacework, tearing into large pawpaw leaves.

SANDY: You should write a book.

BILL: Tell me you got some footage!

JEFFREY: It's funny about my pictures of the Whan See . . . Not one of them came out. There must have been something in their silvery fur that set off a toxic reaction to my film.

MIA: The whole thing was like a dream except . . .

JEFFREY: Except . . .

SANDY: Oh no, it will be something awful!

MIA: We didn't find out about it until our last night, otherwise we'd still be there.

JEFFREY: Neither of us wanted to leave. We'd have given up everything to stay with them.

MIA: Our careers, our fieldwork, our publications . . .

JEFFREY: Sometimes at night we'd watch them make love, their silvery bodies radiating a kind of shimmering electricity. And everyone would watch: children, parents, grandparents . . .

MIA: But that last evening we saw the flaw . . .

JEFFREY: The sty . . .

MIA: The moral defect.

BILL: *They eat their young!*

(Sandy screams.)

MIA: Our last evening there a girl went into childbirth.

SANDY *(Hands over her ears)*: I can't listen!

MIA: As usual, everyone gathered around to watch, since they had no concept of privacy or modesty.

JEFFREY: No one doctor or midwife was in charge—the delivery was the responsibility of all the women of the tribe.

MIA: As the girl was in the final throes of labor, the older women reached out their hands to help her.

SANDY: It will be awful!

MIA: Finally her moment came, the head appeared. She gave a shrill yelp of pain and joy.

(Sandy gasps.)

And the baby was born.

SANDY: Thank God!

MIA: But the very instant it emerged, they lifted the tiny creature up and . . . and . . .

SANDY *(Hands flying to her heart)*: *Don't!*

MIA: It's too awful.

BILL: *One of the elders popped it in his mouth!*

(Sandy screams.)

MIA: They lifted the tiny creature up and reinserted it back into its mother's womb.

SANDY AND BILL: But that's impossible!

MIA: And they did it again and again and again and again . . .

BILL: Son of a bitch!

MIA: And the mother kept urging them on. As soon as the baby came out, she'd motion them to . . . stuff him back in. It was obviously some sort of ritual. There was a minimal number of reinsertions the mother had to withstand.

SANDY: I don't believe it! It's unnatural.

BILL: Did. You. Get. Any. Footage?

JEFFREY: Only the strongest survive.

BILL: If you got any of that on tape, you could make one hell of a documentary!

SANDY: But why? Why did she do it?

JEFFREY: You have to remember, these were a highly primitive people who took things literally. When a civilized woman has a baby, she too is possessive, only in more subtle ways. She's possessive of her birth experience and delights in retelling it. She's possessive of her baby and tries to keep him helpless for as long as possible. Well, these Stone Age women were just acting out those same impulses by forcing the baby back into the womb. Through fetal reinsertion, you see, the primitive mother could experience her moment of motherhood again and again and again.

MIA: After the fourth insertion, her uterus went into profound shock, and how that baby squealed. It wasn't human after a while, but mangled . . . and drenched . . . like some rodent . . . some furry little . . . hamster.

SANDY: I'm going to be sick.

JEFFREY *(Moving away from them, holding some slides up to the light)*: I've got to go through these slides and make sure I gave Nicky the right ones . . . Let's see . . . oh, yes, Caracas! What's this one of Nepal doing in here?

MIA: After a while they motioned me to join them and pulled me over to where she lay.

SANDY: I wish you'd stop this.

MIA: It was such a beautiful night, the air was so warm . . . I didn't understand what they wanted me to do at first, so I just stood there.

JEFFREY: That's enough, darling . . .

SANDY: I haven't been feeling well today. When I looked in the mirror this morning, I saw an old woman.

MIA: Then someone gripped my hand, guiding it towards the girl's birth canal. I felt something warm and moist. I looked down. I was holding the baby's head. Such a tiny head. It was about the size of a softball and covered with that same silvery fur, except it was wet and matted down. It was so slippery I was afraid I'd drop it, but then this hand closed over mine and brought the baby up against his mother's birth canal, which opened again, receiving him.

SANDY: I've been smelling the sea ever since I got up.

MIA: Her body convulsed, the baby came out again and again: five, six, seven times . . .

JEFFREY: You know what happens.

SANDY: My front teeth feel loose.

MIA: After a while I noticed that I was doing it by myself, no one was helping me, *I* was inserting the baby!

JEFFREY: You get confused.

SANDY: I feel so tired all the time.

MIA: You know what it felt like? Stuffing a turkey. Stuffing a fifty-pound turkey with some little . . . hamster or guinea pig.

SANDY: Oh Nicky . . . my Nicky . . . just look at him!

MIA: And there was this overpowering cinnamon smell. I started laughing.

JEFFREY: Yoo-hoo? . . . Darling?

SANDY: Nicky is four today. My son is four years old.

MIA: And then everyone started laughing, with those light sighing voices, but then something went wrong. The baby stopped moving.

SANDY: You're afraid.

MIA: It went all stiff in my hands.

SANDY: You're afraid to have a baby.

MIA: The mother didn't realize. She kept motioning me to stuff him back in.

JEFFREY: Enough is enough!

SANDY: You're afraid something will be wrong.

MIA *(Increasingly upset)*: I didn't know what to do.

SANDY: We're all afraid, but *it isn't like that*!

MIA: Everyone looked at me, waiting . . .

JEFFREY *(Even more upset, disappearing into his slides)*: Don't say I didn't warn you!

SANDY: Of course there are sacrifices.

MIA: Finally, I laid him in her arms. She bared her breast to him, cupping his tiny head against her, but he didn't move.

SANDY: For the first few years you'd have to stay home.

BILL: You certainly couldn't take an infant into some mud village with no sanitary or medical facilities.

MIA: She breathed into his mouth, she slapped his face, she dug at his closed eyes with sticks, no life anywhere . . .

JEFFREY: You're on your own here! Let's see, where was I? *(Looking at a new slide)* Ah, yes, the Wahai children who speak with their elbows!

SANDY: You'd have to forget about your career for six or seven years.

(Jeffrey starts making strange gestures with his arms.)

BILL: Maybe even longer.

MIA: She understood at last and screamed this scream.

SANDY: It isn't like that, it just isn't like that.

BILL: You should have seen Sandy . . . natural childbirth all the way.

SANDY: It was great!

MIA: Then in one awful moment, she rose, lashed the baby to her chest, spread out her arms and jumped.

JEFFREY *(Looking at another slide)*: The green-eyed hermaphrodites who fixed my glasses! Speaking of which, where *are* my glasses? I must have left them in the car. I'll be right back. *(He exits)*

BILL: She was in labor thirty-two hours.

SANDY: Thirty-six!

MIA: Down they plunged and were lost in the night.

BILL: The woman was magnificent!

MIA: Gone. Swallowed up. *(Staggering)* I don't feel well.

SANDY *(Trying to steady her)*: Oh, Mia, *you* should have a baby!

BILL: It would change your life.

MIA: I'm so dizzy all of a sudden.

SANDY *(Guiding Mia onto the floor)*: You'd better lie down.

BILL *(Helping Sandy)*: Atta girl . . .

MIA: The room is spinning.

SANDY: Take a deep breath. In . . . and out. In . . . and out. In . . . and out . . .

BILL *(Attending Mia as a doctor)*: Her pulse is racing.

SANDY: Come on, breathe! *(Setting up a rhythm) In* . . . and out. In . . . and out . . .

BILL *(Breathing with Sandy)*: *In* . . . and out. In . . . and out . . .

SANDY: Nicky, we need you, too.

(Nicky wakes up and joins in with great concentration and flair. He takes blood pressure, administers shots, writes on charts.)

Don't worry, we're right here. *We won't leave you!*

BILL: In . . . and out. In . . . and out. In . . . and out . . .

NICKY: Blood pressure: a hundred and fifty over two hundred and seventy-seven. Heart racing, irregular cardiovascular pattern.

SANDY: Don't stiffen up . . . relax and breathe . . . relax and breathe . . .

(Sandy breathes with Bill.)

It's the most beautiful experience a woman can have. Breathe in . . . and out . . . In and out . . .

(Mia starts breathing in time with Sandy.)

Good girl . . . That's right . . . Hold it . . . Let it out slowly . . .

MIA: *Oh! Something's happening!*

NICKY: Pulse: sixty over eighty. Blood pressure: two hundred and thirty over ninety-eight. She should be dilated about seven centimeters by now.

(They all breathe faster.)

MIA *(Screaming in pain)*: Oh! . . . Oh! What's happening to me? I don't want this . . . please . . . I . . . Oh!

SANDY *(Holding her hand)*: You're doing beautifully. The first is always the hardest.

MIA: In and . . . Oh! . . . Oh! Help me!

BILL: The first is always the hardest.

NICKY: The first is always the hardest.

SANDY: But the most rewarding.

BILL: Certainly the most rewarding.

NICKY: Absolutely the most rewarding.

MIA: Can't you do something? Can't you stop it? God! . . . Oh! Stop it!

BILL *(Struggling to hold her down)*: You'd better give me a hand, she's fighting.

NICKY: If you don't cooperate with us, you'll have to be put to sleep and miss everything.

SANDY: That's right, you'll miss everything.

SANDY, BILL AND NICKY: You don't want to miss everything, do you?

NICKY: Blood pressure: Two hundred and fifty over six. Lungs congested . . . I want this woman on a respirator!

SANDY: You've got to relax!

BILL: We'll have to put her to sleep.

SANDY: Push, hold, breathe . . . Push, hold, breathe . . .

MIA *(Screaming)*: I . . . don't . . . Stop . . . Please! Oh! Oh! You can't . . . Stop! Help! HELLLLLLP! I . . . Oh . . . Ahhhh . . . Ahhhh! *(She passes out)*

JEFFREY *(Rushing into the room. He turns on the lights and the encroaching jungle vanishes)*: What's going on in here?

(Sandy, Bill and Nicky freeze.)

(Rushing to Mia's side) I SAID WHAT ARE YOU DOING
TO MY WIFE?

(Sandy, Bill and Nicky leap away from her.)

SANDY: Nothing, nothing . . .
BILL: We were just . . .
JEFFREY: Darling, speak to me!

(Dead silence.)

SANDY: Well . . .
BILL: Well . . .
SANDY: I guess some women just can't have children.
BILL: You can't pass a camel through the eye of a needle.
NICKY: One man's meat is another man's poison.
SANDY: A rolling stone gathers no moss.
BILL: All work and no play makes Jack a dull boy.
NICKY: No pain, no gain!
JEFFREY: WHAT THE HELL ARE YOU TALKING ABOUT?
SANDY: Your pathetic wife!
JEFFREY: Excuse me?
SANDY: The woman on the floor who's afraid to have children.
JEFFREY: "Afraid to have children"? My dear Sandy, you don't
    have a clue about that woman and her feelings for children.
    Not. One. Fucking. Clue!
SANDY: Sorry, sorry . . .
BILL: We were just . . .
JEFFREY: I said, *drop it*!

(An awful silence.)

SANDY: So . . . what do you say we bring out Nicky's cake?!
NICKY *(Racing to the table)*: My cake, my cake, my cake . . .
BILL: Hats, everybody . . . *hats*! *(He starts passing out party hats)*
SANDY *(Approaching Mia)*: Rise and shine . . . It's time to get up.
BILL *(Offering her a hat)*: Mia?
NICKY: She's not moving.

JEFFREY (*Carrying her over to a chair at the table and setting her down*): Let me.

(*Mia sits upright for several seconds and then slumps over. Sandy and Nicky scream.*)

SANDY: What have we done?

BILL (*Lightly slapping Mia's face*): Come on, Mia . . . wake up . . .

SANDY: Oh, Bill . . .

BILL (*To Sandy*): Get her some water! (*Lifts Mia up, holding her under the arms*) Come on, let's walk her.

SANDY (*Sprinkling water on Mia*): Mia? Mia?

NICKY: She's dead, she's dead!

SANDY: She's not dead, she just passed out. She's not moving, Bill.

BILL: I know she's not moving. What do you think I am, *blind*?

SANDY: You don't have to yell!

NICKY: Mia's dead, Mia's dead!

SANDY: Can it, Nicky!

BILL: Maybe we should lie her down on the floor again.

SANDY: Oh, Mia, I'm sorry.

NICKY: You killed her!

BILL: We didn't kill her, she just fainted.

NICKY: I *saw* you kill her!

BILL: She should carry medication!

SANDY (*To Bill*): Prop her up again, she's so scary this way.

BILL (*Leaning Mia against a chair*): There!

NICKY: *You killed her!*

BILL: Stop it, Nicky, or it's back to your room!

NICKY: How could you *kill* somebody on my birthday? Even I wasn't that bad.

JEFFREY (*To all of them*): HANDS OFF! LEAVE HER ALONE!

(*Sandy, Bill and Nicky jump away from Mia.*)

SANDY: I came on too strong.

NICKY: I didn't *kill* anybody!

BILL (*Raising his hand to him*): Nickyyyyyy!

(*Mia slides down to the floor again with a thud. Sandy and Nicky scream.*)

(Peeling back Mia's eyelids) Someone get some smelling salts!

JEFFREY *(In an awful voice)*: I said, take your filthy hands off of her!

NICKY *(Starting to cry)*: I'm scared.

SANDY: What do we do now?

JEFFREY: Finish the party so we can go home and forget the whole thing.

(Slight silence.)

BILL: Cake! Cake! Let's bring out the cake!

NICKY: I don't want any cake.

BILL: Of course you want cake, it's your birthday. Get the cake, Sandy.

SANDY: How can we eat cake when she's . . .

BILL: I said, *get the cake*!

(Sandy exits.)

NICKY *(Crying)*: I don't like this anymore.

(Jeffrey carries Mia back to her chair. She slumps over the table again. Silence. Sandy enters carrying the cake, candles blazing.)

BILL: Isn't that some cake? Come on . . . let's sing!

(Bill and Sandy sing "Happy Birthday" to Nicky. Sandy then sets the cake down in front of him.)

Come on, Nick, let's hear your wish.

(A long silence.)

NICKY *(Concentrates, takes a deep breath)*: I wish I had a brother. *(And then blows out the candles)*

BILL *(Stunned)*: Good old Nick, you never know what he's going to say next.

SANDY *(More stunned)*: My Nicky . . .

BILL: That's quite a wish.

NICKY: I wish I had . . . three brothers!

SANDY: But what about poor Mommy?

NICKY: I want three brothers to play with.

JEFFREY: All children need siblings.

BILL: That's all we need, three more kids.

JEFFREY: It would do Nicky good to have siblings, I should know.

NICKY: I'm lonely.

JEFFREY: The only child is more prone towards psychosis in the later years.

NICKY *(Stamping his feet)*: I want three brothers for my birthday!

JEFFREY: Forensic studies show that sixty-seven percent of all serial killers were only children.

SANDY: He's overtired. We shouldn't have let him come down from his room this afternoon.

BILL: Next time you'll stay in your room!

(Mia slides to the floor with a thud.)

NICKY: I want five brothers! No, I want eleven brothers . . . thirty-seven brothers . . . a hundred brothers . . . six hundred brothers . . . nine hundred brothers!

SANDY: Oh, Nicky . . .

NICKY: I want nine hundred brothers!

SANDY: But don't we have fun together? We play Babies and Rabbit Says . . . Daddy makes videos of us.

NICKY: I want nine hundred brothers!

SANDY: I'd like to have more babies, but I can't.

NICKY: Why not?

SANDY: We've been trying.

BILL: Ever since you were born.

NICKY: Is your baby hole broken?

BILL: Not exactly.

(Jeffrey starts packing up to leave.)

SANDY: There's nothing Mommy loves more than having babies, you know that.

BILL: We've been to special doctors.

NICKY: I want someone to play with!

SANDY: They can't seem to find any reason why we can't conceive again, it's just one of those things.

NICKY: I want to share my room with nine hundred brothers!

BILL: They say if she and the daddy try too hard the eggs will get scared and run away.

SANDY: "Scared and run away"? What are you talking about?

NICKY: I want a sister!

BILL *(Under his breath)*: You know . . . the pressure.

SANDY *(Likewise)*: Like *you're* the only one who feels pressure!

NICKY: Sisters are fun.

BILL: Hey, I'm the man.

SANDY: *Are* you?

NICKY: I want lots of sisters . . . with braids!

BILL: I'm doing the best I can.

NICKY: I want nine hundred sisters with long gold braids. Plus . . .

JEFFREY: The barren woman of the Gabon Tua tribe is considered a witch.

NICKY: *Plus* nine hundred brothers!

SANDY: It's just such a wonderful feeling . . . life fluttering inside you . . .

JEFFREY: The barren Tot woman is taken out and drowned.

SANDY *(Near tears)*: Sometimes I imagine I can feel you turning inside me . . .

BILL: We haven't given up, Nicky. We're still trying.

JEFFREY: In Arabic cultures, the barren woman is . . .

BILL: *Will you shut up?!*

SANDY: When I looked in the mirror this morning, I saw an old woman who could only conceive once.

JEFFREY *(Lifting Mia up under her arms)*: Well, we'd better get a wiggle on, we've got a plane to catch at the crack of dawn.

BILL: You can't leave yet, we haven't shown you our video of Nicky.

JEFFREY: We're flying to the tip of South America.

SANDY: My hair is falling out and I could only conceive once.

JEFFREY: A tribe of toddlers who can breathe underwater is waiting for us. *(Making strange watery sounds)*

(Mia comes to, making little mewing sounds.)

BILL *(Blocking his way)*: Not so fast . . . you said you'd see our video.

NICKY: I want to see the video, I want to see the video!

SANDY: Just stay another half hour.

BILL: We saw your slides. Fair is fair.

(Bill starts setting up the video.)

NICKY: *I want to see the video! I want to see the video!*

JEFFREY: We have two stopovers, one in Los Angeles and one in Rio. We're talking thirty-six hours in the air.

MIA *(Staggering around the room)*: Ohhhhhhhhh . . .

SANDY: Nicky was counting on you watching with us.

MIA: I feel as if I've been run over by a train!

JEFFREY *(Shaking Nicky's hand)*: Well, Nick, it was a great party. We'll send you postcards, lots of postcards. You can peel off the stamps for your collection. It must be pretty substantial by now.

BILL: You can't leave now, we're ready to roll.

NICKY *(Through an imaginary megaphone)*: Showtime!

SANDY: Showtime!

JEFFREY *(Kissing Sandy)*: Thanks for everything, Sandy. *(Cuffing Bill)* Keep the faith, Bill.

BILL: You'd better keep the faith, buddy boy, it's a jungle out there!

(Silence.)

MIA *(Lurching around the room)*: Ohhh . . . I'm so dizzy.

NICKY *(Grabbing her around the waist)*: Don't go!

MIA: I just had the most amazing dream. *(To Nicky)* It was about you!

NICKY: Me?

MIA: It was so strange . . .

SANDY AND BILL: Tell us, tell us!

JEFFREY *(Looking at his watch)*: You'd better make it quick, we've got to be at the airport by four a.m.

MIA: I dreamed I had a baby . . . and the baby was you. But instead of being normal size, you were tiny, only this big. *(Measuring with her thumb and forefinger)* And you were carved out of *ivory*.

SANDY: I love it! I love it!

NICKY (*Snuggling close to Mia*): More, more!

MIA: You were so small, I was afraid I'd lose you, so I wrapped you in cotton and put you in a soap dish.

BILL: Hear that, Nick? I guess she was hoping some of that soap would rub off on you!

NICKY: Shhhhhhhh!

MIA: Then suddenly I was in the middle of a forest . . . It was several weeks later and I'd lost you.

SANDY AND BILL: Oh no!

MIA: I was frantic. I started scouring the underbrush looking for you. Scary animals rustled around me, but I wasn't afraid.

JEFFREY (*Looking at his watch again*): Darling . . .

MIA: Then I saw this snow white cake in the distance. It was ten feet high and blazing with candles.

SANDY AND BILL: Nicky's birthday cake . . .

MIA: It started to glow with a great light. All the scary animals came out of hiding and started walking towards it. They paraded two by two, and then the cake turned into a kind of Noah's ark . . . this huge frosted ship. The next thing I knew, I was on board, still holding the empty soap dish. I started looking for you again . . . I raced along the deck and down through the galleys, past the lions, hippos and snakes but there was no sign of you, so I climbed up to the crow's nest and searched the horizon. I could see for miles . . . the ocean was everywhere . . . I gazed down at the ship. It had become very small, small enough to fit in a bottle . . . It was a perfect ivory miniature just like you. Then I realized . . . you were the ship, I'd never lost you. Sometimes you were a tiny baby, sometimes you were a cake, but you were always with me . . . On land, sea and in the air . . . You were my talisman, my magic charm . . . my boy . . .

(*Silence.*)

SANDY (*Moved to tears*): Oh, Mia . . .

BILL: Whoa . . .

JEFFREY (*Taking Mia's arm*): Darling . . .

NICKY (*To Mia*): I wish *you* were my mommy!

(*A shocked silence.*)

SANDY *(Stricken)*: *Nicky!*

BILL: What did you say?

NICKY *(Throwing his arms around Mia)*: I wish *you* were my mommy!

(A shorter silence.)

MIA *(Trying to pull away)*: Nicky, Nicky . . .

JEFFREY: Well . . . *tempus fugit.*

(Silence.)

SANDY *(Teary to Nicky)*: But what about Daddy and me?

NICKY: I want to be carved out of ivory.

BILL: He's overtired.

NICKY: I want to live in a soap dish.

SANDY: We won't have a son anymore.

NICKY: I want to be a birthday cake.

BILL: The poor kid didn't get any sleep last night.

MIA *(Heading toward the door)*: We'd better go . . .

NICKY: Stay! . . . Please!

MIA: We can't.

NICKY: Pretty please?

JEFFREY: It's getting late.

NICKY *(Struggling to hold on to Mia)*: Pretty, pretty please? With figs and kumquats on top!

JEFFREY: Our plane leaves in six hours.

NICKY *(Bursting into a flood of tears)*: Don't go! Don't!

MIA *(Extricating herself)*: There, there, be a brave boy.

JEFFREY: We'll send stamps, lots of stamps! One finds consolation in the strangest things these days.

MIA: Good-bye . . . good-bye . . . good-bye . . . good-bye . . . good-bye . . .

(And Jeffrey and Mia are gone. Silence.)

NICKY: They left.

SANDY: They left.

BILL: Ingrates!

NICKY: How could they leave?

BILL: That's Jeffrey and Mia for you. Always on the move. *(Imitating Jeffrey)* "Our plane leaves in six hours . . ." Big deal!

SANDY *(Imitating Mia)*: "I haven't even packed yet!" Well, don't forget your smelling salts!

BILL *(Imitating Jeffrey)*: "Get a wiggle on, darling, the Squawk children are waiting for us."

SANDY *(Imitating Mia)*: "They're half human and half parrot. Their heads and bodies are like yours and mine, but they have wings instead of arms and are covered with feathers . . . shocking pink feathers, the color of bubble gum." *(She squawks)* "You should see them flying through the trees! They look like fuzzy pink bedroom slippers!" *(Squawking more)* These are the children Jeffrey and Mia choose to spend their time with. Not normal boys and girls blowing out birthday candles and making wishes, but mutants, freaks . . . It's pathetic! I feel sorry for them!

(Pause.)

NICKY: Losers!

BILL: JERKS!

NICKY *(Running to the door, yelling after them)*: ASSHOLES!

SANDY AND BILL *(Shocked)*: Nicky!

NICKY *(Yelling louder and louder)*: DICKHEADS! BUTT-WADS!

BILL *(Pulling Nicky back inside, shutting the door)*: That's enough.

NICKY: *SCUMBAGS!*

(Silence.)

SANDY: What a day.

BILL: Unbelievable!

SANDY: Now what?

NICKY: I want to see my video. I want to see my video.

BILL: Well, shit on them, we'll see it without them!

SANDY *(Hand flying to her mouth)*: Oh no, my front tooth just fell out! Look! *(She flashes a smile with a blacked-out tooth)*

BILL: I don't need some . . . dried-up anthropologist to see my video. He fancies himself this great documentarian, but he didn't get any footage of those fucked-up monkey people. Not. One. Shot. All he's left with is his academic mumbo jumbo. There's no gathering in the family room to see a show, no sharing popcorn with Daddy's special lemonade . . . The guy's an island unto himself. To say nothing of his whacko wife . . . I feel sorry for them. I really do.

SANDY: I'll have to call the dentist tomorrow. I can't walk around like this. *(Smiling again)*

BILL *(Dimming the lights)*: All right, folks. Ready for one hell of a show?

NICKY: Showtime, showtime!

SANDY *(Showing Nicky)*: Look at Mommy's tooth, Nicky. What do you think?

(Bill sings a fanfare and starts the video.)

It looks so tiny lying in my hand.

NICKY: Will the whole video be just me?

SANDY: The other one's loose too.

(Light from the TV screen flickers across their faces. It becomes increasingly dappled as if they're at the ocean.)

BILL: Hey, Nicky!

NICKY: Hey, Daddy!

BILL: Hey, Sandy!

NICKY: Hey, Mommy!

SANDY: Nicky on his fourth birthday . . . My Nicky . . .

BILL: Four years old!

NICKY: Look! Look! Look! Look!

SANDY: Smell that air! The sea's all around us . . .

(We hear waves break in the distance. Bill and Nicky start laughing at the screen.)

(Wrapping her arms around Nicky) Four years ago today, you made us the happiest family in the world! Where did you come from? And how did you get here? *Our* Nicky . . . our boy . . . It's a miracle . . . a miracle!

(The lights focus on them in an endless embrace. The sound of the ocean gets louder and louder.)

Approaching
Zanzibar

Production History

Approaching Zanzibar received its world premiere in April 1989 by the Second Stage Theatre in New York City. It was directed by Carole Rothman. The set design was by Heidi Landesman, costume design was by Susan Hilferty, lighting design was by Dennis Parichy and sound design was by Gary and Timmy Harris. The production stage manager was Pamela Edington. The cast was as follows:

WALLACE BLOSSOM	Harris Yulin
CHARLOTTE BLOSSOM	Jane Alexander
TURNER BLOSSOM	Clayton Barclay Jones
PONY BLOSSOM	Angela Goethals
RANDY WANDS	Jamie Ross
PALACE ST. JOHN	Maggie Burke
FLETCHER ST. JOHN	Damien Jackson
SCOTTY CHILDS	Jamie Ross
JOY CHILDS	Aleta Mitchell
AMY CHILDS	Damien Jackson
DALIA PAZ	Aleta Mitchell
OLIVIA CHILDS	Bethel Leslie
DR. SYBIL WREN	Maggie Burke

Characters

WALLACE BLOSSOM, a composer, forty-nine

CHARLOTTE BLOSSOM, his wife, forty-five

TURNER BLOSSOM, their son, a prodigy, twelve

PONY BLOSSOM, their nearsighted daughter, nine

RANDY WANDS, a new father, forty-three

PALACE ST. JOHN, a hearty grandmother, sixty-three

FLETCHER ST. JOHN, her deaf grandson, eleven

SCOTTY CHILDS, Charlotte's brother, a landscape architect, forty-eight

JOY CHILDS, his new wife, African-American TV newscaster who's seven months pregnant, twenty-eight

AMY CHILDS, Scotty's athletic daughter, played by a boy, eleven

DALIA PAZ, Olivia's Mexican nurse, twenty-eight

OLIVIA CHILDS, Charlotte's aunt, an eminent site-specific artist, eighty-one

DR. SYBIL WREN, her doctor, with a severe limp, sixties

Author's Note

I always envisioned a set made of fabric, mimicking Olivia's evanescent installations. A lighter than air affair that could rise and fall, shimmer and change shape with the twist of a few hidden ropes. It worked beautifully under Heidi Landesman's artful hands in the world premiere at Second Stage.

Act One

Scene 1

The Blossoms are driving toward Falling Waters, West Virginia, in a station wagon. It's the first week of August, around ten in the evening. Wally's at the wheel and Charlotte sits next to him. Turner and Pony are piled in the back along with all their gear. Pony wears glasses. They're all singing "Ninety-nine Bottles of Beer on the Wall" with flagging energy.

ALL:
> Forty-four bottles of beer on the wall,
> Forty-four bottles of beer,
> If one of those bottles should happen to fall,
> Forty-three bottles of beer on the wall.
>
> Forty-three bottles of beer on the wall,
> Forty-three bottles of beer,
> If one of those bottles should happen to fall,
> Forty-two bottles of beer on the wall.
>
> Forty-two bottles of beer on the wall,
> Forty-two bottles of beer,

If one of those bottles should happen to fall,
Forty-one bottles of beer on the wall . . .

CHARLOTTE: STOP . . . STOP . . . I CAN'T TAKE IT ANYMORE!

WALLY, TURNER AND PONY:
Forty-one bottles of beer on the wall,
Forty-one bottles of beer,
If one of those bottles should happen to fall,
Forty bottles of beer on the wall.

CHARLOTTE: Pleeeease?

TURNER AND PONY *(Softly)*:
Forty bottles of beer on the wall,
Forty bottles of beer,
If one of those bottles should happen to fall . . .

WALLY: Your mother asked you to stop.

TURNER AND PONY *(Softer)*:
Thirty-nine bottles of beer on the wall,
Thirty-nine bottles of beer,
If one of those bottles should happen to fall . . .

CHARLOTTE: Kids?! . . .

TURNER AND PONY *(Barely audible)*:
Thirty-eight bottles of beer on the wall . . .

WALLY: IF YOU DON'T STOP RIGHT THIS MINUTE, I'M
PULLING OVER TO THE SIDE OF THE ROAD!

*(They keep humming. The sound of screeching brakes as Wally
veers over to the side of the road. They all lean to the right.)*

CHARLOTTE: LOOK OUT,   TURNER AND PONY:
LOOK OUT!   We stopped, we stopped!

*(A silence. Wally straightens the wheel and eases back onto the
road.)*

WALLY: Thank you.

(Charlotte sighs deeply. Silence as Wally drives.)

PONY: Are we there yet?

WALLY: We just started, for Christ sakes! We have two thousand more miles to go!

CHARLOTTE: Why do they always have to push us to the breaking point? Why? . . . It's not fair.

(Pause.)

WALLY *(Suddenly whirls around, glaring at the kids)*: Answer her! WHY DO YOU ALWAYS HAVE TO PUSH US TO THE BREAKING POINT, HUH? . . . HUH?! . . .

PONY: I didn't do anything.

TURNER: Don't look at me. Pony was the one who—

CHARLOTTE: WALLY, EYES ON THE ROAD, PLEASE!

PONY: Right, right, it's always *my* fault.

WALLY *(Turning back toward the road)*: Sorry, sorry . . .

TURNER *(To Pony)*: You were the one who kept singing.

PONY: You were singing, too.

CHARLOTTE *(To Wally)*: You're already breaking the speed limit as it is.

TURNER *(To Pony)*: That's not true.

WALLY *(To Charlotte)*: Are you complaining about the way I'm driving?

TURNER *(To Pony)*: I stopped when Dad asked me to.

PONY: You did not!

TURNER: I did so!

PONY: Did not!

TURNER: Did so!

WALLY *(To Charlotte)*: Hello? . . .

PONY: Did not!

(Faster and faster:)

TURNER: Did so!

PONY: Did not!

TURNER: Did so!

CHARLOTTE *(To Wally)*: I just wish you wouldn't go so fast.

PONY: Did not, did not, did NOT!

WALLY: Since when is sixty-five fast?

TURNER *(Shoving Pony)*: DID SO!

PONY: OW . . . OW . . . TURNER PUSHED ME!

CHARLOTTE: The speed limit is fifty-five.

WALLY: Would you like to drive?

(Pony bites Turner's arm.)

TURNER *(Leaping out of his seat)*: YIIIIII! PONY BIT ME!

CHARLOTTE: All I said was: you're breaking the speed limit. *(Turning around)* KIDS, PLEASE?! . . .

WALLY: I happen to be a safe driver.

(Turner gives Pony a noogie.)

PONY *(Leaping out of her seat)*: OW, OW . . . TURNER GAVE ME A NOOGIE, TURNER GAVE ME A NOOGIE!

(They start wrestling.)

PONY: I'm going to get you, Turner. Hold still! Will you hold still? Turrrner . . . ?!

TURNER: Oh . . . so you want to fight do you? . . . All right, Pony . . . say your prayers!

(The wrestling gets more ferocious.)

CHARLOTTE *(Whirling around)*: KIDS, WE ASKED YOU TO BEHAVE!

WALLY *(Also whirling around)*: ALL RIGHT, WHAT'S GOING ON BACK THERE?

CHARLOTTE *(Grabbing the wheel)*: LOOK OUT, LOOK OUT!

(They all veer to one side as the tires squeal.)

WALLY *(Grabbing it back)*: GIVE ME THAT WHEEL!

(They veer to the other side.)

CHARLOTTE: WALLY, WE ALMOST WENT OFF THE ROAD!

(The kids keep slugging each other.)

WALLY: JESUS CHRIST, CHARLOTTE . . .
CHARLOTTE: What are you trying to do . . . ? *Kill us?*
WALLY: . . . YOU DON'T GRAB THE STEERING WHEEL OUT OF SOMEONE'S HANDS!
CHARLOTTE: We were going off the road!

PONY: I hate you, I hate you, I hate you, I hate you, I hate you, I hate you, I hate you . . .	TURNER: If you hurt my hands, I'll smash you. I really mean it, I'll smash you!

(Wally pulls over to the side of the road and slams on the brakes. Everyone lurches forward and then back.)

CHARLOTTE: Wally, what are you . . . ?
WALLY: *All right, that's it! That's it!*

(A horrible silence.)

(Calm and collected) I can take a hint. If you don't like the way I'm driving, *you* drive! *(He gets out of the car, slams his door and marches over to the passenger side)*
CHARLOTTE: Wally . . . ?!

(He opens the door and pushes Charlotte over.)

Wally, what are you . . . ?
WALLY: Come on, move over, move over!
CHARLOTTE: *Wallace . . . ?!*
WALLY: I said . . . MOVE! *(He slams the door closed)*
CHARLOTTE: I didn't say I wanted to drive.
WALLY: Well, someone's got to drive if we want to make it to Rushing Rivers or wherever the hell it is . . .
CHARLOTTE: Hey, hey, *you* were the one who took the wrong turn off 81 . . .
WALLY: So now that's my fault too.
CHARLOTTE: And it's not Rushing Rivers, it's *Falling Waters*!

WALLY: Why we had to stop at Hershey, Pennsylvania, I'll never understand.

CHARLOTTE: Come on, you loved every minute of it!

WALLY: At the rate we're going, the campsite will be filled and we'll have to stay in a motel.

CHARLOTTE: Who had to go back in line a second time to watch the chocolate Kisses being poured and wrapped, hmmmm?

WALLY: It's so typical. Our first day on the road and we'll have to stay in a motel! Pay a hundred and fifty bucks to sleep in some gummy room with a broken air conditioner!

CHARLOTTE: We won't have to stay in a motel.

WALLY: If you'd been looking at the map instead of the god-damned speedometer all the time, I wouldn't have taken that turn!

CHARLOTTE: Okay, okay . . .

(Pause.)

CHARLOTTE: I just hate it when you speed. Especially with the kids in the car. It's just asking for trouble!	WALLY: I don't believe we're doing this . . . *Driving* to New Mexico. How did you ever talk me into it?

(Pause.)

If I hadn't grabbed the wheel, we'd all be lying dead in a ditch!	Do you know how many more states we have to go through . . . ?

(Pause.)

CHARLOTTE: Is that how you want to start our vacation? All being piled into body bags at the side of the road?

WALLY: . . . Virginia, North Carolina, Tennessee, Alabama . . .

CHARLOTTE: We're not going anywhere *near* Alabama!

WALLY: Kentucky, Missouri, Arkansas, Oklahoma . . .

CHARLOTTE: She's dying, honey.

WALLY: There are about a hundred and fifty states between New York and New Mexico.

CHARLOTTE: I want to say good-bye.

WALLY: The airplane was invented for a reason, you know.

PONY: Mommy . . . ?

WALLY: Texas alone is the size of China.

CHARLOTTE: But I don't fly.

WALLY: Why do you have to take it out on us?

CHARLOTTE: Turner's never played for her. I want her to hear him.

PONY: Mommy . . . ?

WALLY: It'll take us seventy-five years to get there.

CHARLOTTE *(Opening her window)*: God, it's hot in here!

WALLY: We'll all be in walkers!

CHARLOTTE: Who's always complaining that we never take a vacation?

PONY: *Mommy . . . ?*

WALLY *(Putting on a creaky old voice)*: "Well, hi there, Livvie, we finally made it! That *is* you, isn't it, Liv? I don't see so good anymore."

PONY: Mommy, what's Livvie dying of?

TURNER: God Pony! . . .

WALLY *(Still playing aged)*: "Hey there, Char, want to pass me my ear trumpet? I don't hear so good neither."

CHARLOTTE: We'll finally get to see the country . . . swim in fresh-water streams, camp out under the stars . . . *go fly-fishing*!

WALLY: Well, at least I convinced you to leave Spit and Wheat Germ behind in a kennel.

PONY: Oh Spit! . . .

TURNER: Spitty, Spitty, Spit!

PONY: I MISS SPIT!

CHARLOTTE: We're going to have a great time! I can feel it!

PONY: I MISS SPIT, I MISS SPIT, I MISS SPIT, I MISS SPIT, I MISS SPIT! . . .	TURNER: SPITTY, SPITTY SPIT! SPITTY, SPITTY SPIT! SPITTY, SPITTY SPIT! . . .

(They start barking.)

CHARLOTTE: We'll get to spend some time with Scotty and Joy. We haven't seen them since the wedding. *(Turning around)* Remember Joy, kids?

WALLY: She is one classy lady. I don't know how Scotty ever nabbed her.

CHARLOTTE *(To the kids)*: Come on, quiet down.
WALLY *(As a rallying cry)*: We'll get to see Amy again!
CHARLOTTE *(Groaning)*: Please!

(Pony and Turner are now baying, yelping, panting and making other assorted canine sounds.)

CHARLOTTE *(Whirling around)*: KIDS, PLEASE! DADDY AND I ARE TRYING TO HAVE A CONVERSATION!

WALLY *(Likewise)*: JESUS CHRIST GUYS, WILL YOU PIPE DOWN? THIS ISN'T A KENNEL!

(Silence.)

CHARLOTTE: God! . . .
WALLY: Give us a break!
CHARLOTTE: I mean, after a while . . .

(Silence.)

PONY *(In a tiny voice)*: Mommy . . . ?
WALLY: There *are* other people in the car, you know.
CHARLOTTE: Daddy and I have *some* rights . . .

(Silence.)

WALLY *(To Charlotte)*: So, are we going to sit here all night, or what?
PONY: Mommy . . . ?
CHARLOTTE: Oh right, right. Sorry. *(She swings back onto the road)*
TURNER: Where are we, anyway?
PONY: Mommy . . . ?
WALLY: *Who knows!*
PONY: I have to pee.
TURNER: You just went fifteen minutes ago.
CHARLOTTE: Why didn't you say something when we were stopped? *(Opening her window wider)* God, I'm burning up!
WALLY: So guys, is everyone ready for . . . *(Trumpet-fanfare sound)* Gamey Amy?!

CHARLOTTE *(Laughing)*:   TURNER: PONY: She's
Oh no!   Spare me!   so weird! . . .

WALLY: Boy Wonder of the Western World!

CHARLOTTE *(Trying not to laugh)*: Come on, don't be mean.

PONY: Mommy . . . ?

WALLY: The only eight-year-old girl I know who can throw a shot put fifty yards.

CHARLOTTE: Honey, she's eleven!

WALLY: And already shaving! *(He mimes using an electric razor)*

PONY: Mommy?

(Turner joins Wally shaving.)

CHARLOTTE *(Trying not to laugh)*: Come on, guys!

PONY: I have to pee, I have to pee!

WALLY: Charlotte, the girl's got sideburns and a mustache!

PONY: EWWWWWW!   TURNER: Gross, gross!

CHARLOTTE: She's just very athletic. Look at her mother.

WALLY: That's a marriage I'll never understand. Your brother and Inge Trim . . .

CHARLOTTE: She was blond, Swedish and a world-class track star.

TURNER: How many Olympic medals has she won?

WALLY: About three hundred. The woman lives to compete. I've never seen anything like it. She had Amy running a four-minute mile by the time she was seven.

CHARLOTTE: Honey . . . ?!

WALLY: And remember that craze with pole-vaulting? Amy would start tearing up the driveway with this special broomstick and then BOIIIIINGGGGG . . . she'd suddenly be flying over the family car!

CHARLOTTE: *Wally . . . ?!*

WALLY: Inge Trim . . . She had calves like a weightlifter.

PONY: I like Joy better.

CHARLOTTE: We all like Joy better. Scotty should have married her in the first place.

PONY: She's so beautiful.

CHARLOTTE: And *kind*! . . .

WALLY: She's also the first black newscaster in Oklahoma City, which is no small feat.

CHARLOTTE: She's wonderful. Amy adores her.

WALLY: Poor Amy.

CHARLOTTE: Poor Amy!

WALLY: Where was it she just won that big hang-gliding contest? . . . Colorado? Wyoming? Arizona? No, wait, I remember, it was in Salt Lake City.

TURNER: Hey, let's play Geography again!

PONY *(Clapping her hands)*: Geography, Geography, Geography!

CHARLOTTE: Oh, not again!

WALLY: Great idea!

PONY AND TURNER: Geography, Geography, Geography!

WALLY: Alabama!

TURNER: Arkansas! That ends in S, Pone.

PONY: I know, I know . . . South Dakota!

TURNER: Mom . . . ?

WALLY: It's your turn, Char.

CHARLOTTE *(Opening her window more)*: Sorry, sorry, I need more air.

TURNER: We're waiting . . .

CHARLOTTE *(Fanning herself as she drives)*: Okay, okay . . . what did you say?

WALLY, TURNER AND PONY: SOUTH DAKOTA!

CHARLOTTE *(Recoils from the blast)*: Arizona!

WALLY: Annapolis!

TURNER: Salem!

PONY: Mississippi!

WALLY: Islip!

TURNER: Islip? Where's Islip?

WALLY AND CHARLOTTE: Long Island.

WALLY: Go on Turner. You start with P.

TURNER: Um . . . Princeton!

(Faster and faster:)

PONY: New Mexico!

CHARLOTTE: Ohio!

WALLY: Oklahoma!

TURNER: Atlanta!

PONY: Alabama!

TURNER: Daddy already said Alabama. You're out, you're out.

WALLY AND CHARLOTTE: You're out, you're out!

PONY: No fair, no fair!

TURNER: Pony's out.

WALLY AND CHARLOTTE *(With an edge)*: Pony's out, Pony's out!

PONY *(Near tears)*: No fair, I'm always out first. It's not fair.

Scene 2

Luray, Virginia, two days and 134 miles later. It's eight in the morning and pouring rain. The Blossoms are huddled around the door of their tent in their pajamas, glumly staring out.

WALLY: Well, there goes our hike up White Oak Canyon Trail.

CHARLOTTE: Just our luck!

PONY *(Yelling out at it)*: LOUSY STINKY RAIN!

TURNER *(Leaning out the door, with his hands out, impressed)*: Whoa, look at it come down!

CHARLOTTE *(Pulling Turner back in)*: Get back in here, you'll get soaked!

WALLY: Well, at least it stopped thundering and lightning.

(A great crash of thunder and lightning shivers around them.)

PONY: HELP . . . HELP! . . .   TURNER: FAR OUT!

CHARLOTTE *(Terrified, drags them away from the door)*: LOOK OUT, LOOK OUT!

WALLY: Me and my big mouth!

CHARLOTTE *(Drops to the floor with her arms over her head)*: Quick, down on the floor.

TURNER: Mom . . . ?

WALLY: Take it easy, Charlotte.

CHARLOTTE *(Rocking back and forth)*: Our Father who art in Heaven, hallowed be thy name. Thy kingdom come, thy will be done on earth as it is in Heaven. Give us this day our daily bread . . .

TURNER: It was just a little thunder.

PONY (*Suddenly all smiles*): That was neat!

(*They stare at Charlotte as she continues to pray.*)

WALLY (*Goes over to Charlotte, offering her his hand*): Honey . . . ?

CHARLOTTE (*Being pulled to her feet*): Sorry, sorry. You know me and thunderstorms . . .

TURNER: Did you know that fireflies are immune to lightning? It just bounces right off them.

WALLY: Where did you hear that?

TURNER: Salvatore Argenti told me.

CHARLOTTE: God, it looks as if a bomb went off in here!

WALLY: Salvatore Argenti . . . ?

CHARLOTTE: Come on guys, what do you say we start straightening up? (*She begins folding a brightly woven blanket*)

TURNER: He told me during our master class last month.

CHARLOTTE: Wal, want to give me a hand with this?

WALLY: He did? Where was I? (*He helps Charlotte fold*) This is really beautiful. You know you're a damned good weaver.

CHARLOTTE: Why, thank you.

WALLY: I wish you'd take it more seriously.

CHARLOTTE: Honey, I don't have time anymore what with the kids . . .

TURNER: He said that because they're already filled with light, they can never be hurt by it. It's the same with electric eels . . .

CHARLOTTE (*Voice lowered*): He was using it as a metaphor about prodigies.

WALLY: Right, right, I remember.

TURNER: They can't be electrocuted.

(*Pony runs to a corner of the tent and stands on her head.*)

CHARLOTTE: Too much talent never destroyed anyone.

PONY: HEY, EVERYBODY LOOK AT ME!

TURNER: Pony, one of these days your brains are going to fall out. They're just going to start oozing out your ears.

WALLY (*Starts folding a sleeping bag*): It's the goddamned world that mucks everything up. You're plodding along writing your trios and suites and . . . FOOM . . .

TURNER: Blub, blub, blub . . .

WALLY: . . . suddenly the melodies elude you.

PONY: It's so neat seeing everything upside down.

WALLY: A great silence descends . . .

CHARLOTTE *(Also folding a bag)*: Careful, Pony, or you'll break your glasses again. Come on, kids, pitch in.

WALLY: Thank God for teaching.

PONY: Your mouths look so funny when you talk . . . *(She exaggerates her jaw movements)* Ba ba ba ba ba ba ba . . .

WALLY *(Moving on to the kids' sleeping bags)*: So . . . how did everybody sleep last night?

CHARLOTTE: Don't ask. *(Mopping her brow)* God, it's hot in here!

PONY: You look like marionettes . . . Ba ba ba ba ba . . .

CHARLOTTE *(To Wally)*: I heard the baby again.

WALLY: Honey, it's just a dream.

PONY: Come on, Turn, join me. It's so fun. Ba ba ba ba . . .

TURNER: Yeah? . . . *(He stands on his head next to her)*

CHARLOTTE: Wally, I heard it!

WALLY: People don't abandon babies in the wilderness. They leave them in bus terminals or movie theaters.

CHARLOTTE: It was sobbing and sobbing as if its little heart would break.

TURNER: This *is* neat! *(Imitating them)* Ba ba ba ba ba . . .

CHARLOTTE: I almost went out to look for him.

WALLY: Him? How do you know it's a boy?

CHARLOTTE: Because I saw him.

WALLY: You *saw* him? When did you see him?

CHARLOTTE: The night before last.

WALLY: But we were in West Virginia.

(Turner and Pony flop back down to their feet to listen.)

CHARLOTTE: It's weird, he's been following us . . . I finally went out and looked for him last night. I found him nestled in a bed of dandelions under a hawthorn bush . . . He's a sort of changeling with bright blue eyes and berries in his hair. He has pointed ears and the rosiest cheeks you've ever seen. They look like little hearts pulsing under his skin . . . I know, I know, I sound like a lunatic, but I've seen him. He smells like cinnamon and has this wonderful rippling laugh like a grown man . . .

TURNER *(Suddenly freezing)*: SSSSHHHHHHHH!
CHARLOTTE *(In a whisper)*: What is it?
TURNER: Nobody move.
CHARLOTTE: *Turner . . . ?!*
TURNER: Listen.

(Dead silence.)

CHARLOTTE *(In a whisper)*: I don't hear anything.
WALLY: Neither do I.
TURNER: Shhhhh! Quiet!

(Pony starts to whimper in fear.)

WALLY, CHARLOTTE AND TURNER *(Whispered)*: Pony . . . !

(She stops. Dead silence.)

TURNER *(Barely audible)*: There it is again.
WALLY: *What?*
TURNER: The earth is turning.
WALLY: What are you talking about?
TURNER: Shhhh!

(Silence.)

PONY *(In a whisper)*: I hear it.
WALLY: It's something outside the tent.
PONY *(Barely audible)*: It's bears. Big. Black. Bears!
WALLY: An animal of some kind.
CHARLOTTE: Oh, I hear it, too!
WALLY, TURNER AND PONY *(To Charlotte)*: SSHHHHHH!
TURNER: It's the humming of the spheres . . .
WALLY: Raccoons!
CHARLOTTE *(In a whisper)*: It's someone with a limp.

(Pony whimpers.)

TURNER: . . . suns and planets moving through space . . .
CHARLOTTE: They're coming closer!

PONY *(Clinging to Charlotte)*: It's the boogeyman, it's the boogeyman!

WALLY *(Prepared for the worst)*: Stand back!

TURNER *(Transported)*: It sounds like people singing . . .

(They freeze as we all hear a wondrous faraway sound. Charlotte gasps.)

PONY: I hear it, I hear it!

CHARLOTTE *(Enchanted)*: Oh, Turner . . .

TURNER: What did I tell you?

WALLY: Only you . . .

CHARLOTTE *(Murmuring)*: Turner, Turner . . .

Scene 3

The Blossoms have just reached a spectacular lookout high up in the Blue Ridge Mountains. It's a perfect afternoon one day and 122 miles later. Standing with them are Randy Wands with his three-week-old baby, William, strapped to his chest. They're all gazing at the view, frozen with awe. Nothing happens for several moments.

Charlotte takes a deep breath. Wally focuses his camera. Turner beats his chest. Pony plucks a nearby wildflower. Silence.

CHARLOTTE: Oh, Wally . . .

(Turner yodels like an ape.)

WALLY *(Snaps his picture)*: Got it!

RANDY *(Turning so William can see the view)*: Well, William, what do you think?

(Pony eats the flower.)

WALLY: The Blue Ridge Mountains . . .

CHARLOTTE: Look! . . . *(She sighs deeply)*

RANDY *(To William)*: Pretty impressive, eh what?

WALLY: . . . one of the oldest land areas on earth.

(Turner beats his chest and yodels again. Pony joins him.)

We're talking over four hundred million years here. The Fertile Crescent was still underwater.

RANDY *(To the others)*: This is his first time up here.

CHARLOTTE: You can see forever.

RANDY: You think this is something, you ought to see it after a snowfall. It's like standing on top of the North Pole. White . . . white . . . white!

CHARLOTTE *(Hands over her ears)*: Kids, please?!

(Turner and Pony stop.)

RANDY: Forget the sledding! . . . My wife and I have already bought him one of those aluminum numbers that looks like a satellite dish. Woooosh! . . . I can't wait! My daddy used to bring me up here when I was little. We'd ease down on that old Flexible Flyer and go belly whopping all the way to Nashville and back. My mother'd have to pry us off with a crowbar . . . and then summers we'd come up here with chili dogs and soda and play our harmonicas. He was good, he was real good. When he got going, the bears would come popping out of those bushes and start stomping their feet like there was no tomorrow! . . .

(He pulls out a harmonica and plays a few lively measures.)

PONY: My brother plays, too.

RANDY: No kidding?

PONY: He's a prodigy. His name is Turner Blossom.

TURNER: *Pony . . . ?!*

WALLY: Now, Pony . . .

RANDY *(Handing him the harmonica)*: Well, come on, let's hear you do your stuff!

TURNER: I play the guitar.

PONY *(More and more braggy)*: The classical guitar. He's been touched by God.

(She plucks another wildflower and starts eating the petals.)

TURNER *(Blazing with embarrassment)*: Pony?!

WALLY *(To Pony)*: Easy, honey . . . and take that flower out of your mouth. What is this with suddenly eating flowers all the time?

PONY *(She quickly swallows it)*: He goes to Juilliard and everything.

TURNER *(To Pony)*: Will you stop it?

PONY: He's even played with symphony orchestras.

TURNER *(Lunging after her)*: I'm going to kill her!

WALLY *(Trying to restrain him)*: Easy, easy . . .

PONY: My daddy's a composer. His name is Wallace Blossom.

WALLY: All right, Pony, cool it.

PONY: He teaches at Juilliard.

RANDY: Well, you sound like quite a family.

PONY: He wrote *The Atlantic Suite*.

(A pause.)

RANDY *(Trying to place it)*: The Atlantic Suite . . . ?

PONY *(Eager)*: Have you heard it?

WALLY: Pony, enough is enough!

PONY: It's played all over the world.

WALLY: Rio and Tokyo are hardly the whole world, and that was three years ago.

CHARLOTTE *(To Wally)*: Now, now . . .

RANDY: Well, William, it looks as if we've stumbled into some pretty fancy company here.

(Charlotte sneaks a look at William.)

WALLY: No, make it four . . . four and a half, to be more accurate. And at the rate I'm going, it'll be twenty years before I come up with something else. *(He goes and stands by himself)*

CHARLOTTE: Wally . . . ?

RANDY: So, where are you folks from?

CHARLOTTE: Hastings, New York. *(To Wally)* Honey . . . ?

RANDY: Say, you wouldn't know Panda Orenstein, would you?

CHARLOTTE: Panda Orenstein . . . ?

RANDY: Tall, red hair . . . she drives a green pickup truck . . . ?

CHARLOTTE: I know a Panda Vogel, but not a Panda Orenstein. Sorry.

RANDY: Great legs! I was real sweet on her once. Whoooie, that Panda Orenstein was something else! *(Pause)* So, where are you heading?

CHARLOTTE: Taos, New Mexico. *(She glances at William again)*

RANDY: *New Mexico?!*

CHARLOTTE: We're driving across the country to visit my aunt.

PONY: Olivia Childs, the famous artist who builds fabric mounds and circles in the desert.

TURNER *(Turning his back)*: I don't know her.

RANDY *(To Charlotte)*: Your aunt is Olivia Childs . . . ? *(To William)* Did you hear that, William, these people are related to Olivia Childs.

PONY: She just finished a circle of one thousand kites.

RANDY: Right, right, I read about it in the paper. What's it called . . . ?

CHARLOTTE AND PONY: *Ring of Prayer.*

RANDY: That's right, *Ring of Prayer* . . . a giant circle of snow white kites.

WALLY *(Rejoining them with his camera)*: Come on guys, I want to take a picture of you up here.

RANDY: How does she come up with that stuff? Decorating the desert with sails and parachutes and wedding veils . . . ?

CHARLOTTE: Her pieces mark sacred Indian sites.

RANDY: But don't they blow away?

CHARLOTTE: That's the whole point. Her work celebrates its vulnerability to nature . . . Prayer is eternal, but our shrines are made of air.

WALLY *(Waving at his family)*: Scrunch together!

CHARLOTTE *(Gazes at sleeping William and whispers)*: What a beautiful baby.

RANDY: Why thank you.

CHARLOTTE *(Touching William's face)*: His *skin* . . . !

WALLY *(Motioning to Charlotte)*: Come on, guys, let's have a little cooperation here.

CHARLOTTE *(To Randy)*: How old is he?

RANDY: Just three weeks.

WALLY: *Sweetheart . . . ?*

CHARLOTTE: Can't you see I'm involved in something else?

WALLY: If we want photographs of this trip, someone's got to take them.

CHARLOTTE *(To Wally)*: All right, all right. Come on, kids, Daddy wants to take a picture of us.

RANDY: Well, I hope you have a great time with that aunt of yours. She sounds like quite a woman.

PONY: She's dying of cancer.

CHARLOTTE: *Pony . . . . ?!*

RANDY: I'm so sorry, that's the worst . . .

CHARLOTTE *(Pulling the kids closer)*: Tell me about it.

WALLY *(Shaking his head)*: Please!

RANDY: . . . the worst!

(Charlotte heaves a deep sigh. Palace St. John, a hearty woman in her sixties, and Fletcher, her deaf grandson, join them and gaze out at the view.)

CHARLOTTE *(Nodding toward Wally)*: He lost both his parents last year. Both!

PONY: She may not even be alive when we get there.

RANDY: To every thing there is a season, and a time to every purpose under Heaven.

(An uncomfortable silence.)

(Undaunted) A time to be born, and a time to die, a time to plant and a time to pluck up that which is planted . . .

WALLY: Okay, guys, say "cheese."

(They mournfully say "cheese.")

Come on, smile!

(They try again, forced.)

CHARLOTTE: Honestly dear, your sense of timing . . . !

(Fletcher approaches Wally and reaches for his camera with authority.)

PALACE: Let my grandson take it so you can be in it, too. He's a whiz with cameras.

WALLY: Yeah? *(He hands it to him)* Well, thanks a lot.

(Charlotte suddenly rips open her blouse and starts fanning herself.)

CHARLOTTE: God, it's hot up here!
WALLY: Charlotte . . . ?
TURNER: Mom . . . ?!

(Fletcher snaps away.)

RANDY: Take it off, take it off!
WALLY: . . . What *are* you doing?
RANDY *(Laughing)*: I love it, I love it!
CHARLOTTE *(Fanning herself with both hands)*: Well, I guess these are the hot flashes my doctor was warning me about, though I still say I'm much too young to be going through this.
WALLY *(Indicating she's exposed)*: Honey . . . ?
CHARLOTTE *(Quickly buttons herself back up, laughing)*: Oh, sorry, sorry . . . *(To Fletcher)* Sorry.

(Fletcher starts arranging everyone into a classic family portrait.)

WALLY *(Hushed)*: She's right, the boy *is* good!
PONY: This is so fun!
WALLY *(To Charlotte)*: Now we'll really have something to show for this crazy escapade of ours.

(Fletcher suddenly pulls Pony away from the others and places her in her own special row in front. He then snaps the picture and hands the camera back to Wally.)

Thanks a lot, that was terrific.
CHARLOTTE: Yes, you're really wonderful. Say thank you, kids.
TURNER: Thank you.
PONY: More, more!
CHARLOTTE: Now, Pony.
PONY *(Pulling on Fletcher)*: More, more! . . .

PALACE *(Hugging him)*: Yes, Fletcher has quite an eye . . .

RANDY: Well, William, we better head back home or Mom and the twins will think we've run away to join the circus.

CHARLOTTE *(Gazing at William again)*: Kids, you've got to come see this baby, he's awake now.

PONY *(Joining her)*: Ohhh, he's so cute!

PALACE: He's just beautiful.

RANDY: Here, let's get you out of this thing so everyone can get a good look at you.

WALLY *(Chucking William under the chin)*: Well hi there, bright eyes, what's happening?

CHARLOTTE: He's precious.

RANDY: Say thank you, William.

CHARLOTTE: Just precious!

PONY: Look at his fingers, they're like candy corns.

WALLY *(Talking baby talk and making faces)*: Is someone trying to smile, hmmm? Yes, yes, yes! . . . *(He makes more faces)*

RANDY: Well, William, is everyone admiring you?

WALLY: Yes! You can do it. Let's see those rosy gums . . .

RANDY *(Lowering his head into William)*: Willie, Willie, Willie! *(He makes loud buffling noises into the baby's stomach)*

WALLY: YES! LITTLE BABY. Ba ba ba ba ba! Little cheeks! What have you got in here . . . ? Tennis balls?

TURNER *(Pulling on Wally's sleeve)*: Easy, Dad, easy . . .

WALLY *(Recovering)*: Sorry, sorry . . .

CHARLOTTE: He really is spectacular.

PONY: Aren't you afraid he's going to break?

PALACE: Babies are very strong.

FLETCHER *(Signs to Palace)*: What day was he born?

PONY: *He's deaf?!* . . .

(The Blossoms and Randy stare open-mouthed at Fletcher.)

CHARLOTTE AND WALLY *(Catching themselves; to Pony)*: Shhhhh!

PONY *(In a whisper)*: Sorry, sorry . . .

CHARLOTTE *(Quietly)*: Honestly, Pony!

(An awkward silence.)

PALACE: He wants to know when his birthday was.

RANDY *(Too loud)*: JULY 7TH!

PALACE *(Signs back to Fletcher)*: July 7th.

CHARLOTTE: July 7th? That's Livvie's birthday! *(To Randy)* Olivia Childs. She just turned eighty-one. Did you hear that, Wally? The baby was born on the same day as Livvie. What a coincidence!

FLETCHER *(Signs to Palace)*: What time was he born?

PALACE: He wants to know what time he was born.

RANDY: Six-thirteen a.m. ELEVEN POUNDS, THREE OUNCES.

PALACE *(To Randy)*: You don't have to yell, he can't hear you anyway.

RANDY *(Mortified)*: Right, right . . . *(To Fletcher)* Sorry about that.

PALACE *(Signs to Fletcher)*: Six-thirteen a.m. Eleven pounds, three ounces.

PONY: Ohhh, I want him, I want him!

WALLY: He's a great baby.

(A silence as they all gaze at William.)

FLETCHER *(Touches William's head and signs)*: He will be a leader of men.

PALACE: He says William will be a leader of men.

FLETCHER *(Signs)*: Your son was born under a highly elegant and aristocratic confluence of the planets.

(Palace translates. Everyone gapes at Fletcher.)

(Signs) Because he was born on the seventh day of the seventh month, he's a totally evolved Cancerian who'll operate in large social dimensions.

(Palace translates.)

RANDY: Oh, William, listen! . . .

FLETCHER *(Signs)*: His whole being cries out for the common good.

(Palace translates.)

(Signs) He'll not only lead, he'll also create—forging bold new philosophies of tolerance and trust.

(Palace translates.)

RANDY: You hear that, William?

FLETCHER *(His signing gets more and more expansive)*: Like a precious jewel flung into a pond, his imprint will shiver and reverberate long after he's gone.

(Palace translates.)

(Signs with foreboding) But be warned . . .

(Palace translates.)

CHARLOTTE: Oh no . . .

RANDY: What, what?

FLETCHER *(Signs)*: He will have to pay a price for these gifts . . .

(Palace translates.)

WALLY: I knew it!

CHARLOTTE *(Hands over her ears)*: I can't listen.

RANDY: What, what? Tell me!

FLETCHER *(Signs)*: His natal moon is in Scorpio, the demon sign . . .

(Palace translates.)

(Signs) Just as he moves to better mankind, the scorpion's poison will flood his senses . . .

(Palace translates.)

RANDY: Stop, stop!

FLETCHER *(Signs)*: He'll be racked with jealousy and desire . . .

(Palace translates.)

RANDY: Please!

FLETCHER *(Signs)*: But all is not lost . . .

(Palace translates.)

(Signs) Because of your son's fortunate trine aspect, he will vanquish the powers of darkness and walk in eternal light.

(Palace translates. Silence.)

RANDY: Did you hear that, William? You're going to be a great man. I knew it, I knew it! *(He covers him with kisses)*

CHARLOTTE: Ohh, that was amazing, just amazing!

TURNER: How does he know all that?

PALACE: Fletcher's a psychic. He can read destinies through any medium . . . astrology, cards, palms . . .

PONY *(Pulling on Charlotte's arm)*: Oh, have another baby, Mommy. Have another baby!

RANDY: It's the way he expressed it.

PALACE: Yes, Fletcher's quite a boy. *(She signs to him)* They're all very impressed with you.

PONY: It would be so fun.

TURNER: Yeah, have another.

RANDY *(Puts William back in his carrier)*: Well, William, we'd better make tracks or Mom will be calling the ranger station.

PONY *(Pulling on Charlotte)*: Please?

TURNER: Please?

RANDY *(Shakes Palace's hand)*: It was a pleasure meeting you folks, and as for your grandson here, he's real special, real special! *(He squeezes Fletcher's arm, then waves to the Blossoms)* Be good. *(And he's gone)*

PONY: We'd help you take care of it.

CHARLOTTE: What's all this about having babies all of a sudden?

TURNER: Come on . . .

PONY: Ohhh, maybe it would be twins!

TURNER: Or triplets!

WALLY: Hey, hey, give your poor mother a break here.

PONY: Oh triplets! Go for it, Mommy!

CHARLOTTE *(Laughing)*: Please!

PALACE: I had five myself. *(She signs to Fletcher)* Her kids want her to have more babies.

FLETCHER *(Signs)*: Babies are great.

PALACE *(Speaking and signing at the same time)*: Babies *are* great, but they're a lot of work. *(To the others)* There are long stretches of time I have absolutely no memory of.

PONY: It would be so neat. Babies in the kitchen, babies in the hall, babies rolling down the stairs . . . *(Clinging to Charlotte)* Goo goo, gaa gaa . . . goo goo, gaa gaa . . .

TURNER *(Likewise)*: Babies in the yard, babies pouring out of the faucets . . . waa waa, waa waa . . .

WALLY: Come on, kids, cool it.

CHARLOTTE: I'm afraid it's too late.

PALACE: It's never too late. My mother had me when she was forty-seven. She didn't even know she was pregnant. She thought she had the flu.

PONY: Please? Pretty please?

CHARLOTTE: I can't.

PALACE: Who says you can't?

WALLY: Her body says she can't.

(Charlotte breaks away from them.)

PALACE: Oh, I'm so sorry.

(Signing, she leads Fletcher away.)

Come on, sweetheart, I'll explain later.

PONY: What's wrong with Mommy?

(Charlotte weeps and weeps.)

TURNER: Mom, are you okay?

CHARLOTTE: Oh, Wally, I can't bear it . . . I'll never feel life moving inside me again . . .

WALLY *(Arms around the kids)*: Hey, hey, you've still got Turner and Pony . . .

CHARLOTTE *(Racked)*: No, no, you don't understand . . .

WALLY *(Not moving)*: Honey, honey . . .

CHARLOTTE: It's like . . . like part of me's dying . . . The best part.

Scene 4

Wally and Turner are fly-fishing side by side in a mountain stream in Asheville, North Carolina. It's late afternoon the next day, 250 miles later. Wally's wearing beat-up old hip boots and his fishing hat. Turner's barefoot in shorts and a light jacket. A liquid calm prevails.

WALLY: This is heaven . . . heaven!

TURNER: You said it.

WALLY: No one here except you and me. *(Pause)* And of course the fish.

TURNER: Fish are great.

WALLY: Fish *are* great! *(He casts)* Boom!,

TURNER: They're so weird! What are they, anyway?

WALLY: Souls. Departed human souls.

TURNER: Come on . . .

WALLY: We begin life in water, so it's where we end up.

TURNER: Where did you get that? *(He casts with too much force)*

WALLY: Common sense. Our souls have to go somewhere. Oceans and streams are the only places left with any room, so they turn into fish. No, no, just flick your wrist like this. *(He demonstrates)* See? Flick!

(Turner does a sloppy repeat.)

Don't *throw* it out. Just toss it out. It's all in the wrist. *(He demonstrates again)* Flick . . . flick . . . flick!

TURNER: Wait a minute, are you saying that all those trout darting around down there were once people?

WALLY: You got it. *(He casts again)* See that?

TURNER: That we'll be cooking up some bank robber or dead housewife for dinner?

WALLY: I hardly moved my arm at all. Bank robber, Indian brave, Joan of Arc . . . it could be anyone.

TURNER: And that I'm going to end up as a guppy or goldfish? That I'll spend all eternity swimming around in some kid's grimy fish tank? . . .

WALLY: Not necessarily . . . you could get lucky and end up as a swordfish or twelve-ton tuna swimming off the coast of Bali.

And it's not forever. You keep changing species . . . stingray
one year, smallmouth bass the next . . .

TURNER *(Casts so violently, he accidentally throws his pole into
the water)*: Whoops!

WALLY: JESUS, TURNER!

TURNER *(Scrambles to pick it up)*: Sorry, sorry . . .

WALLY: I SAID: DON'T THROW IT!

TURNER: I'm sorry.

WALLY *(Reaching it first)*: That's a two-hundred-dollar rod and
reel you've got there!

TURNER: I'm really sorry.

WALLY *(Wipes it off)*: Son of a bitch! *(A silence as he inspects it)*
Well, you were lucky this time.

TURNER: It just flew out of my hands.

WALLY *(Handing it back to him)*: Okay, here you go.

TURNER *(Doesn't take it)*: No, I think I'll just watch.

WALLY: Come on, take it.

TURNER: I like watching you.

WALLY *(Forcing it on him)*: Will you take it?!

TURNER: Okay, okay . . .

WALLY: I've finally got a chance to teach you something I'm really
good at, so take advantage of it!

TURNER: Okay.

(Silence.)

WALLY: I happen to be an ace when it comes to fly-fishing.

TURNER: I know.

(Silence.)

WALLY: So pay attention.

TURNER: Okay, I'm with you.

WALLY *(Picking up his rod again)*: It's like making music. The
whole thing is to stay loose. *(He casts)* See that?

TURNER: Nice!

WALLY: Boom!

TURNER: Very nice, Dad.

WALLY: Just put it right out there!

TURNER *(Prepares to cast)*: All right fish: Say your prayers.

WALLY: And . . .

TURNER *(Casts much better)*: Boom!

WALLY: Yes!

TURNER: I did it!

WALLY: It's all about the fine art of letting go.

TURNER *(Reeling in the line)*: This is fun.

WALLY: It's like when I was writing *The Atlantic Suite.* I could do no wrong. The melodies just kept coming. Adagios and obbligatos unfurled all around me. Cadenzas shivered overhead, fanfares swelled underfoot . . . I wrote them down as fast as I could. It was amazing. Incredible! *(He casts again)* Boom!

TURNER: Or my spring recital at Juilliard. I was in a trance. It was so weird, I had the feeling my fingers had turned into a flock of parakeets or canaries . . . I kept expecting to see all these feathers floating out over the audience. *(He makes eerie sound effects, then casts beautifully)*

WALLY: Then, poof, it was all over. Granddad and Mamie both got sick, I was put in charge, and ashes, ashes, we all fall down. Though I can't blame everything on them. I just lost it, that's all. It can happen to anyone. The trick is to accept it and go down gracefully. Right, old buddy? Blub, blub, blub . . . *(Casts too vehemently and gets the line tangled)* Whoops!

TURNER: Hey, I think I got it!

WALLY *(Struggling to untangle it)*: Shit!

TURNER: Watch, Dad!

WALLY: Goddamnit!

TURNER *(Casts perfectly)*: Boom!

WALLY *(Making a worse and worse mess of it)*: What's wrong with this fucking line?

TURNER: Did you see that?

WALLY: I knew that guy sold me the wrong weight!

TURNER: Dad . . . ?

WALLY: Stupid asshole!

TURNER: I can do it now.

WALLY: You can do *what*?

TURNER: Cast.

WALLY: Well, any idiot can cast if they have the right line!

TURNER: Want to see?

WALLY *(Doubled-up over his reel)*: Do you believe this?!

TURNER *(Casts perfectly)*: And . . . boom!

WALLY *(Tearing the line off the reel)*: We drive thirty miles to go fishing in this great secluded mountain stream and what happens? . . . The goddamned line breaks on me! . . . *Unbelievable!*

TURNER *(Offering him his rod)*: Here, use mine.

WALLY: I don't want yours.

TURNER: Come on, take it . . .

WALLY: I said: *I don't want it!*

TURNER: But you were doing great.

WALLY: No, *you* were the one that was doing great, not me.

TURNER *(Trying to press it on him)*: Come on, Dad...

WALLY *(Pulls his line every which way, then finally flings his rod into the water)*: Oh fuck it! Just fuck the whole goddamned thing!

TURNER *(Offering his rod again, eyes filling with tears)*: Dad . . . ?!

Scene 5

Midnight, two days and 70 miles later. The Blossoms' tent is nestled in a moonlit clearing high up in the Smoky Mountains. Everyone's asleep except for Charlotte, who's sitting stock-still, straining to hear something. It's pitch black and eerie, woodland sounds abound. A baby suddenly cries.

CHARLOTTE *(In a whisper)*: Wally . . . ? *Wally?*

WALLY *(Half asleep)*: Uuuhhhh . . .

CHARLOTTE: Listen!

WALLY: Uuuhhhh . . .

CHARLOTTE: There it is again.

> *(The crying stops and then resumes, sounding less and less like a baby.)*

> *(Getting out of her sleeping bag)* It's the baby.

WALLY *(Waking up)*: Hey, where are you going?

CHARLOTTE: He's been crying all night.

WALLY *(Grabbing her arm, amorous)*: I was just dreaming about you.

CHARLOTTE: I'll be right back.

WALLY: Hey, hey, not so fast! *(He tries to pull her into his sleeping bag)*

CHARLOTTE *(Resists, laughing)*: Honey . . . ?!

WALLY: Come here.

CHARLOTTE: What are you doing?

WALLY: Trying to get you into my sleeping bag.

(The crying becomes more and more catlike.)

CHARLOTTE: Wait! . . . Listen!

WALLY: Sweetheart, it's a stray cat! *(Nuzzling against her)* Mmmm, you smell so good!

CHARLOTTE *(Resisting)*: Wally . . . ?!

WALLY *(Pulling her into his bag)*: Come on, get in here. I never get to be alone with you anymore.

(Thuds and crashes as he tries to haul her in.)

CHARLOTTE: Honey, there isn't room! . . . Gosh, you're right, that does sound like a cat!

WALLY: Mmmmm, you're so warm! *(A crash)* Whoops!

CHARLOTTE: Shhh! You'll wake the kids.

WALLY *(Trying to pull off her top)*: Come on, let's get this off. *(He accidentally pokes her in the eye)*

CHARLOTTE: Ow!

WALLY: Sorry, sorry . . .

CHARLOTTE: You hit me in the eye.

WALLY: I'm sorry. There. Is that better?

CHARLOTTE *(She starts to giggle)*: I don't believe this!

WALLY: Here, lift up a little.

(Pony moans in her sleep.)

CHARLOTTE *(Sitting up like a bolt)*: What was that?

WALLY *(Trying to get at her legs)*: What have you got on here?

CHARLOTTE: Shhh!

WALLY: Hiking boots?

CHARLOTTE *(In a whisper)*: Turner, is that you?

WALLY: Since when did you start wearing hiking boots to bed?

(He drops one to the ground)

(Pony moans again.)

CHARLOTTE: Turner . . . ?

WALLY: Goddamned sweatpants! *(He gets them off)* Ahhh, this is more like it!

CHARLOTTE: Take off your shirt.

WALLY: Talk to me, talk to me.

(They embrace, laughing and groaning. Pony moans again.)

CHARLOTTE: Honey, we're waking up the kids.

WALLY: Fuck the kids!

CHARLOTTE: WALLY?!

WALLY: What do you think families did in the old days when everybody slept in one room?

CHARLOTTE: This isn't the old days.

WALLY: Our Founding Fathers didn't have separate bedrooms and look how well they turned out! Mmmm, you're so soft! I'd forgotten how soft you were!

CHARLOTTE *(Trying to break away)*: I just can't in front of them . . .

(Wally croons with pleasure.)

PONY *(Whimpering in her sleep)*: Stop, stop! I didn't do it, I didn't do it!

(Charlotte struggles to get out of the bag.)

WALLY: Hey, where are you going?

PONY: No, no . . . put it down . . . Melinda's in the kitchen with the ocean player.

CHARLOTTE: Turner's having a nightmare.

WALLY: Kids have nightmares. And that isn't Turner, it's Pony. *(Getting out of his sleeping bag, pulling her with him)* Come on, let's get out of here!

CHARLOTTE: Wallace . . . ?!

WALLY: Let's take a walk.

CHARLOTTE: But what about the kids?

PONY: Eeewwwww, there's a spider, look out, look out!

WALLY: They're asleep.

CHARLOTTE: And what if they wake up?

WALLY: They won't.

CHARLOTTE: How do you know?

WALLY: Because they never wake up in the middle of the night.

CHARLOTTE: Wally, you've lost your mind!

WALLY (Grabbing her arm): Come on, let's go.

CHARLOTTE: Honey, you don't leave two small children alone in the middle of the Smoky Mountains!

WALLY: Don't we have any rights around here?

CHARLOTTE: I don't believe this!

WALLY (Getting madder and madder): I mean, isn't this our vacation, too?

CHARLOTTE: Shhh shhh, not so loud!

WALLY: What about us for a change? You and me?

CHARLOTTE: Oh God . . . !

WALLY: You only care about them!

CHARLOTTE: That isn't true.

WALLY: It is so! It's always the kids this, the kids that . . .

CHARLOTTE (Trying to hush him): Honey, please . . . ?!

WALLY: See what I mean? (Heading for the door) Look, you can stay chained to them if you want, but I'm taking a walk!

CHARLOTTE (Following him to the door): Wally . . . ?

WALLY: I don't even care if you come with me or not. (And he's gone)

CHARLOTTE: Honey, please! Now what do I do? . . . (She lurches back and forth between the door and the sleeping kids) Oh shit! (Then grabs a blanket and flashlight and rushes to the door) Wally, wait up! (Running back to the kids) Please God, don't wake up . . . Just . . . don't! (And she's gone)

(A long silence. Then spooky sounds start up: wings flap, the baby cries and cries, an albino bat gives birth to kittens. Pony moans in her sleep. A lion roars close by.)

PONY (Wakes like a shot): What was that?

(Silence. Then all the sounds combine into a terrifying cacophony.)

(In a whisper) Mommy?

(The sounds get louder.)

Mommy . . . ?!

(And louder.)

(Frozen) It's bears!

(Dead silence.)

MOOOOOOOOOOOOOOMYYYYYY???!
TURNER *(Wakes instantly)*: What's happening?
PONY: It's bears. Big black bears!

(Silence.)

TURNER: I don't hear anything.

(The lion roars again.)

(Whispering) Dad . . . ?
PONY *(Whispering)*: Mommy . . . ?
TURNER: Is that you?
PONY: Can I get in with you?
TURNER: It's so dark in here.
PONY *(Creeping out of her sleeping bag)*: Where are you?
TURNER *(Likewise)*: Who has the flashlight?
PONY: Mommy . . . ?
TURNER *(Running into Pony)*: Dad . . . ?
PONY: No, it's me, Pony.
TURNER: *Pony . . . ?*
PONY: What?
TURNER: Oh no!
PONY: *Turner . . . ?*
TURNER: Where are they?

TURNER: DAD . . . ?   PONY: MOMMY? . . .
DADDY . . . ?   MOMMMYYYYYYY?

(Silence.)

PONY: *The bears got them, the bears got them!*
TURNER: Will you shut up?
PONY: I want Mommy, I want Mommy!
TURNER: Come on, quiet down or they'll get us, too!

(An instant silence.)

PONY *(Jumping)*: What was that?
TURNER: What was what?
PONY: *That!?*
TURNER: I didn't hear anything.
PONY: It sounded like snakes.
TURNER: Will you stop it?
PONY: It's snakes, it's snakes!
TURNER: Wait a minute, let me get my circus light.

(He turns on the kind of little glow-stick sold at circuses and starts waving it, drawing liquid circles in the air.)

PONY: Oh neat! Let me try.
TURNER: Use your own.
PONY: I don't know where it is.
TURNER: Look in your sleeping bag. *(He keeps waving it)*
PONY: Hey, I found it, I found it! *(She turns it on and copies Turner)* This is fun.
TURNER: I wish we had sparklers.
PONY: Oh, sparklers would be great!

(They wave away until the tent starts to glow.)

Hey, why don't you play your guitar.
TURNER: Now?
PONY: It would be neat.
TURNER: Yeah?

PONY: Yeah, we'll have a sound-and-light show. I'll do them both and you play that really beautiful piece that I love.

TURNER *(With enthusiasm)*: Okaaay! *(He hands her his light and starts taking his guitar out of its case)*

PONY: Are you scared of seeing Livvie?

TURNER: Why should I be scared?

PONY: Because she's dying of cancer.

TURNER: So?

PONY: She'll look all strange. Her teeth will be black and she'll be wearing a wig.

TURNER: How do you know?

PONY: I heard Mommy and Daddy talking.

(Turner starts playing Bach's Suite no. 1 in G Major. Pony listens for several measures, then resumes waving the lights as Turner plays.)

What if she dies in front of us? What if she turns blue and starts gasping for air? . . . *(She makes lurid strangling sounds)* What if she wants to be alone with one of us? What if we're locked in the room with her and she comes after us . . . ? What if she falls and dies right on top of us? . . .

(There's a sudden awful noise outside.)

(Dropping the lights) IT'S HER, IT'S HER . . . SHE'S COMING TO GET US!

(Turner continues playing.)

HELP . . . HELP! . . .

TURNER *(Stops playing)*: Jeez, Pony!

PONY: She's coming to get us, she's coming to get us!

TURNER: She lives over two thousand miles away!

PONY: Mommy, Mommy . . . !

TURNER *(Rising)*: I'm getting out of here, you're crazy!

PONY: Hey, where are you going?

TURNER *(Heading for the door)*: I want to see what's going on.

PONY: You can't go out there.

TURNER: Who says?

PONY: The bears will get you! *(In a frantic whisper)* Turner . . . ?!
TURNER *(Pulls back the tent flap and steps outside)*: Ohhh, look
at all those stars!

(Moonlight pours through the door.)

PONY: Turner, get back in here!
TURNER: The sky's full of shooting stars. Quick, Pone, you've got
to see this!
PONY *(Whimpering)*: I want Mommy, I want Mommy . . .
TURNER *(Returning for Pony)*: They're amazing. Come on, give
me your hand.
PONY: Where are we going?
TURNER: Just follow me.

*(He leads her to a clearing outside the tent. The sky is ablaze
with shooting stars.)*

(Putting his arm around her shoulder) Well, what do you
think?
PONY: Ohhhhh, look!
TURNER: Isn't it incredible?
PONY: Look at all those stars!
TURNER *(Pointing)*: Oh, one's falling, one's falling!
PONY: There are millions of them . . .
TURNER: Did you see that?
PONY: . . . billions and zillions of them!
TURNER: Come on, let's get closer.
PONY: Ohhh, they're so bright!

*(Arms around each other, they walk deeper into the starlit
night.)*

TURNER: Hold on tight now. I don't want to lose you.

Act Two

Scene 1

It's four days and 700 miles later. The Blossoms are in a sailboat scudding across a lake in Oklahoma City with Charlotte's brother, Scotty Childs; Joy, his new wife, who's African-American and seven months pregnant; and Amy, his daughter from his first marriage. Amy's at the tiller wearing a Little League shirt and cap. She looks suspiciously like a boy. The grown-ups are drinking champagne and laughing. Pony's sitting close to Joy, waiting to feel the baby move, and Turner's sunbathing on the deck. The wind slaps against the sails as they skim over the water. It's one of those idyllic summer days you remember for a lifetime.

SCOTTY *(Laughing)*: Wait, wait, there's more . . .

JOY: You and Charlotte packed a fourteen-inch cast-iron frying pan . . . ?

SCOTTY: . . . a fourteen-inch cast-iron frying pan, an orange-juice squeezer, an electric toaster . . .

JOY: But, Scotty, how did it all fit in a doll's trunk?

ALL *(Roaring with laughter)*: It didn't!

CHARLOTTE: *Plus* . . .

WALLY: Plus a gallon of milk, a bottle of maple syrup . . .

TURNER: Three jars of peanut butter . . .

PONY: Four-and-a-half bananas . . .

AMY: Five bags of marshmallows . . .

CHARLOTTE: And Horatio, my life-size pink teddy bear!

JOY *(Laughing)*: Stop, stop! . . .

WALLY *(Hopping up with his camera)*: Nobody move! I've got to get a picture of this! *(He starts snapping away)*

SCOTTY: And of course . . . the crucial carton of eggs.

CHARLOTTE: Yes, don't forget the eggs.

TURNER, PONY AND AMY: The eggs, the eggs, the eggs!

WALLY *(Snapping away)*: OH YES!

CHARLOTTE: Which all smashed when I tried to shut the lid.

AMY: *Yuck!*

PONY: Eeewy gooey, eeewy gooey.

JOY: This is the saddest story I've ever heard.

SCOTTY: What do you mean?

CHARLOTTE: It's not sad.

JOY: Running away from home to fry eggs on top of a mountain . . . ?

SCOTTY: We were city kids. *(Tilting the champagne bottle)* A little refill, Char?

CHARLOTTE: We wanted to join Livvie out West. She'd built herself this canvas dome high up in the Tetons. It was the shape and color of a giant apricot. It was that crazy dome that inspired Scotty to move out here and become a landscape architect. *(Holding out her glass)* Please!

SCOTTY *(Pouring)*: It's true. I still remember the pictures of it. It was a cross between a hot-air balloon and a mad scientist's observatory . . .

WALLY *(Taking more pictures)*: What a day! . . . It's days like this that make you feel you can do anything.

CHARLOTTE: She wanted to be close to the sky . . .

WALLY: Swim the Atlantic, ride bareback on a zebra, write music that will leave audiences sobbing in their seats. It's all just . . . *out there,* swaying within reach.

CHARLOTTE: This was in her painting days before she moved to the desert . . . which she says is even closer to the sky.

WALLY: The thing is to seize it! *(He roars with resolve)*

JOY: I understand wanting to run away to join her . . .

WALLY: Thrust out your arms and partake!

JOY: But to fry eggs . . . ?

SCOTTY: She made *great* eggs. *(Lifting the bottle toward Wally)* Wallace?

CHARLOTTE: She made *great* eggs!

WALLY: Please! *(Extending his glass)*

(Scotty fills it.)

JOY: When I ran away from home, it was to CBS in Chicago because I wanted to be a newscaster so badly.

CHARLOTTE: You were just more realistic, that's all. *(Mopping her brow)* Gosh, it's hot out here!

JOY: The only problem was, it was over five hundred miles away, and it took me four days to get there.

WALLY *(Drinks in great gulps)*: Crawl out of your hole and partake!

CHARLOTTE: But look how it paid off! I mean, here you are interviewing kings and presidents all over the place.

JOY *(Jumps, hand over her stomach)*: WHOA!

PONY: I felt it, I felt it! *(She presses her head against Joy's stomach)* Again, again!

CHARLOTTE: Our dream was to make it out West and fry eggs with wild-and-woolly Livvie . . . *(She fans herself)*

SCOTTY: We would have walked across Siberia to be with her.

WALLY *(Flings his head back and closes his eyes)*: Ahhhh!

CHARLOTTE *(With affection)*: Look at Wally! . . . *(Taking his hand)* Having fun, sweetheart?

WALLY: This is the life.

(Charlotte leans against him and sighs happily.)

Everything is music. All you have to do is listen.

PONY *(Pressing her head into Joy's stomach)*: Neato! I can hear it breathing. *(She breathes loudly)*

JOY: *Her*, not it! She's a girl. Your mommy wove her the most amazing quilt covered with dragonflies . . .

PONY: It's a girl? How do you know it's a girl?

JOY: Because I had a special test. Really, Charlotte, you could show your things in art galleries . . .

WALLY: That's what I keep saying.

JOY: They're so beautiful.

CHARLOTTE: Please! It's just a hobby.

PONY: What kind of a test?

JOY: A test where they take out some of the fluid the baby is living in.

PONY: Ewwwww, ewwwwwwww!

JOY: It doesn't hurt.

CHARLOTTE *(Quietly to Scotty, shifting away from Wally)*: So, when did you see Livvie last?

SCOTTY: Amy and I flew up two weeks ago. She's becoming quite a little pilot.

CHARLOTTE: You go all the way to Taos in the Cessna?

SCOTTY: It's a snap. With favorable winds we can make it in three hours.

JOY: Babies live in special sacs filled with water.

CHARLOTTE: And how was she?

SCOTTY: Not good.

WALLY *(To Charlotte)*: Come back, come back.

PONY: Then how do they breathe?

JOY: Through gills. They start out like fish.

AMY: Ewwwww . . . ewwwww!

CHARLOTTE: Yeah, she sounded pretty rocky on the phone the other day.

SCOTTY *(Voice lowered)*: It's just a matter of days.

CHARLOTTE *(Hands over her ears)*: Don't . . .

SCOTTY: You'll make it in time, don't worry.

CHARLOTTE: Oh Scotty . . . !

SCOTTY: I know, I know. *(He takes her hand)*

CHARLOTTE: Well, racing to finish *The Ring of Prayer* in a-hundred-and-two-degree heat didn't help. Sybil was furious with her.

SCOTTY: What would we do without that woman? She's not only a great doctor, but she and Sinclair are the only ones Livvie will listen to.

CHARLOTTE: I don't know which I dread more—getting there too late or having to see her suffer.

SCOTTY: The worst is over, it's just a matter of letting go.

CHARLOTTE: Stop . . .

JOY *(To Pony)*: You see, nature is very logical. Since life began in water, we begin in water, too. When a baby's tiny it looks just like a fish. Then it grows hair and lungs and turns into an egg-bearing mammal . . .

PONY: Wow . . . !   AMY: Gee . . . !

PONY: You mean, I was a fish?
JOY: We all were! *(She makes fish faces and laughs)*
PONY *(Yelling over)*: HEY, TURNER, DID YOU KNOW WE
    ALL STARTED OUT AS FISH?
TURNER: No, we *end up* as fish, silly.

(A silence.)

SCOTTY: Hey, Amy, how about giving someone else a turn?
AMY: Sure, anyone want to sail?
PONY *(Raising her hand)*: Oh me, me!
SCOTTY: Turner?
TURNER: I don't know how.
AMY: Come on, I'll teach you. It's easy.
SCOTTY: She's an ace, she's been sailing since she was two. Go
    on, give it a whirl.

(Turner joins Amy.)

PONY *(Softly to Charlotte)*: Amy is so weird. Are you sure she's
    not a boy?
CHARLOTTE: Now Pony . . .
AMY *(Showing Turner)*: This is the tiller. It's like a steering wheel,
    except you move it in the opposite direction you want to go.
    (She moves it from side to side) See? It's a cinch.
JOY: The girl's amazing. She's captain of the track team, she plays
    first base for Little League, and don't ask me where this came
    from—but she's a crackerjack at archery!
CHARLOTTE: Well look at her mother . . .
SCOTTY: You look at her!
WALLY: What's old Inge up to these days?
AMY *(Handing over the tiller)*: Now you try.
SCOTTY: Running marathons, if you can believe it.
PONY: Mommy . . . ?
WALLY: You're kidding.
SCOTTY: She's gone off to Calcutta to train.
WALLY: Calcutta?
JOY: No, no, Kenya. He mixes them up on purpose.

SCOTTY: So, to continue our saga . . .

PONY: Mommy . . . ?

JOY: Yes, do, do!

CHARLOTTE: It just gets worse, believe me.

WALLY: Hey, Turn, how're you doing?

TURNER: Great!

AMY: He's a natural!

PONY: *Mommy?!*

WALLY AND CHARLOTTE *(Angry)*: What is it, Pony?

PONY: This is fun.

SCOTTY: Good girl! That's just what I like to hear . . . *(He tousles her hair)* So, after Char smashed the eggs trying to close the doll's trunk, we realized we had too much stuff. We decided not to bring anything.

PONY *(Snuggling up to Joy again)*: You're so pretty.

JOY: Why thank you, honey.

PONY: I love your hair. *(She starts playing with it)*

JOY: Ugh, you can have it! *(To the others)* What I can't get over is that your parents let you go.

CHARLOTTE: They were very liberal.

JOY: If I lived in New York City and Amy suddenly announced she was going to run away from home to fry eggs on top of the Tetons, I wouldn't let her out the door!

SCOTTY: Well, there were two of us, remember.

JOY: But you were only eight and eleven . . .

PONY *(Still involved with Joy's hair)*: Can I brush it?

JOY: . . . you were just babies! *(Starts rummaging around in her bag)* Sure, I think I've got a brush in here someplace . . .

TURNER: LOOK EVERYBODY, I'M SAILING, I'M SAILING!

CHARLOTTE *(Waving to him)*: Yay Turner . . . !

AMY: Tomorrow I'm going to teach him how to windsurf. That's *really* fun!

WALLY *(Getting out his camera and taking more pictures)*: Wait'll they see this back at Juilliard . . . Turner at the helm. And suddenly he's surrounded by a herd of killer whales.

AMY *(Pointing into the distance)*: Thar she blows!

JOY *(Finds a brush and gives it to Pony)*: Here you go.

PONY *(Brushing away)*: Ohhh, it's so curly! I wish I had hair like this!

JOY *(With disgust)*: Please!

AMY *(Grabbing Turner)*: Look out, look out, one's right underneath us! Man the lifeboats! *(She starts running up and down)*

AMY AND TURNER: MAN THE LIFEBOATS! MAN THE LIFEBOATS!

SCOTTY: Easy, Amy, easy. *(Pause)* So . . . we announced our plans on a bright Sunday morning in April. Father said it was fine with him, and he gave us a couple of dimes in case we wanted to call from the road. Mother just warned us not to talk to strangers . . .

JOY *(To Scotty)*: Incredible!

CHARLOTTE *(Fanning herself)*: And never to accept anything from them.

JOY *(Noticing Charlotte's discomfort)*: Hey, are you okay?

CHARLOTTE: Particularly soda. *(To Joy)* It's this brutal Oklahoma sun.

SCOTTY: She said wicked people sometimes pour poison in it when you're not looking so they can rob you. She then told us to be back by one-thirty for lunch because . . . *(A weighty pause)*

SCOTTY AND CHARLOTTE: "We're having chocolate sundaes for dessert!"

CHARLOTTE: Oh, Scotty, I wish you didn't live so far away!

SCOTTY *(Reaching for the bottle)*: Hey, how about another bottle of champagne?

WALLY *(Putting his camera away)*: Sounds good to me! *(He suddenly starts humming the woodwind section of a melody that's come to him)*

SCOTTY *(Uncorking the bottle as he talks)*: We headed into Central Park, figuring that was the best place to start looking for mountains.

CHARLOTTE: I would have followed him anywhere, *anywhere*!

JOY *(To Pony)*: Would you like me to brush *your* hair? It's so pretty. It shines like corn silk.

PONY: Sure!

JOY: My little sister and I used to do this for hours . . . Hours! *(She brushes Pony's hair into a series of fancy styles)*

SCOTTY: And before we knew it, we were standing in front of the lion's cage at the zoo. *(Lifting the bottle in Charlotte's direction)* Char?

CHARLOTTE: Please!

SCOTTY *(Fills her glass, then moves toward Wally)*: Maestro?

WALLY: Let 'er rip! *(He keeps humming his melody)*

(Charlotte starts sprinkling herself with drops of champagne.)

SCOTTY *(Pouring)*: That's my man! If you come up with some new quartet or symphony on this boat, *I* expect some of the credit now . . .

WALLY: You got it. *(Tilts his glass to him and drinks)* Ahhhhh . . .

JOY *(To Pony)*: How about we sweep it all on top of your head and make you look like a princess?

PONY: Ohhh, that feels so good. Isn't Joy beautiful, Mommy?

CHARLOTTE *(Guiltily stops dousing herself)*: Very.

JOY: Please! I'm a blimp!

CHARLOTTE: In fact, Joy's one of the most beautiful women I know.

SCOTTY: Hear, hear . . . So, there we were watching the lion pace back and forth when this man suddenly comes up to us and says, "You children aren't out here all alone, are you?"

JOY: Oh God . . . !

CHARLOTTE: Naturally we don't answer him since Mother told us not to talk to strangers . . . *(She pours more champagne into her glass)*

SCOTTY: But then he looks really concerned and asks, "Have you lost your mother and father . . . ?"

JOY *(Skeptical)*: Right, right . . .

CHARLOTTE: No, he seems genuinely concerned, so we say, "No, we're running away from home."

JOY: Oh no!

SCOTTY: So *he* says, "You're running away from home, are you? Where are you going?"

JOY: I can't listen to this!

CHARLOTTE: So, *we* say, "To the top of a mountain to fry eggs with Livvie!" *(To Scotty)* We really *were* crazy, you know. *(She dunks her hand in her glass and sprinkles more champagne over herself)*

SCOTTY: And *he* says, "Gosh, that sounds like fun. Can I come with you?"

JOY: Stop . . .

CHARLOTTE: So we say, "Sure." *(Pause)* This is really great champagne.

JOY: These things really scare me.

WALLY *(Draining his glass)*: This *is* great champagne!

SCOTTY *(Handing him the bottle)*: Help yourself, I've got lots more onboard . . .

WALLY *(Refills his glass)*: Ahhh, just what the doctor ordered . . . You were absolutely right, Char, this has turned out to be a terrific trip, really terrific! *(He lets out a roar and tilts the bottle Charlotte's way)* How about some more?

CHARLOTTE: Thanks . . . So, there we are telling this guy about all our plans while the lion keeps pacing back and forth in his cage . . . *(She douses her arms and shoulders directly from the bottle)*

SCOTTY: We're going on and on about how we're going to hook up with our crazy Aunt Livvie who paints twelve-foot canvases of clouds and sky, when he suddenly says, "You know, we're standing in a very vulnerable spot in relation to this lion because of the wall behind us. If he suddenly decides to take a leak, it's going to hit the wall and ricochet all over us like a loose fire hose."

JOY: Scotty, this is getting weird.

SCOTTY: The guy then launches into this lecture about the great force with which lions pee, and how the wall behind us will just act as a conductor. So Char and I start to get a little nervous. I mean, this is *not* the sort of conversation we're used to . . .

(Charlotte is now pouring the champagne all over herself.)

When all of a sudden, the lion looks us straight in the eye, lifts his leg, and lets fly the most horrendous piss you've ever seen! We are talking broken water main here . . . It comes streaking past us at ninety miles an hour, slams into the wall just as the guy predicted and—SPPPPLATTTTTT!—we are drenched! I mean, soaked from head to foot!

JOY *(Laughing)*: Oh no.

CHARLOTTE *(Pouring the champagne over her head)*: It was unbelievable!

WALLY: *Honey . . . ?!*

SCOTTY: Charlotte, what are you doing?

(A silence as they all stare at her.)

CHARLOTTE *(Guiltily hides the bottle behind her)*: Oh, sorry, sorry . . . I was a little hot.

WALLY: Then you go in for a swim. You don't waste good champagne.

SCOTTY: Hey, how often do I get to see my little sister?

CHARLOTTE *(Mopping herself off)*: Sorry, this is a new thing with me. It's like I'm on fire all the time.

WALLY: Jesus.

JOY: That's some story . . . !

SCOTTY: It's not over yet.

JOY: Oh no.

SCOTTY: We made it back to the apartment just as Mother was filling our milk glasses.

JOY *(Laughing)*: I don't believe a word of this.

CHARLOTTE: Father took one look at us and said, "Good Lord, what happened to you on top of that mountain? It looks as if a lion peed all over you!"

(She and Scotty roar with laughter.)

JOY: He followed you.

CHARLOTTE *(Still laughing)*: He followed us.

WALLY: It's such a wonderful story.

SCOTTY: Father worked in mysterious ways.

CHARLOTTE: You can say that again. *(Pause)* We had a great childhood.

SCOTTY: A great childhood!

CHARLOTTE: The best.

WALLY *(To Turner)*: HEY SKIPPER, HOW'S THE WHALE SITUATION?

TURNER: We scared them all away.

WALLY: That's my boy! Just look at him. The kid can do anything, anything! *(He roars with pride)*

TURNER: Let's us get a boat!

CHARLOTTE: Oh, Turner, Turner . . . Why do I love little boys named Turner so much?

JOY *(Has finished Pony's hairdo)*: There, you're done. You're one beautiful little girl, you know that? *(She gives her a big kiss)*

PONY *(Prancing up and down)*: Look at me, look at me!

TINA HOWE

Scene 2

Early evening, two days and 230 miles later. Thirty miles east of Amarillo, Texas. Turner and Pony come running out of the Panhandle Diner. They head for the car—Pony pretending she's Wally, and Turner pretending he's Charlotte.

PONY *(Sliding behind the wheel)*: COME ON GUYS, GET A WIGGLE ON!

TURNER *(Gets in next to her)*: It would be nice to reach a campsite before dark for once!

PONY *(Yelling out her window)*: KIDS . . . ? *(To Turner)* What's your cash situation like?

TURNER *(Yelling out his window)*: LET'S GET MOVING! *(To Pony)* Eighty-five cents.

PONY: Great, that's just great! I have a dollar fifty! *(Pretends to turn on the ignition)* Well, let's just hope we've got enough gas to make it to Armadillo.

TURNER: Amarillo, *Amarillo*!

PONY: Jesus, Char, what are those kids up to? We paid the check ten minutes ago. *(Yelling out the window)* PONY . . . ?!

TURNER: TURNER . . . ?!

PONY *(Softly)*: What do you say we take off without them?

TURNER: Now you're talking! Come on, step on the gas!

PONY *(Making accelerating sounds)*: Those kids are history!

(Charlotte and Wally come streaming out of the diner—Charlotte pretending she's Turner and Wally pretending he's Pony.)

WALLY: Mommy, Mommy, Mommy . . . ?!

CHARLOTTE *(Getting into the car behind Turner)*: They're leaving without us!

WALLY *(Clambering in next to her)*: Mommy, Mommy, Mommy . . . !

PONY: Shit!

TURNER: They caught up with us.

PONY: Just our luck!

TURNER *(Turning around, all smiles)*: Hi kids.

PONY: Son of a bitch!

WALLY: No fair, Turner's in my seat!

CHARLOTTE: I am not!

WALLY: You are so!

CHARLOTTE: Am not!

WALLY *(Starts pounding on Charlotte)*: Give me my seat back!

CHARLOTTE *(Hitting back)*: Cut it out, Pony!

WALLY: OW, OW, TURNER'S HITTING ME, TURNER'S HITTING ME!

TURNER: Careful of his hands now . . . Come on, Wally, do something! I can't take this anymore.

(Charlotte and Wally keep slugging each other.)

PONY: *You* can't take it? . . . What about me? I'm having a fucking nervous breakdown!

WALLY: You're so mean, you're so mean . . . OW . . . OW . . . No fair!	CHARLOTTE: I'm going to kill you, Pony, I really mean it!

(It escalates.)

TURNER: KIDS, KIDS . . . ENOUGH IS ENOUGH!	PONY: IF YOU DON'T STOP IT RIGHT THIS MINUTE, I'M GETTING OUT OF THE CAR!

PONY: THAT'S IT! . . . WE'RE TURNING AROUND AND GOING BACK HOME!

TURNER: Sweetheart?

PONY: This vacation is over!

WALLY: I'm sorry, we'll be good, we'll be good.

PONY: It's too late.

TURNER: But what about Livvie?

WALLY: Daddy's mad. I hate it when Daddy's mad.

PONY: Livvie, Livvie . . . everything's always Livvie. You're on the goddamned phone with her every other day!

CHARLOTTE: Don't worry, he'll get over it.

TURNER: I had another one of my dreams last night. I finally found the baby I keep hearing crying outside the tent.

PONY: Oh no, not another one of your crazy dreams!

TURNER: I picked him up and brought him inside to show you.

WALLY: I've got to pee.

CHARLOTTE: So do I!

TURNER: And he was enormous! So big I could hardly carry him.

WALLY: *Mommy?!*

TURNER: Except it wasn't a baby and it wasn't a boy.

CHARLOTTE: We've got to pee!

PONY: Easy kids, easy . . .

TURNER: It was Livvie. She'd been buried alive . . .

WALLY AND CHARLOTTE: We've got to pee, we've got to pee, we've got to pee!

PONY: Buried alive . . . ? *(Whirling around)* I said: CAN IT!

(They do.)

Thank you. *(To Turner)* And . . . ?

TURNER: She was all covered with mud and leaves and stuff and she was roaring with laughter, saying, "Hubba-hubba, hubba-hubba." Shaking and sputtering, with tears rolling down her face, saying it over and over again, "Hubba-hubba, hubba-hubba, hubba-hubba!" *(Pause)* It was terrifying.

WALLY: I miss Spit and Wheat Germ!

WALLY AND CHARLOTTE *(In a loud wail)*: Spitty, Spitty, Spitty, Spit!

PONY *(Under her breath)*: This is a fucking madhouse!

TURNER *(Softly)*: Wally, I *wish* you wouldn't use that kind of language in front of them!

PONY: I mean, after a while . . .

WALLY: Mommy . . . ?

TURNER *(Fanning himself)*: Jeez, it's hot in here!

PONY: . . . how much can a guy take?

CHARLOTTE: Dad, can I move up front with you?

WALLY: Mommy?

PONY *(To Charlotte)*: No, you can't move up front with me!

TURNER *(Taking off his shirt)*: I don't know about the rest of you, but I'm burning up!

CHARLOTTE: Please?

PONY: I said, no!

(Turner starts fanning his naked chest.)

WALLY: Mommy . . . ?

PONY *(To Turner)*: Charlotte, what *are* you doing?

TURNER: I'm hot!

WALLY: *Mommy . . . ?!*

TURNER AND PONY: WHAT IS IT, PONY?

WALLY: This is fun! *(He grabs a candy bar out of Charlotte's pocket)* Nyah, nyah, I've got your candy bar. Anyone want some?

CHARLOTTE *(Trying to snatch it back)*: Hey, that's mine!

(They start fighting.)

Ow, ow, watch my hands . . . ! *(She lifts them up and examines them)* Jeez, Pony!

PONY *(Suddenly gets out of the car, slamming the door behind her)*: I CAN'T TAKE THIS ANYMORE, YOU DRIVE!

TURNER: Honey . . . ?

CHARLOTTE *(Starting to get out)*: Great! Now I can sit up front!

WALLY *(Pulling her back)*: Oh no you don't! It's *my* turn to sit up front! *(Starts slugging her)* TURNERRRR?!

(They fall into another fight.)

PONY *(Storms to the back of the car and gets in behind the driver's seat, pushing Wally over and Charlotte out)*: MOVE!

CHARLOTTE *(Falling with a crash)*: OW!

WALLY: Daddy, what are you doing?

CHARLOTTE *(Dashes over to Turner's door and starts pushing him toward the driver's seat)*: Move over, Mom! *(Back to Wally)* Nyah nyah, I got here first!

TURNER *(Being pushed behind the wheel)*: Turner . . . ?!

WALLY *(Storms out the backseat after Charlotte)*: Oh no you don't . . . ! *(And gets into the front seat, shoving Charlotte behind the wheel and Turner out onto the ground)*

TURNER: Hey . . . ? What's going on?

CHARLOTTE: Jeez, Pony!

WALLY: No fair, no fair!

PONY: This is more like it, now I have the whole backseat to myself!

TURNER *(Comes around to the back and pushes Pony over)*: That's what you think! Move over!

(Turner slams his door, Wally slams his, Pony slams hers and Charlotte slams hers.)

CHARLOTTE *(To Wally)*: Hi, Pone.
WALLY *(To Charlotte)*: Hi, Turn.
PONY: GREAT IDEA! LET THE KIDS DRIVE!
TURNER *(Stunned)*: What?
CHARLOTTE *(Turning on the ignition)*: Far out!
WALLY: Go for it, Turner!
TURNER *(To Pony)*: They can't drive!
PONY: Who says?
TURNER: Honey, you've lost your mind.
PONY: I don't know why we didn't think of this before. It solves everything!
CHARLOTTE *(Gunning the gas pedal)*: And . . . we're off!

Scene 3

Taos, New Mexico, two days and 345 miles later, around noon. The Blossoms have just been ushered into Olivia Childs's bedroom by Dalia Paz, her Mexican nurse. Pony clings to Charlotte's skirt, terrified. Turner's next to her, carrying his guitar. Olivia's four-poster bed dominates the room. It's shrouded with masses of fabric, making it look like a gauze cathedral about to lift off the ground. A vase of orchids sits on her bedside table and an oxygen hookup is nearby.

DALIA: Come . . . she is expecting you. *(She sweeps across the room and lifts the gauze around the bed; to Olivia)* Ya llegaron, señora. [They are here, miss.]

(Olivia doesn't stir.)

She sleeps and sleeps. *(Waving them closer)* Please . . .

(Wally and Charlotte gingerly step forward.)

PONY *(Being pulled with them)*: No, no, no, no . . .

CHARLOTTE *(Taking Olivia's hand)*: Livvie . . . ? Livvie? It's me, Charlotte.

(Pony keeps whimpering.)

DALIA: Your family is here, señora. Wake up, wake up. They want to see you.

CHARLOTTE *(Softly)*: How are you feeling?

DALIA *(To Olivia)*: Vamos, abre los ojos. Han venido de muy lejos. [Come, open your eyes. They have traveled a long way.]

CHARLOTTE: That's all right, let her sleep.

DALIA: No, no she sleeps too much. ¡Despiértate, despiértate! ¡Estás muy caprichosa! [Wake up, wake up! You're being very naughty!]

CHARLOTTE: We can come back later.

DALIA *(Angry, to Olivia)*: ¿Así es como te vas a comportar cuando tu familia te viene a visitar? [Is this how you behave when your family comes to see you?]

(Nothing.)

PONY: She's dead, she's dead!

CHARLOTTE:	WALLY: Can it,	TURNER: God, Pony!
PONY . . . ?!	Pony, just can it!	

CHARLOTTE *(To Dalia)*: She's too young to understand.

DALIA *(Not understanding)*: Please?

CHARLOTTE: I said . . . she doesn't understand.

(Dalia looks at her blankly.)

(Embarrassed) She thinks she's dead.

DALIA *(Upset)*: Oh no, no, señora! She is not dead! Don't say such things. She is sleeping.

CHARLOTTE: I know, I know . . .

DALIA *(Mimes sleeping for Pony)*: She is sleeping.

CHARLOTTE *(Voice lowered)*: She's too young to understand, she's just a baby.

DALIA: Yes, she sleeps like a baby. She's my little angel. *(She strokes Olivia's forehead and murmurs)* ¿Y en dónde estás ahora, mi querida? ¿Nadando en una playa azúl como un pescadito, o volando más alta que las nubes como una grande águila? [And where are you now, my precious one? Swimming in the clear blue ocean like a little fish? Or flying high above the clouds like a great eagle?]

(Silence as the Blossoms stare at the floor.)

(Noticing Turner's guitar) You play the guitar?
TURNER: Yes.
DALIA: I play, too.
TURNER: Yeah?
DALIA *(All modesty)*: Just a little.
TURNER: That's great.
DALIA: Not great just . . . so-so . . .
TURNER: Come on, I'll bet you're really good.
DALIA *(Blushing)*: No, no . . .
WALLY: Play for us!
TURNER: Yes, do! *(He hands her his guitar)* Come on . . .
CHARLOTTE: We'd love to hear you.
DALIA *(Stroking it)*: What a beautiful guitar.
CHARLOTTE: And it might help wake her up.
DALIA: It's been so long, so long . . . I used to play and dance in the hills . . .

(She bends over it, takes a deep breath and starts playing and singing a spectacular flamenco song complete with hand slapping and Gypsy yelps. The Blossoms stare at her, open-mouthed, then gradually thaw, snapping their fingers and tapping their feet. Wally suddenly starts to dance. Charlotte joins him in a torchy duet. Then the kids join in, feigning a bullfight. They get more and more carried away.)

(Finishes in an inspired burst and hands the guitar to Pony) Gracias.

(The Blossoms break into wild applause.)

TURNER *(Staring at Dalia)*: That was amazing!
WALLY: Spectacular!

(Olivia moans.)

DALIA: She's awake! *(She goes over to her)* Señora, ellos llegaron. [Senora, they are here.]
OLIVIA *(Groggy)*: Music . . . I heard music.
DALIA *(Propping Olivia up)*: Anda, anda . . . Abre tus ojos. [Up, up . . . Open your eyes.]

(Olivia is raised to a sitting position. She's very old and frail to the point of transparency. She opens her misty eyes. The Blossoms gasp.)

PONY *(In a whisper)*: She's alive!

(Olivia abruptly shuts her eyes and sinks back into her pillows.)

TURNER *(To Pony)*: Now look at what you did.
PONY *(Terrified)*: I'm sorry, I'm sorry . . .
CHARLOTTE: Oh, Wally, I didn't think she'd be this bad.
DALIA *(Pulling her back up)*: Señora, no seas caprichosa. Quieren verte. Han venido de muy lejos. [Señora, don't be naughty. They want to see you. They've come a long way.] Open your eyes!

(Olivia opens her eyes and looks around blankly.)

See? They're here!
OLIVIA *(To Dalia)*: Who are these people?
CHARLOTTE *(Leaning over her)*: It's me, *Charlotte*!
DALIA: Your family, my angel!
CHARLOTTE *(Taking her hand)*: Oh, Livvie, it's so good to see you again. You look wonderful.
OLIVIA *(Peering at Charlotte)*: Scotty?
CHARLOTTE: No, it's me, *Charlotte*. Scotty's in Oklahoma City.
WALLY *(To Olivia)*: You look great!
CHARLOTTE: Doesn't she?
OLIVIA *(Suddenly spies Turner)*: Amy!

CHARLOTTE: No, no, this is Turner.

OLIVIA *(Stretching out a bony arm)*: Amy, Amy, come closer and let me get a good look at you.

(Pony whimpers in terror.)

CHARLOTTE: Livvie, it's me, *Charlotte*. This is my son, *Turner*!

OLIVIA *(Gesturing more frantically)*: Closer, I can't see you!

PONY *(Clutching Wally)*: Daddy, Daddy . . . !

CHARLOTTE *(Shepherding them closer)*: Come on, kids, you're too far away . . .

WALLY *(Pulling her forward)*: Pony . . . ?!

PONY *(Digging in her heels)*: No, no, no . . .

CHARLOTTE *(To Olivia)*: See, it's me, Charlotte, and here are my two children, Turner and Pony . . .

OLIVIA *(Snatches Turner's hand)*: Amy . . . ! Come, give your poor old great-aunt a kiss like a good little girl. *(She makes lurid kissing noises)*

(Turner freezes and Pony whimpers.)

Don't be frightened, I won't bite.

(Turner leans over and gives her a quick peck on the cheek. Pony's whimpering gets louder.)

WALLY *(Under his breath)*: Stop it, Pony! Just . . . stop it!

OLIVIA *(Gazing at Turner)*: I can't get over how much she looks like a boy.

CHARLOTTE *(Getting the giggles)*: Oh God . . .

OLIVIA: Why do you cut her hair so short and dress her this way?

DALIA: Señora, this *is* a boy!

WALLY *(Under his breath, referring to Dalia)*: Obviously she hasn't met Amy!

(He and the kids start to giggle.)

CHARLOTTE *(Chastisingly)*: Wally!

OLIVIA *(Pulling Turner closer)*: You're such a pretty little girl. Why don't you let your hair grow?

CHARLOTTE: Livvie, this is my son, *Turner*! He's going to play for you later.

OLIVIA: Ah yes, you play baseball, don't you?

(The Blossoms' giggles increase.)

TURNER: Come on, guys . . .

PONY *(Swinging Turner's guitar)*: Batter up . . . Play ball!

OLIVIA *(Notices Pony for the first time)*: And who is this?

TURNER: My sister.

OLIVIA *(Seeing her with the guitar)*: So you were the one playing the music just now...

DALIA: That was me.

TURNER: No, I'm the one that plays.

OLIVIA: I didn't know you had a sister that played the guitar. Well, well . . .

DALIA: No, señora, *I* was playing . . . *(To the others)* She gets confused sometimes.

OLIVIA *(To Pony)*: You play very well.

PONY: Thank you.

(Olivia suddenly falls back into her pillows, eyes closed, mouth open. Silence.)

CHARLOTTE: Maybe we ought to let her rest a while, I'm afraid we're tiring her out.

WALLY: Good idea.

CHARLOTTE *(Starts moving toward the door, voice lowered)*: Come on, kids, we'll come back later.

DALIA *(Fussing over Olivia)*: Duerme, mi ángel. Volverán. [Sleep my angel. They'll be back.]

WALLY *(Herding the kids toward the door)*: Quietly, quietly . . .

PONY: Shhhhhhhhh . . .

CHARLOTTE *(Whispering to Dalia)*: We'll see her after lunch.

DALIA *(Crooning to Olivia)*: Descansa, mi querida. Vuelve a tus sueños. [Rest, my sweet one. Go back to your dreams.]

(The Blossoms start tiptoeing out the door. Olivia suddenly sits up, thrusting out an arm.)

TINA HOWE

OLIVIA *(In an agonizing cry)*: NO, NO, DON'T GO! DON'T LEAVE ME!

Scene 4

Later that evening, around nine. A bedside lamp glows eerily in Olivia's room. She's being examined by her doctor, Sybil Wren, a hearty woman in her sixties who has a severe limp. Wally, Charlotte and Dalia stand nervously in the doorway. Turner and Pony are spread out in the hall playing Hearts.

SYBIL *(Stethoscope on Olivia's chest)*: All right now, take a deep breath.

(She takes a shallow one.)

Hold it.

(She does.)

Okay, you can let it out.

(She does.)

Again.

(They go through it again.)

Good, now cough.

(She coughs weakly.)

Again.

(And weaker still.)

And once more.

(It's barely audible.)

Oh, Liv, what are we going to do with this poor tired-out old body of yours?

OLIVIA *(In another world)*: No, no, just back up the truck over by the canyon . . .

SYBIL: How's the pain?

OLIVIA *(Agitated)*: Why would I bring candles? The shovel's under the porch. OW, OW . . . STOP IT! THAT HURTS!

SYBIL: I know, I know . . .

OLIVIA: STOP IT, YOU'RE CRUSHING MY CHEST! *(She whimpers)*

(Sybil kisses Olivia's brow, puts away her stethoscope, snaps her bag shut.)

SYBIL *(To the others)*: I almost thought she'd lick it.

CHARLOTTE *(Leaning against Wally, weepy)*: I can't bear it, I just can't . . .

WALLY: Oh, honey . . .

SYBIL: She's such a crafty old bird.

(Dalia lurches out of the doorway with her hands over her face.)

CHARLOTTE *(Suddenly breaks away, weeping)*: Oh, Wally, it all goes so fast . . .

SYBIL: She's always got one more trick up her sleeve.

WALLY: Honey . . . ?

CHARLOTTE: I'm sorry, I'm sorry, I just can't keep up . . .

SYBIL *(To Olivia)*: Come on, show us your stuff.

CHARLOTTE: You dance through childhood, race through the teenage years, fall in love a couple of million times, bear some delicious bald babies, and then . . . whhhhhhst, it's all over . . . Don't you ever feel like digging in your heels and shouting: "SLOW DOWN GUYS AND LET ME GET THE LAY OF THE LAND FOR A MINUTE!" . . . *(She pauses and looks around the room)* It's nine o'clock in the evening . . . the children are playing cards in the hall . . . there's a sweet smell in the air. What is it? Pistachios! The whole room smells of pistachios . . . ! Livvie's sleeping with her mouth open. Look at her. Poor thing, she looks like an old man . . . Just slow down and take it all in . . . Sybil's wearing silver earrings, Wally's got a bruise on his arm, someone's heart is beating like crazy . . . Shhh! Listen! . . . Lub dub, lub dub, lub dub, lub dub . . . It's *my* heart! Nobody move . . . The moment's holding . . . *(In a whisper)* It's perfect . . . perfect! . . .

(A silence.)

OLIVIA *(Babbling)*: The children are in the meadow flying kites . . . There's Franklin in his pinafore. Wait for me . . . wait for me! . . .

SYBIL: It's funny, I've been feeling real anger lately . . .

CHARLOTTE: Oh, Wally . . . !

SYBIL: I keep thinking about that first project I went on with Liv when I lost my leg. You know, her eight-mile highway of sails that wound around Chaco Canyon. The reason I lost it was because she was so intent that they all fly at precisely the same height. And that was no small task when you consider she used over three thousand sails rigged on forty-foot masts . . . It was beautiful as hell, but backbreaking work. We were a crew of one hundred and fifty . . .

OLIVIA *(Overlapping)*: Come on, Franklin, it's my turn . . . Oh no, Boxer's loose, Boxer's loose! Bad dog, go back to Mummy!

SYBIL: I was rehoisting the last one five-and-a-half inches higher, and she just serenely backs the truck over me . . . I mean, here I take off time from medical school to help her on the project, and she runs over my leg for five-and-a-half lousy inches. Do you believe it?

OLIVIA: Wait, wait, I've got a stone in my shoe . . .

SYBIL: Well, the woman has me bewitched, I'd follow her anywhere. It's just lately I've been feeling this deep resentment. I mean, it's hard enough being a female doctor out here, but then to be a one-legged one on top of it . . .

CHARLOTTE AND WALLY: Sybil . . . !

(Turner and Pony suddenly appear at the door.)

CHARLOTTE: Oh, hi, kids!

(A pause.)

SYBIL: I'm not complaining, I'm not complaining. I have a wonderful life. Sinclair's a great husband and we have two fabulous children . . . It's just there's so much more I wanted to do.

(Turner and Pony edge over toward Wally.)

WALLY: Yeah, I know what you mean. Our feelings play strange tricks on us. *(Putting an arm around each)* Oh, hi, guys. This has been a tough year. The last thing I wanted to do was drive to New Mexico to watch another relative die. But the closer we got, the better I began to feel. I mean, look at us . . . we drove over two thousand miles and we're still talking to each other. We had a few laughs and saw some dynamite scenery. It was a great trip, a great trip! And here's poor Livvie hanging on by a thread, and I'm still raring to go. Charlotte's in another world, the kids are terrified, and you're furious . . .

PONY *(Gazing up at him)*: Hi, Daddy.

WALLY: Hi, Pone, what's happening?

OLIVIA *(Moaning in her sleep)*: Amy, Amy, I want to see Amy . . .

CHARLOTTE: What's she saying?

OLIVIA *(Garbled)*: The little girl who played the music . . .

WALLY: I think she wants to see Turner again.

OLIVIA *(Beckoning toward the kids)*: Closer . . . come closer!

WALLY: Go on, Turner, she's calling you.

(Turner starts to approach her.)

OLIVIA: No, the other one. Bring me the other one.

CHARLOTTE *(Nodding in Pony's direction)*: Her?

WALLY: Pony?

TURNER: My sister?

OLIVIA *(Pointing directly at her)*: THAT ONE! The little girl with the glasses!

(They all stare at Pony, who goes rigid.)

WALLY: Well, Pone, I guess you're the one she wants this time.

PONY *(Frozen, barely audible)*: No, no, no, no . . .

SYBIL: Don't be afraid, she won't hurt you. *(Pushing Pony toward her)*

WALLY: Come on, Pone, there's nothing to be afraid of.   CHARLOTTE: Honey, she just wants to look at you.

PONY *(In a frantic whisper)*: Turner, you promised you wouldn't leave me alone with her . . . Turner . . . ?!

WALLY: Atta girl . . .   CHARLOTTE: Honey, you're embarrassing us!

SYBIL: I was the same way at her age, exactly the same . . .

(Olivia starts to chuckle in a terrifying way.)

PONY *(Eyes closed)*: She'll die on me, she'll die on me . . .
CHARLOTTE *(Horrified)*: PONY . . . ?
PONY: HELLLLLLLLLLP!

(Turner looks on helplessly.)

OLIVIA *(Sounding more and more like a witch)*: Yes, *she's* the one I want . . .
PONY *(Flinging her arms around him)*: SAVE ME, TURNER . . . SAVE ME!

(Wally and Charlotte pry her away.)

TURNER: I'm sorry, Pone, I'm sorry . . .
SYBIL: Don't be scared, she's gentle as a lamb . . .

(Charlotte drags Pony, head bowed and eyes closed, to Olivia's bedside. A long silence as Olivia glares at her. No one breathes. Olivia suddenly stages a little show. She bleats like a lamb, howls like a coyote and crows like a rooster. She then rips off her wig, revealing a bald pate. Everyone screams. Dalia comes running into the room. Dead silence.)

OLIVIA: I just wanted to make sure you were paying attention.

SYBIL: Typical, typical.

DALIA *(Crossing herself)*: Santa María de la Cruz!

CHARLOTTE: Livvie!

WALLY: Whoa! You nearly gave me a heart attack!

(Olivia then pulls off her bald pate, revealing a crop of sparse white hair, which she coyly fluffs into place.)

TURNER *(Starts applauding her)*: Wow! Way to go!

PONY: That was really neat!

OLIVIA: There, this is more like it.

SYBIL: See what I have to deal with? You can't trust her for a minute.

OLIVIA: Now there's a little life around here!

PONY: Again, again!

SYBIL *(To Olivia)*: And here we were practically administering last rites. You are very naughty!

OLIVIA: Well, a dying old lady's got to have some fun.

PONY: More, more!

CHARLOTTE: You're too much, too much!

PONY: Gee, you're really neat!

OLIVIA *(Sighs deeply and shuts her eyes)*: All right, now everybody leave the room.

DALIA *(Protesting)*: Señora . . . ?!

OLIVIA *(Pointing a stern finger)*: I said, go!

DALIA: But someone has to stay with you.

OLIVIA: You heard me. I want to be alone.

SYBIL *(In a whisper, moving toward the door)*: Come on, we'll wait outside the door.

OLIVIA *(Highly agitated)*: GO, GO, GO!

SYBIL *(Shepherding them all out)*: All right, all right.

(They all tiptoe toward the door.)

OLIVIA *(Pointing at Pony)*: Except for her! I want the little girl to stay.

PONY *(Amazed)*: Me . . . ? You want *me*?

OLIVIA: Yes. You stay!

PONY *(Happy)*: All right!

(Everyone stares at Pony.)

You heard her, we want to be alone.

SYBIL *(Starting to move)*: Okay okay, but if you need us, we'll be right outside.

DALIA: What about changing your bedclothes?

OLIVIA: *I said GO!* And shut the door behind you.

PONY: Yes, shut the door behind you.

(Everyone leaves. Dalia shuts the door. A silence.)

OLIVIA *(Closes her eyes, then opens them and smiles)*: There, this is more like it. Sit down, sit down.

(Pony pulls up a chair next to her and sits.)

(Casually plucks an orchid out of her vase and starts eating it) Mmmmm . . .

(Pony watches, amazed.)

Would you like to try one?

PONY: Could I?

OLIVIA *(Handing it to her)*: Please!

PONY *(Takes a cautious bite)*: Mmmm, I've never had this kind before. *(She eats with rising gusto)*

OLIVIA: They're orchids.

PONY *(Finishing it off)*: It's so sweet!

OLIVIA: An old admirer sends them to me from Hawaii. Here, have some more.

(She hands Pony a few and takes more herself. They munch away, smiling at each other and wiping their mouths.)

PONY *(Between swallows)*: How old are you?

OLIVIA: Eighty-one.

PONY: *Eighty-one . . . ?* Gosh, that's so old!

OLIVIA: And how old are you?

PONY: Nine.

OLIVIA: *Nine . . . ?* Is that all? I thought you were thirteen or fourteen . . .

PONY: No, just nine.

OLIVIA: I'm amazed!

PONY: When's your birthday?

OLIVIA: July 7th.

PONY: Oh, that's right. We just met a baby that was born on the same day. He was so cute. *(Pause)* What's your favorite color?

OLIVIA: White. And yours?

PONY: Blue.

OLIVIA: Blue's all right.

PONY: And what's your favorite animal?

OLIVIA: The snowy owl. And yours?

PONY: *Horses!*

OLIVIA: Horses. Of course!

PONY: Do you have a lucky number?

OLIVIA: One.

PONY: *One?* That's so weird.

OLIVIA: What's yours?

PONY: Four.

OLIVIA: How come?

PONY: I don't know, it just is.

(Silence.)

OLIVIA: I like your glasses. Could I try them on?

PONY: Sure. *(She takes them off and hands them to her)*

OLIVIA *(Putting them on)*: Ohhhh, these are great! Everything's so clear!

(A silence as she gazes around the room.)

PONY: How do you go to the bathroom if you have to stay in bed all day?

OLIVIA: In a bedpan.

PONY: What's that?

OLIVIA: A kind of portable toilet. Would you like to see it?

PONY *(Thrilled): Could I?!*

OLIVIA: Sure. *(She whips it out from under the covers and holds it aloft)* What do you think?

PONY: Oh, that's neat!

OLIVIA *(Handing it to her)*: Here, sit on it, it's like a little throne.

PONY *(Puts it on the seat of her chair and sits on it)*: Wow . . . ! *(She makes a peeing sound)* Pssssss . . .

OLIVIA *(Offers her the first wig she had on)*: Now put this on for the full effect . . .

PONY *(Puts it on and tucks her hair inside)*: Psssssss psssssss . . .

OLIVIA *(Starts laughing and clapping her hands)*: Perfect, perfect! *(She suddenly has a seizure and grabs for the oxygen mask)* Air . . . air . . . *(She gropes wildly to get it on)* Help me, I can't get it on, I can't get it on . . .

PONY *(Rises and gropes for the unit)*: Wait, I can't see . . .

OLIVIA: Air . . . air!

(She finally gets it on. Her breathing becomes more labored. She takes several more deep breaths and is restored. She removes the mask and hangs it up. She gazes at Pony and smiles. A silence.)

PONY: What happened?

(Olivia shuts her eyes and sighs.)

Are you okay?

OLIVIA *(Drifting off to another world)*: Come, let's move into the shade. I don't like all these bees.

PONY: I thought you were dying.

OLIVIA *(Waving her hands at the invisible bees)*: Shooo shoo . . .

PONY: Death is so scary. Aren't you scared? I don't want to die.

(Olivia keeps shooing away the bees.)

I get so scared thinking about it, I can't sleep. Every night I touch my bedside light forty-four times and hold my breath for as long as I can and pray, *"Please God, don't let me die! I'll be good, I'll be good!"* And then I start imagining what it will be like . . . You know, being dead in a coffin, being underground all alone in the dark . . .

OLIVIA: What's that smell? I know, it's cloves . . . Cloves!

PONY: . . . with mice and, and spiders, and worms crawling over me . . . and, and dead people moaning all around me . . . and trying to call Mommy and Daddy but they can't hear me because I'm so far underground . . .

(Olivia breathes heavily.)

(Getting more and more upset) And, and then I start thinking about being there forever and ever and ever and ever until my body's a skeleton . . . a clattery skeleton with grinning teeth and no eyes, and I touch my night-light 144 times so it will go away, and then 244 times, and 444 times, and I get crying so hard Mommy has to come in and hold me . . . And, and . . . Oh no, it's starting to happen now . . . Could I get in bed with you? *(Climbs in next to her, whimpering)* I don't want to die, I don't want to die . . .

OLIVIA *(Waking, groggy)*: I just had the most beautiful dream . . .

PONY *(Clinging to her)*: Hold me, hold me!

OLIVIA: No, it was a reverie because it actually happened. Yes . . . it happened a long long time ago.

PONY: Tighter!

OLIVIA: I was on a train . . . *(She reaches for a nasal cannula that feeds her more oxygen)* Wait, just let me put this on, it helps me remember. *(Still in Pony's glasses, she puts it on)*

PONY *(Reaching out for her)*: Hold me!

OLIVIA *(Breathing easily)*: Ahhh, that's better, much better . . . I was on a train . . .

PONY *(Burying her head against Olivia, wig still on)*: I don't want to die, I don't want to die!

OLIVIA *(Putting her arms around her)*: There, there, no one's . . . going to die . . . I was on this horrid train on my way to the Sahara Desert . . . Yes, there was something about the Sahara Desert back then . . . I wanted to get lost in it, fling myself facedown in it . . . I'd been studying painting in Paris for the year. How could I have forgotten? I was all of twenty. Mercy, this was a thousand years ago. During my wild days. *(She roars)* What I put my poor parents through! Well, you'll do it, too, you'll do it all, just wait and see . . . Poor thing, you're shivering . . .

PONY *(Whimpering)*: I don't want to die, save me, save me!

OLIVIA: What's all this talk about dying all of a sudden? . . . I was on a train somewhere between Paris and southern Spain . . . we'd stopped at some godforsaken town in the middle of nowhere, and standing on the platform was the most beautiful man I'd ever seen—tall, with olive skin and a thrilling mouth. He wore a white suit and was pacing up and down the platform carrying this enormous bouquet of poppies that stained his face crimson. I couldn't take my eyes off him. He was like something out of *The Arabian Nights.* I kept expecting to see peacocks and jeweled elephants stamping in the distance. Finally he caught my gaze . . . I pressed my face against the window and whispered, "My name is Callisto!" *(She laughs)* Do you believe it? I used to call myself Callisto in those days . . . The train suddenly started up. We pulled out of the station. I watched him get smaller and smaller. Then I fell into a deep sleep. I began having nightmares . . . I was being chased down this long tunnel . . . I started to scream. Someone grabbed my hands. I opened my eyes. It was him! He'd jumped on the train at the last minute and was sitting across from me, eyes laughing, poppies blazing . . . He didn't speak a word of any language I knew, but he held me spellbound. I never made it off the train. He wrapped me in his flying carpet and wouldn't let me go. You've never seen such feverish carryings-on . . . He rocked me over mountains, sang me through rain forests and kissed me past ancient cities. Oh, what a ruckus we made! Well, you'll do it, too, you'll do it all, wait and see. We ended up in Zanzibar, island of cloves. *(She removes her nasal cannula)* I was so full of him, I thought my heart would burst. Zanzibar! *(She starts to rise, reaching for Pony's hands)* Come on, jump with me . . .

PONY *(Taking her hands and bouncing):* This is such a bouncy bed.

OLIVIA: It was there that he taught me how to live on orchids and read the stars . . . Zanzibar, say it!

PONY: Zanzibar! Hey, let's play Geography!

(They start jumping together.)

OLIVIA: We visited the wonders of the world without taking a step . . . Baghdad!

PONY: Detroit!

OLIVIA: Vienna!

PONY: Alabama!

OLIVIA: Nicosia . . .

PONY *(Stops jumping)*: No, no you're not playing right. Alabama ends with A, so you've got to name a place that starts with A!

OLIVIA: Addis Ababa! *(She resumes jumping)*

PONY: That's right! Arizona!

OLIVIA: Athens!

PONY: Sacramento!

(They jump higher and higher.)

OLIVIA: Oslo!

(Dalia, Charlotte, Wally and Turner come bursting in. They skid to a stop when they see the two of them bouncing on the bed; Olivia still in Pony's glasses, Pony, in Olivia's wig.)

DALIA: Señora, señora . . . ?

PONY: Ohio!

CHARLOTTE: Livvie?!

WALLY: What's happening?

OLIVIA: Odessa!

TURNER: Pony, what have you got on your head?

PONY: We're playing Geography! *(She rips off the wig and flings it in the air)*

OLIVIA: *Odessa!*

PONY: Albuquerque!

CHARLOTTE *(Starts laughing)*: It's a miracle, a miracle!

SYBIL *(Comes streaking in)*: Finally . . .

PONY: Albuquerque!

SYBIL *(Laughing)*: You see, you see . . . ?

OLIVIA: Egypt!

SYBIL: What did I tell you!

CHARLOTTE: Look at her go!

WALLY: Unbelievable!

TURNER: She's great, really great!

CHARLOTTE: Go Livvie!

WALLY: Jump!

OLIVIA: I said Egypt! What's the matter with you? Are you deaf?

PONY: Oh, sorry, sorry . . . um . . . Tallahassee!

OLIVIA: Equador!

PONY: Rhode Island!

WALLY: *Jump!*

OLIVIA *(Starts to weaken)*: Denmark.

PONY: Kansas!

OLIVIA *(Weakening more)*: Shanghai!

SYBIL *(Easing Olivia down to the edge of the bed)*: Easy, easy . . .

OLIVIA: I said . . . Shanghai!

PONY: Islip! It's in Long Island.

OLIVIA: Paradise!

PONY: Paradise.

OLIVIA: Come on, say it loud and clear.

PONY: Paradise!

OLIVIA: Again!

PONY *(Bouncing higher)*: Paradise!

OLIVIA: And again!

(Pony jumps higher and higher. She starts doing wondrous spins in midair.)

PONY: Paradise . . . Paradise . . . Paradise!

ALL *(Massing around the bed, overlapping, continuous and euphoric)*: Paradise . . . Paradise . . . Paradise . . . Paradise . . . Paradise . . . Paradise . . . Paradise . . .

(The light around Pony becomes more intense. Hair flying and nightie billowing, she looks like a reckless angel challenging the limits of Heaven.)

END OF PLAY

One Shoe Off

Production History

One Shoe Off received its world premiere in May 1993 by the Second Stage Theatre in New York City. It was directed by Carole Rothman. The set design was by Heidi Landesman, costume design was by Susan Hilferty, lighting design was by Richard Nelson and sound design was by Mark Bennett. The production stage manager was Jess Lynn. The cast was as follows:

LEONARD	Jeffrey DeMunn
DINAH	Mary Beth Hurt
TATE	Daniel Gerroll
CLIO	Jennifer Tilly
PARKER	Brian Kerwin

Characters

LEONARD, once an actor, fifties

DINAH, his wife, a costume designer, forties

TATE, an editor, forties

CLIO, his wife, an actress, thirties

PARKER, a director, fifties

Act One

Scene 1

The ground floor of Leonard and Dinah's Greek Revival farm-house in rural upstate New York. A slow-moving disintegration is at work; things are starting to fragment and sink into the ground. Rooms are drifting into each other, leaving moldings, doorjambs and window frames stranded. The staircase, upper-most walls and ceiling vanish in midair. Grass, weeds and tangled shrubbery are encroaching indoors. Saplings and full-grown trees have taken root in the corners, giving the place the look of a sur-real ruin. It's early November, around six in the evening. Leonard and Dinah are in their bedroom trying to decide what to wear. Dinah's in her slip and Leonard's in his underwear and a shirt. Both are barefoot. The bed and floor are littered with cast-off outfits. The wind howls outside.

LEONARD *(Holding up an old sports jacket)*: What do you think?
DINAH *(Looking at herself)*: It's hopeless . . .

   (The wind rattles the windows.)

LEONARD: Fucking wind.
DINAH: . . . hopeless!

LEONARD: Just listen to it.

(They stand motionless, lost in their own worlds.)

DINAH: *I don't know what to wear!*
LEONARD: One of these days it's going to blow the house down. That's all we need, to have the goddamn house flattened.
DINAH: Look at me!
LEONARD: You look great.
DINAH: But I'm still in my slip.
LEONARD *(Nuzzling her)*: Mmmm, you're so warm!
DINAH *(Resisting)*: Honey . . . ?
LEONARD: You're like a little furnace.
DINAH: They'll be here any minute.
LEONARD: So?
DINAH: I've got to get dressed.
LEONARD: Who says?
DINAH *(Heading into her closet)*: I hate this, I just hate it! *(She crashes around inside)*
LEONARD *(To himself)*: Forget it, she's out of here. *(He puts on the sports jacket)*
DINAH *(Emerges wearing a beribboned shepherdess dress)*: What do you think of this? *(She strikes shepherdess poses)*
LEONARD *(Engrossed in his jacket)*: I've always loved this jacket.
DINAH *(Starts herding imaginary reindeer)*: On Dasher, on Dancer, on Cupid and Vixen . . .
LEONARD *(Holding up two pairs of pants)*: Which pants do you think go better?
DINAH: On something and something and Donner and Blitzen.
LEONARD: The gray?
DINAH: Wait a minute, those are reindeer, not sheep! What's wrong with me?
LEONARD: Or the brown?
DINAH: Good old reindeer . . .
LEONARD *(Switching them back and forth)*: What do you think? Helloooo? You there . . .
DINAH: What *is* it about reindeer?
LEONARD: Bo Peep?
DINAH: They're so . . . what's the word . . . ? *(Pointing to the gray pants)* Nice pants!

TINA HOWE

LEONARD: Yeah . . . ?

DINAH: They look great, but then you look great in everything.

LEONARD: Hey, hey, what do you say? Forget the brown and go with the gray! *(He puts them on)*

DINAH: Isolated, that's it.

LEONARD: *Isolated* . . . ? What are you talking about?

DINAH: Reindeer. You never see them with other animals . . . *(Pause) Oh honey, he's coming, he's finally coming!*

LEONARD: You're not planning to *wear* that, are you?

DINAH: After all this time.

LEONARD *(Disappearing into his closet)*: And now for a tie . . .

DINAH *(Catching a glimpse of herself in the mirror)*: God, look at me, I look like something out of the circus! *(She wriggles out of the dress)*

LEONARD: Which do you think would go best? The maroon one you gave me for my birthday or the one with the crickets?

DINAH: You're so lucky, you always look great. It's not fair.

LEONARD *(Emerging with several ties)*: Or how about the paisley one I spilled on?

DINAH: That's why I married you, come to think of it. You could wear a shower curtain and look good.

LEONARD *(Holding it up)*: Then there's this striped number Po-Po gave me last Christmas.

DINAH *(Putting her arms around him)*: Five hundred years later and you still take my breath away, it's uncanny!

LEONARD: Awww.

DINAH *(Suddenly pulling away)*: He's going to cancel. You know Parker, he always cancels at the last minute.

LEONARD: I still don't understand why you had to invite those creeps over. Claribel and Thaddeus, or whatever their names are . . .

DINAH: Clio and Tate.

LEONARD: The guy's an asshole.

DINAH *(Heading back into her closet)*: How can you say that?

LEONARD: Easy—he's an asshole.

DINAH: But you don't even know him.

LEONARD: So why did you invite him over?

DINAH *(Emerges wearing a fringed cowgirl outfit)*: What do you think of this? *(She strikes cowgirl poses)*

LEONARD: It's going to be a disaster.

DINAH: Remember how he used to pick you up and carry you around?

LEONARD: Who?

DINAH: Parker.

LEONARD: Parker . . . there's another one.

DINAH: I always loved that.

LEONARD: Dinah, what is that you're wearing?

DINAH *(Whipping it off)*: I know, I know, don't even say it.

LEONARD: Stay in your slip!

(Dinah screams with frustration.)

I mean what kind of name is that? Theo . . . ?

DINAH: Tate, *Tate*!

LEONARD: It's so pretentious, he sounds like an English butler. Can't you tell them not to come?

DINAH *(Picking up a variety of cast-off outfits and holding them up to herself)*: No.

LEONARD: Why not?

DINAH: I just *can't*!

LEONARD: You know I don't like having people over.

DINAH: They're new here, they don't know a soul.

LEONARD: So?

DINAH: I'm trying to be nice.

LEONARD: What about being nice to me?

DINAH: What are you talking about. I *am* nice to you.

LEONARD: The evening's going to be a disaster.

DINAH: Don't worry, it will work out. Parker's cool, he can handle anything. He's a director.

(The wind howls again.)

LEONARD: You hear that . . . ?

DINAH: Remember *Cyrano* . . . ?

LEONARD: Fucking wind!

DINAH: I've never seen so many crazy people onstage at once.

LEONARD *(Sitting down on the bed)*: I can't take this anymore!

DINAH: What was the name of that lovesick actress who cried all the time?

LEONARD: Meg Benedict.

DINAH: *Eggs Benedict*, always in tears! Poor Parker, I've never seen anyone so besieged. Not that he seemed to mind. You know Parker and women.

LEONARD: Don't laugh, but I've always thought you had a thing for him.

DINAH: *Me?*

LEONARD: Your whole face lights up whenever you talk about him. I may be going out on a limb, but I've always suspected something once happened between the two of you.

DINAH: Between Parker and me?

LEONARD: That's what I said. What is this, an echo chamber?

DINAH: Pull yourself together woman and *get dressed for God's sake*! *(She throws down the last of the cast-off outfits and heads back into her closet)*

LEONARD: I'm right, aren't I? Something did happen between you.

DINAH: Between who?

LEONARD: Between Parker and you. Jesus . . .

DINAH *(Emerging in a green cocktail dress dripping with beads and sequins)*: My lizard dress! What do you think? *(She darts her tongue in and out)*

LEONARD: I think you need professional help.

DINAH: *I have nothing to wear!*

LEONARD: What do you mean, you have nothing to wear? Look at all this stuff.

DINAH *(Taking the dress off)*: But it's not mine.

LEONARD: You designed it.

DINAH: For shows, not myself. I can't dress myself, I don't know who I am. It's tragic.

LEONARD: I wouldn't go that far.

DINAH: You're so lucky, you look great in everything.

LEONARD: I'm not lucky, I have shitty luck.

DINAH: You don't have shitty luck.

LEONARD: The worst.

DINAH: Don't say that! It's just asking for trouble.

LEONARD: You're right, I'm sorry.

DINAH: If you go around saying you have the worst luck, you'll *get* the worst luck. I mean, think of all the terrible things that could happen. Colon cancer, Parkinson's disease . . .

LEONARD: I'm sorry, I'm sorry . . .

DINAH: A sudden stroke, cholera . . .

LEONARD: *Cholera?* . . .

DINAH: You ought to sink down to your knees and thank God for your blessings, I'm serious! *(Shutting her eyes and praying)* Thank you, God, for giving us so much. Good health, beautiful children . . .

LEONARD: We only have *one* child, Po-Po. God, I wish we saw her more often. *(Wailing)* Po-Po, Po-Po, I want Po-Po.

DINAH: Half an acre of land, exciting careers . . .

LEONARD: Speak for yourself, I haven't worked in eleven years.

DINAH: Food in the icebox, wonderful friends . . .

LEONARD: What friends? We don't have any friends.

DINAH: You're right, we *don't* have any friends, I forgot. *(Pause. She looks around the room)* Jeez, look at the place . . .

LEONARD: We used to have friends. The minute the going got tough, they were out of here. Take Parker, for example, the man hasn't called in five years.

DINAH: Six.

LEONARD: You'd think we had the plague or something. Arrogant son of a bitch.

DINAH: It's a mess! *(She pulls a rake out from under the bed and starts raking drifts of fallen leaves into piles)* Come on, give me a hand.

LEONARD: Who does he think he is, suddenly inviting himself over after six years of avoiding us? The prodigal son! *(He grabs another rake and joins her)*

DINAH *(Raking away)*: I can't keep up anymore.

LEONARD: It never occurs to him that *we* might have plans, that *we* have a life . . .

DINAH: Look at this, we're being buried alive!

LEONARD: You've been planning to invite our new neighbors over for months now, months. What are their names again?

DINAH: Clio and Tate.

LEONARD: They sound like a pair of goldfish. *(He stops raking and starts making fish faces)*

DINAH: They *do* sound like a pair of goldfish, how funny. You're right, the evening's going to be a disaster, we don't even know these people. There's no telling how they'll get along with Parker or what kind of shape he'll be in when he gets here. *How did we get into this? (Pause)* You know the trouble with us? We lack courage.

LEONARD: What are you talking about?

DINAH: Do you think we'll ever have to forage in the woods?

LEONARD: *Forage in the woods?*

DINAH: WE DON'T HAVE ANY MONEY!

LEONARD: Oh, that . . .

DINAH: Things are starting to get scary. *(She picks up a ChapStick and starts reading the ingredients on the side)* Petrolatums, padimate, lanolin, isopropyl, myristate, cetyl alcohol . . .

(The telephone suddenly rings. Both race to get it.)

DINAH: It's probably Parker! I'll get it, I'll get it!   LEONARD: The telephone! I've got it, I've got it!

LEONARD *(Gets there first and grabs the receiver)*: Hello?

DINAH: Who is it?

LEONARD: Hey, Parker, son of a bitch!

DINAH: I knew it.

LEONARD: You're still coming, aren't you?

DINAH *(Trying to horn in)*: Hi, Parker . . .

LEONARD: Slow down, slow down, I can't understand a word you're saying.

DINAH: It's me, Dinah . . .

LEONARD *(Struggling with Dinah)*: Easy, honey, easy! *(To Parker)* Where are you? . . . What . . . ? I can't hear you over the sirens . . .

DINAH *(Yelling into the phone)*: We can't wait to see you!

LEONARD: Dinah, please! *(Back to Parker)* I'm sorry, you were saying . . .

DINAH: Hey, I was in the middle of a . . .

LEONARD *(To Dinah)*: Can't you see I'm talking?

DINAH *(Imitating his rhythm)*: Nya, nya, nya, nya, nya nya!

LEONARD *(To Parker)*: Sorry, sorry, I'm back . . . What are all those sirens in the background? . . . Slow down, slow down, I can't hear you. *(Listening for a while)* No! . . . Sweet Christ!

DINAH *(Going ashen)*: What happened?

LEONARD: Oh no.

DINAH: *Is he all right?*

LEONARD *(To Dinah)*: Stop, stop!

DINAH: WHAT HAPPENED?

LEONARD *(Back to Parker)*: Right, I understand . . . Hey, we'll do it another time . . . Right, I will . . . You, too. *(He gazes at the receiver)*

DINAH: Is he okay?

LEONARD *(Hanging up)*: Good-bye.

DINAH: *What happened? (Pause)* Tell me! Honey, please?

(Leonard covers his face with his hands.)

I'm *dying*!

LEONARD *(Recovered)*: I don't believe a word of it. Not. One. Word.

DINAH *(Shaking him)*: A word of *what*?

LEONARD: What does he take me for? A half-wit?

(Dinah mews with frustration.)

The man's a congenital liar.

(Dinah's mewing intensifies.)

A mobile home breaking loose from its trailer and careening all over the highway . . . ? Three cars totaled and five people dead before it finally crashes into a truck in the opposite lane . . . Get real!

DINAH: He's not coming?

LEONARD: He said it missed him by inches, *inches*!

DINAH *(In a tiny voice)*: He's not coming?

LEONARD: Wreckage and twisted bodies everywhere . . .

DINAH: I knew he'd cancel, I knew it.

LEONARD: He stayed with the victims until help came, but now he's so shaken up he has to go home.

DINAH: He does it every time.

LEONARD: I've heard excuses to get out of evenings, but *this* takes the cake.

(There's a knocking at the door.)

DINAH: It's Parker, he came after all!

LEONARD *(Full of affection)*: That son of a bitch, he almost got us that time.

DINAH *(Heads toward the door)*: I'll get it, I'll get it!

LEONARD: Coming, coming . . .

DINAH *(Suddenly skids to a stop)*: Oh no, I'm still in my slip! *(She rushes back into the bedroom)*

LEONARD *(Skidding to a stop)*: Whoops, I don't have any shoes on! *(Calling) Just a minute, just a minute! (He follows Dinah into the bedroom)*

(The front door opens a crack, the wind howls.)

CLIO *(Offstage)*: Hello . . . ?

TATE *(Offstage)*: Anybody home . . . ?

CLIO *(Creeping into view)*: Are you there?

LEONARD *(To Dinah from the bedroom)*: Flipper and Whosis!

DINAH: Oh no, I forgot all about them.

CLIO: Yoo-hoo, we're here!

Scene 2

A split second later. Clio and Tate come tiptoeing into the living room. Clio is breathtakingly beautiful, dressed in actressy clothes. Tate is rugged looking, wearing casual weekend gear. Because they've left the front door open, the wind howls louder than ever. Dinah and Leonard are still in their bedroom.

TATE *(Calling)*: Louis . . . ?

CLIO *(Correcting him in a whisper)*: Lawrence.

TATE *(Whispering back)*: Who *are* these people, anyway?

CLIO: Lawrence and Diana.

TATE: How did you get us into this?

CLIO: Or is it Dianne?

TATE: You know I don't like going out on weekends.

CLIO *(In a singsong)*: Hellooooo . . . ? It's us . . .

TATE *(Pulling on her arm)*: Come on, let's get out of here while we've still got a chance.

CLIO *(Calling)*: Lawrence . . . ? Dianne . . . ? *(To Tate)* No, I was right the first time, it's Diana. Or is it Delilah? Oh God . . .

TATE *(Pulling harder)*: I want to go home, I don't like this.

CLIO: You don't like anything.

TATE: I don't like going out on weekends, you know that. It's my one chance to get caught up on my work.

CLIO: Work, work, work . . . Can't you ever take a break?

TATE *(Turning to go)*: You can stay if you want, but I'm leaving.

CLIO *(Taking in the room)*: Holy mackerel . . .

LEONARD *(Suddenly comes rushing into the room)*: Come in, come in . . .

TATE *(Skids to a stop, under his breath)*: Shit!

CLIO: This is amazing!

LEONARD: We were just . . .

TATE: Too late!

LEONARD *(Pumps Tate's hand)*: Tad!

TATE: Louis!

CLIO *(Correcting Tate)*: Lawrence.

LEONARD *(Correcting Clio)*: Leonard.

CLIO *(Correcting Leonard)*: Tate!

LEONARD *(Pumps Clio's hand)*: Clara!

TATE *(Correcting Leonard)*: Clio!

LEONARD: Whoops!

TATE *(Softly to Clio)*: Thanks a lot, I'll remember this.

CLIO: I'm sure you will.

LEONARD: So glad you could make it. Come in, come in. Let me take your coats.

(They overwhelm him with coats, mufflers, hats and mittens.)

(Dropping and retrieving them) Whoops . . . sorry, I've got it, I've got it . . . Good old wintertime . . . nothing like it . . . Whoops, there we go . . . *(He exits trailing their outerwear after him)*

TATE: Well, this is quite some place . . .

CLIO: It's wild.

TATE: Great trees.

LEONARD: Please!

CLIO: Just wild!

TATE: How do you get them to grow indoors?

LEONARD *(Returning)*: You mean, how do you get them to stay *outdoors*?!

CLIO: It's such a great idea.

(Silence.)

LEONARD *(Rubbing his hands together)*: So . . . ?

(The wind howls with rising fury.)

TATE: Oh sorry, I'm afraid we forgot to shut the ding. *(He rushes over to it and slams it shut)*

CLIO *(Under her breath to Tate)*: The *door*!

TATE: That's what I said.

CLIO: No, you said, the "ding" . . .

TATE: The *ding*?

CLIO: Never mind. *(To Leonard)* What *is* it with the wind around here . . . ?

LEONARD: Don't get me started.

CLIO: I've never heard anything like it.

(Tate opens the door again.)

Toto, what are you . . . ?

TATE *(Slams and opens it obsessively, finally slamming it for good)*: There we go, I just wanted to make sure it was shut tight.

CLIO: Well, we all have our little . . .

TATE: Why waste precious heat if you don't have to?

(Silence. Then, Dinah pokes her head in the room. She's still in her slip.)

CLIO: Dianne!

TATE: Delilah!

LEONARD *(In a whisper)*: You're still in your slip.

CLIO *(Whispering to Tate)*: What's her name?

TATE *(Whispering back)*: How should I know?

LEONARD *(Whispering to Clio)*: Dinah.

CLIO AND TATE: *Dinah!*

DINAH *(Trying to enter the room but stay hidden at the same time)*: Don't pay any attention to me . . .

TATE *(Starts singing)*:
Someone's in the kitchen with Dinah,
Someone's in the kitchen, I know-ow-ow-ow . . .

CLIO AND TATE:

>Someone's in the kitchen with Dinah
>Strumming on the old banjo.
>They're strumming fee, fie, fiddly-i-o . . .

DINAH: I just wanted to see what everyone was wearing. *(To Clio)* Ohh, what a great dress.

CLIO: What, this old thing?

DINAH *(Dashing out of her room)*: I'll be right back.

CLIO: I've had it for years.

LEONARD *(To Dinah)*: Hey, where are you going?

TATE: Stay in your slip, you look great.

LEONARD: She does look great, doesn't she? *Dinah, come back!*

(Silence.)

CLIO: It's so nice to finally meet you.

TATE: So . . . how long have you lived here?

LEONARD *(Calling after Dinah)*: Honey . . . ?!

CLIO: We've been waving at each other for months now.

LEONARD: Don't mind her, she has a terrible time dressing herself.

CLIO: Don't we all.

TATE: Speak for yourself.

CLIO: I just did.

TATE: Well, well, aren't we in good form this evening.

(Silence.)

LEONARD *(Calling in a strangled voice)*: Dinah, please!

DINAH *(Enters, dressed in a spectacular toga)*: You called?

*(Leonard covers   CLIO: Holy Moses!   (Tate does a wolf
his eyes and moans.)   whistle.)*

DINAH: *Julius Caesar.* It's too much, isn't it?

CLIO: Look at you!

LEONARD: Honey, this is upstate New York, not the Roman senate.

CLIO: That's incredible . . .

DINAH *(Turns to go)*: I *knew* it was too much.

CLIO: Incredible!

LEONARD *(Grabbing her arm)*: Don't go!

CLIO: Look, Zoo-Zoo.

TATE: I see, I see.

CLIO: Where did you get that?

LEONARD: She made it.

DINAH *(Trying to pull away)*: I've got to change.

LEONARD: Don't leave me again!

TATE *(To Dinah)*: You made it?

DINAH *(Struggling with him)*: Leonard . . . ?

TATE: *Why?*

LEONARD: Because she's a costume designer.

CLIO: Of course! I knew your name was familiar!

TATE: Right, right.

CLIO *(Pressing Dinah's hands)*: You're wonderful!

DINAH: Why, thank you.

TATE: Clio's an actress.

DINAH: No kidding.

TATE: Onstage and off.

CLIO *(To Tate)*: What's *that* supposed to mean?

TATE: If the shoe fits, eat it.

(A pause as everyone looks at Tate.)

DINAH: Leonard's an actor, too.

CLIO: No!

LEONARD: Was an actor.

DINAH *(To Leonard)*: Now, now . . .

CLIO: I didn't know that.

LEONARD: *Fucking bastards!*

CLIO *(To Tate)*: Did you know he was an actor?

TATE: I had no idea.

LEONARD: *Sons of bitches!*

DINAH: He was the best, the best.

CLIO: Wow, what were you in?

LEONARD: You wouldn't remember, it was so long ago.

DINAH: *Cyrano, Richard the Second, Uncle Vanya . . .*

LEONARD: *Stupid assholes!*

DINAH *(Putting her hand on his arm)*: Honey . . . ?

LEONARD *(Whirling away from her)*: *Don't touch me!*

(An awful silence.)

DINAH: He also keeps bees.

CLIO AND TATE: Bees . . . ?

LEONARD *(World-weary)*: Dinah . . . ?!

TATE: I love bees!

CLIO: I'm terrified of bees!

DINAH: Leonard's a naturalist.

LEONARD: I thought I was a fatalist.

TATE: My brother keeps bees.

DINAH: He has over five thousand.

CLIO *(Rushing toward the door)*: I'm getting out of here!

LEONARD: They're not in the house, I keep them out back.

DINAH: We'll have to give you some of our honey, it's the best in the area. Leonard markets it all over the state.

LEONARD: Bees are highly civilized, they put us to shame.

TATE: Bees are the best.

LEONARD: They *are* the best!

DINAH: Well, they certainly keep Leonard busy.

CLIO *(Her hands over her ears)*: I don't want to hear.

LEONARD: I could watch them all day.

DINAH: And he often does.

LEONARD: Well, better beekeeping than acting, it's a lot safer.

TATE: I've never understood the impulse to perform.

DINAH: Me either.

TATE: It's always seemed slightly perverse. Oh well, one man's meat is another man's pistol.

CLIO: Poison.

TATE: That's what I said.

CLIO: No, you said "pistol."

(The wind suddenly blows the front door open with a blast. The four freeze in terror. Clio rushes to Tate, who puts his arms around her. Dinah stands rooted to the spot, hand over her heart. Leonard sways on his feet. Then just as suddenly the wind dies down. Clio gasps, Tate releases a long breath, Leonard and Dinah shudder.)

What was that?

TATE: Wee Willie Winkie.

DINAH AND LEONARD: Wee Willie Winkie?

LEONARD: God, there's a name I haven't heard in ages.

TATE:

    Wee Willie Winkie runs through the town,
    Upstairs and downstairs, in his nightgown;
    Rapping at the window, crying through the lock,
    "Are the children in their beds?
    Now it's eight o'clock."

(They all look at Tate. An uncomfortable silence.)

DINAH *(To Leonard)*: So, how about shutting the door?
LEONARD: Right, right. *(He moves to the door)*
TATE *(Joins him)*: Here, let me give you a hand.

(They hurl themselves against the door, slamming it shut.)

    Diddle diddle dumpling, my son John
    Went to bed with his trousers on . . .

LEONARD: So, what would everybody like to drink? We've got
    beer, wine, vodka . . .

TATE:

    One shoe off and one shoe on,
    Diddle diddle dumpling, that's my John . . .

DINAH: Mineral water, ginger ale, orange juice . . .
TATE: Poised for the worst.

(Silence.)

LEONARD *(To Tate)*: Well, what's *your* line of work? *(To Dinah)* Whoops, after you . . .	DINAH: So, what do *you* do, Tate? *(To Leonard)* Oh, sorry, sorry . . .

(Pause.)

LEONARD: Sorry, I was just wondering what *you* . . .	DINAH: So, tell us what you . . . Whoops . . .

(Pause.)

CLIO: Tell them what you do, Dee-Dee!

TATE: Guess.

DINAH: Let's see . . .

LEONARD: Um . . . you write nursery rhymes.

TATE: Close, close . . .

DINAH: You illustrate nursery rhymes.

TATE: You're getting warmer . . .

LEONARD: You *are* a nursery rhyme.

TATE: Bingo!

CLIO: He's an editor.

TATE: You got it!

> The girl in the lane, that couldn't speak plain
> Cried, "Gobble, gobble gobble . . . "

LEONARD: And where do you do this editing?

CLIO: Raven Books.

LEONARD *(Impressed)*: Raven Books? Wow, you don't mess around!

TATE:

> The man on the hill that couldn't stand still
> Went, "Hobble, hobble, hobble."

CLIO *(Putting on a funny voice)*: Hobble hobble, wiggle wobble!

DINAH: She sounds just like Enid Brill.

CLIO: Enid Brill?

DINAH: The woman who gallops around the countryside in her nightgown.

CLIO: *Her!*

LEONARD *(Imitating her)*: She talks through her nose.

CLIO: We see her every morning.

LEONARD: She's certifiable.

DINAH: She's my idol.

LEONARD: Her husband's a crop duster. You'll hear him in the spring. *(He mimes a low-flying plane)*

DINAH: They have eight children.

CLIO: She whips that horse as if her life depends on it.

DINAH: It does, she's fearless.

(Leonard's crop dusting intensifies.)

Wait till you've lived here a few more years, you'll understand. Easy, Leonard, easy . . .

LEONARD *(Recovering)*: Sorry, sorry.

DINAH: You know what she dressed up as at Halloween? You'll never guess *(Pause)* A sieve.

CLIO AND TATE: A sieve?!

DINAH: She pulled the screen out of her back door, molded it over her head in a dome and stuck a broom handle between her legs. The year before she went as a rubber glove. Don't even ask.

LEONARD: Poor Enid Brill.

DINAH: There but for the grace of God go I. Well, I hope everybody likes carrots. *(She heads into the kitchen)*

LEONARD: So, what would you like to drink? We've got beer, wine, vodka, mineral water, ginger ale, orange juice . . .

TATE: Clee-Clee?

CLIO: I'll have some white wine if you've got it.

LEONARD: You're on. And you, Todd?

TATE: Vodka sounds good.

CLIO *(Correcting Leonard)*: Tate, *Tate*!

LEONARD *(Fixing the drinks)*: Coming right up.

DINAH *(Enters carrying a mountain of carrots with their tops still on)*: I'm back, miss me?

CLIO: Holy Moses . . .

TATE: Look at all those chariots!

CLIO: Where on earth did you . . . ?

DINAH: Help yourselves, I'm trying to get rid of them.

(Clio and Tate each gingerly take one.)

They grow all over the house. In the kitchen, the den, the upstairs bathroom . . . Dig in, dig in!

(Clio and Tate each take a tentative bite.)

CLIO: Hey, these are delicious!

TATE: They're so sweet!

(They crunch in tandem.)

DINAH *(Offering the tray again)*: Take more, take more.

(They do.)

LEONARD: You should have tasted the acorn squash from our bedroom last year . . . *(Passing out the drinks)* Chloe? Ted?

CLIO *(Still engrossed with her carrot)*: Ohhhhh . . . these are fabulous! *(To Leonard)* Oh thanks . . .

TATE: Mmmmmm . . . ooooohhhh . . . *(To Leonard)* Much obliged.

(More happy crunching.)

DINAH: Well, I hope you're in the mood for turkey.

TATE: Where did you grow that? Down in the basement with the cranboobies? *(He emits a hoot of laughter)*

DINAH: Whenever we have guests, I do Thanksgiving with all the trimmings. It's the only meal I'm really good at.

CLIO *(Reaching for the platter of carrots)*: More, more . . .

DINAH: Fall, winter, spring, summer, out comes the Butterball and Stove Top stuffing.

CLIO: Tate does Thanksgiving at our house.

LEONARD: Butterball and Stove Top all the way! We love processed food.

CLIO: He's a great cook. We're talking corn chowder, oyster stuffing, zucchini pilaf . . . We can't move for weeks, weeks!

DINAH: An old friend was going to join us tonight, but he canceled at the last minute.

LEONARD: He came up with this incredible cock-and-bull story about a mobile home running amok on the highway . . .

TATE *(To Clio)*: Well, you do Christmas, fair is fair. That is, when you're home.

LEONARD: I mean, people aren't mowed down by houses.

DINAH: They're only buried by them.

CLIO *(To Tate)*: I've never missed a Christmas with you, never!

LEONARD: What does he take us for, total idiots?

CLIO *(To Tate)*: When have I ever missed a Christmas with you?

DINAH: You'd think we'd learn. He sets us up and lets us down . . .

TATE *(To Clio)*: Last year.

DINAH: Sets us up and lets us down.

CLIO *(To Tate)*: My plane was grounded, I was stuck in the airport.

DINAH: Six years and not a word.

TATE *(To Clio)*: For a week?

DINAH: The trick is not to let it get you, right?

CLIO *(To Tate)*: As if you'd notice, you're so wrapped up in your goddamned editing.

TATE *(To Clio)*: Now just one minute . . .

CLIO *(To Tate)*: Words, words, words . . . and they're not even your own.

TATE *(To Clio)*: Nice, Click, very nice.

DINAH: Keep your hand on the tiller and your back to the wind! *(She picks up a nearby bottle of Worcestershire sauce and reads the list of ingredients on the side)* "Water, vinegar, molasses, sugar, anchovies, tamarinds, hydrolyzed soy protein, onions, salt, garlic, eschalots, spices and flavorings"! *(She slams the bottle back down)*

(Silence. Clio and Tate resume munching on their carrots.)

(Gazing at Clio) You are so beautiful.

CLIO: Why, thank you.

DINAH: Your skin . . . *(Reaching out to touch it)* May I?

CLIO: Be my guest.

DINAH *(Caressing her cheek)*: Ohhhh . . . it's so soft. Feel, Leonard, feel . . .

(Leonard hesitates.)

CLIO: Go ahead, it's all right.

LEONARD *(Touching her cheek)*: Mmmmmm . . .

DINAH: Isn't it soft?

LEONARD: Not as soft as yours.

CLIO AND TATE: Awww . . .

LEONARD: I think you have the softest skin in the world.

CLIO AND TATE: Awwwww . . .

DINAH: It's like burlap.

TATE *(Reaching to touch Dinah's face)*: Burlap . . . ?!

DINAH *(Whirling away from him)*: Please?!

(Silence. The phone suddenly rings. Everyone jumps.)

| LEONARD *(Getting there first)*: I've got it, I've got it! | DINAH *(Racing to get it)*: I'll get it, I'll get it! |

LEONARD *(Picking up the receiver)*: Hello?

DINAH *(Trying to wedge in on him)*: Who is it, who is it?

LEONARD *(Into the phone)*: Parker!

DINAH: Parker . . . ?!

LEONARD: Umhmmm . . . umhmmm . . . yeah . . . yeah . . . Wow, that's great! You sure you remember the way? . . . Okay, twenty minutes. See ya. Bye. *(He hangs up. To Dinah)* He's coming.

CLIO: Who?

LEONARD AND DINAH: Parker Bliss.

CLIO: *Parker Bliss?*

TATE: The director?

DINAH: You know him?

CLIO *(To Leonard and Dinah)*: You know Parker Bliss?

LEONARD: He's one of our oldest friends.

TATE: What was the title of that terrifying movie he just made?

DINAH: We've known him forever.

TATE: You know, the one based on the true story about the couple that murdered their children.

LEONARD, DINAH AND CLIO: *Lullabye and Goodnight.*

TATE: *Lullabye and Goodnight!*

CLIO: It was incredible!

TATE: I couldn't sleep for weeks.

DINAH: Us either.

CLIO: The performances he got out of those children. They were just toddlers.

DINAH: Parker's always been great with kids.

LEONARD: Except his own.

CLIO: That scene where their mother dressed them in party clothes before she threw them in the freezer . . .

TATE *(His hands over his ears)*: Don't, don't.

CLIO: The look on that girl's face as her mother leaned down and folded the cuffs of her tiny white socks, just so . . .

TATE: She knew what was going to happen.

DINAH: She knew.

ALL: She knew.

TATE: I couldn't go near our freezer for months.

LEONARD: When Parker called this morning and said he was going to be in our neck of the woods, we insisted he drop by.

DINAH: We figured you wouldn't mind if he joined us.

CLIO: *Wouldn't mind?* I've always wanted to meet him.

DINAH: But then he called right before you came, claiming a mobile home had broken loose from its trailer on his way up.

LEONARD: It totaled three cars and killed five people before it finally crashed into a truck in the opposite lane.

CLIO AND TATE: Oh no!

DINAH: It missed him by inches.

LEONARD: Please! You can't trust a word the man says.

TATE *(With meaning)*:

> Jack and Jill went up the hill
> To fetch a pail of water.
> Jack fell down and broke his crown,
> And Jill came tumbling after.

CLIO: Don't mind him, he's editing a new annotated *Mother Goose.*

TATE *(With brio)*:

> Then up Jack got and off did trot
> As fast as he could caper.
> To old Dame Dob, who patched his nob
> With vinegar and brown paper.

CLIO: Ahh, Tate, ever the brilliant mind.

DINAH: Well, the important thing is he's coming.

CLIO *(Leaning into Tate)*: Actually, you *do* have a brilliant mind, Tic-Tac.

TATE *(To Clio)*: Why thank you, Clicquot.

DINAH: He's coming, he's coming!

LEONARD *(To Dinah)*: I'll believe it when I see it.

DINAH *(Rises, freezing)*: God, look at me! I've got to change!

Scene 3

An hour and a half later. Parker still hasn't shown up. Dinah's slumped in a chair wearing an old-fashioned cotillion dress. Leonard's pacing by the door. He keeps checking his watch. Clio and Tate are asleep on the sofa, a mound of carrot tops at their feet. Several moments pass.

LEONARD: Nine forty-one . . .

DINAH: Honey, please.

LEONARD *(Continuing to pace)*: Nine forty-two.

DINAH: You're driving me crazy!

LEONARD: An hour and forty minutes late!

DINAH: Not so loud, you'll wake them up.

LEONARD: Manipulative son of a bitch!

(Clio groans and stirs.)

DINAH: Gently, gently . . .

LEONARD *(In a strangled whisper)*: Who the hell does he think
he is?

DINAH: He probably got lost.

LEONARD: Tell me another one.

DINAH: He'll show up.

LEONARD *(Resumes pacing, looks at his watch)*: Nine forty-three!

DINAH *(Suddenly rises)*: I can't take this anymore!

(Clio and Tate stir in their sleep.)

LEONARD *(As if seeing her for the first time)*: Honey, what is that
you're wearing?

DINAH: Amanda Wingfield, the dinner party scene with the Gentleman Caller.

LEONARD: Let me out of here!

DINAH *(Striking flirty poses)*: What do you think?

LEONARD: This is a madhouse.

DINAH: Be honest, I can take it.

LEONARD: I want to go home.

DINAH: You *are* home. *(Dashing out of the room)* Hang on, I'll
be right back.

LEONARD: Where are you going?

DINAH: To change.

LEONARD: Not again!

DINAH: I'll just be a sec.

LEONARD: This is getting perverse.

DINAH *(From the bedroom)*: What did you say?

LEONARD: I SAID, THIS IS GETTING PERVERSE!

(Clio and Tate wake like a shot.)

TATE: Perverse? Who . . . ? Where . . . ?

CLIO: Did somebody say "perverse"?

LEONARD *(Waving to them)*: Welcome back to the land of the living.

CLIO *(Groggy)*: Ohh, where am I?

LEONARD: Still waiting for Parker.

(There's a loud crash from the bedroom.)

CLIO *(Jumping)*: What was that?

LEONARD: Easy, Dinah, easy . . .

TATE *(Looking at his watch)*: Good God, look at the time.

(A series of crashes from the bedroom.)

DINAH *(From the bedroom)*: It's all right, it's all right, not to
worry . . .

LEONARD: Poor Dinah, getting dressed always throws her into a
tailspin. It's one of life's ironies—the costume designer who
doesn't know what to wear.

*(Dinah enters swathed in a jingling harem outfit with pointy
gold shoes. Leonard covers his eyes and groans.)*

DINAH *(Brandishing a scarf)*: *Peer Gynt.* What do you think?

CLIO: Heaven, *heaven*!

TATE: What happened to Amanda Wingfield?

CLIO *(Grabbing the scarf)*: I want it!

TATE: I've always been a sucker for faded Southern belles.

LEONARD *(Peeking at Dinah between his fingers)*: Sweetheart . . . ?

DINAH: God, look at it in here! *(She grabs a nearby rake and
starts raking the carrot tops)*

LEONARD: We need to have a little talk.

(Dinah keeps raking as Clio launches into a sexy belly dance.)

TATE: Clee-Clee, this isn't the Casbah!

(Clio dances with rising abandon. Everyone watches, enthralled. Suddenly there's a loud knock on the door. They all jump.)

| DINAH: He's here, he's here! | LEONARD: Well what do you know? | CLIO: It's him! | TATE: At last! |

| DINAH *(Getting there first)*: I'll get it, I'll get it! | LEONARD *(Two steps behind)*: I've got it, I've got it! |

(Parker stomps in, shaking a blizzard of snow off his head and shoulders. He wears work shoes and a parka with an enormous fur-lined hood. He scoops Dinah up in his arms and whirls her around in circles.)

PARKER: Dinah, Dinah . . .

DINAH *(Clinging to him)*: Oh, Parker . . .

PARKER: Sorry I'm so late, I got lost.

CLIO *(Gazing at him in rapture)*: Parker Bliss . . .

TATE: It's snowing?

LEONARD: HEY, PARKER . . . !

TATE: When did it start snowing?

CLIO: I'm going to die.

PARKER *(Showering Dinah's face with kisses)*: Threads, Threads! . . .

LEONARD *(Trying to horn in)*: YOU OLD SON OF A BITCH!

DINAH: I've missed you so!

PARKER *(Thrusts Dinah out at arm's length)*: Hey, sweet thing, let me get a good look at you!

DINAH *(Reaching for him)*: Come back, come back!

PARKER *(Pointing at her dress)*: Peer Gynt, the Olympic Theatre!

DINAH: You got it!

LEONARD: "Anitra, oh thou true daughter of Eve, how can I refuse you? I am but a man."

PARKER *(Bursts out laughing, scooping Dinah back into his arms)*: You're too much, too much!

LEONARD *(To Clio)*: Like I said, we've done a lot of shows together—Washington, Philadelphia, New York . . .

TATE *(Goes to the door and gazes out)*: Boy, look at it come down.

CLIO *(Shivering)*: Oooh, shut the door, Robert, that wind is wicked!

TATE: Robert? Who's Robert?

(Parker squeezes Dinah tighter and roars.)

CLIO *(All innocence)*: Robert?
TATE: You just said, "Shut the door, Robert, that wind is wicked."
CLIO: I did?
TATE: As clear as a bell.
CLIO: You've lost your mind.
TATE: Not my mind, just my bearings. *(He plunges out the door)*
CLIO *(Starts to follow him)*: Toto, where are you going? It's freezing our there!
DINAH *(To Parker)*: Hold me, hold me.
PARKER *(Squeezing her tight)*: It's been so long.
DINAH *(Barely audible)*: My dearest, my darling . . .
CLIO *(Reentering the room)*: Don't mind him.
LEONARD *(Dancing around Parker and Dinah)*: When do I get my turn? I want my turn!
PARKER *(Lifting Dinah off her feet)*: God, I love this woman!
LEONARD *(Trying to pull Parker and Dinah apart)*: No fair, no fair! What about me?
PARKER *(Finally catches Leonard's eye and starts laughing)*: Hey, Handsome, how are the bees?
LEONARD: *Busy!*
PARKER: Come on, get over here.

(They roar and pummel each other.)

(Parker grabs Leonard in a bear hug and kisses him square on the lips) MAA! *(Holding him at arm's length, laughing)* Look at you, you crazy son of a bitch!
LEONARD: I *am* a crazy son of a bitch, aren't I?
PARKER *(Imitating him)*: "I *am* a crazy son of a bitch, aren't I?" Jesus Christ, you never change.

(They start air boxing.)

DINAH *(To Clio)*: Men . . .
CLIO: Please!
DINAH: They're such little boys.

CLIO: You should see Tate when he gets together with his friend Walter. Forget it!

DINAH: Where *is* Tate, by the way?

CLIO: *Who knows!*

(There's a sudden banging on the front door. Leonard and Parker stop air boxing.)

DINAH: Goodness, who can that be?

CLIO: Beats me.

LEONARD *(Heading toward the door)*: Well, there's one way to find out.

DINAH: Careful now, there are all kinds of maniacs out there.

(The knocking gets louder. No one moves.)

PARKER: I'll get it. Let me. *(He opens the door)*

(Tate stands shivering on the threshold, a light mantle of snow dusting his head and shoulders.)

Yes, may I help you?

TATE: Ohhhhh, it's freezing out there!

LEONARD: Todd!

CLIO: Zum-Zum!

DINAH: Tate!

CLIO: There you are!

DINAH: Where have you been?

TATE: I just stepped out for a fresh of breath air.

LEONARD: Come in, come in.

TATE *(Entering, stomping snow off his feet)*: Oooohhhh!

LEONARD *(Introducing him to Parker)*: Todd, Parker. Parker, Todd . . .

TATE *(Extending his hand)*: Parker!

PARKER *(Shaking it)*: Todd!

CLIO *(Touching Parker's arm)*: Tate!

PARKER *(Finally seeing her)*: You!

CLIO *(Staring back)*: Parker Bliss . . .

PARKER: Clio Hands . . .

DINAH: You know each other?

PARKER: *I don't believe it!*
CLIO: I'm speechless.
PARKER: I adore you!

(*Silence as they gape at each other.*)

DINAH: When did you meet?
PARKER: We've never met. *(Takes her hand and kisses it)*
DINAH: Oh.

(*Leonard ushers Parker into the living room.*)

LEONARD: Well, come on in and stay a while. Take off your parka,
    Parker. *(He laughs at his cleverness)*
PARKER *(Rooted to the spot)*: Clio Hands . . .
TATE *(Strides over to Clio, pulling her close)*: Hi, Coco.
PARKER: I must be dreaming.
CLIO: Hi, Totes.
TATE: How're you doing?
CLIO: Fine, fine . . .
PARKER *(To Leonard and Dinah)*: Didn't you see *Tiger Bright*?
LEONARD AND DINAH: *Tiger Bright*?
TATE *(Under his breath)*: Here we go . . .
PARKER: The movie.
LEONARD *(To Clio)*: You were in *Tiger Bright*?
PARKER: She was a vision . . .
LEONARD: I didn't know that.
PARKER: A vision.
DINAH: Gosh.
LEONARD: So, you're a movie star?
CLIO: Hardly, it was my first film.
PARKER: That scene where you danced with the dwarf . . . *(He
    groans)* She smiled this smile . . . her lips started to tremble,
    or should I say melt . . . No one in the theater could breathe.
    (While gesturing, he accidentally brushes Clio's breast) It was
    as if she'd handed us her soul.
TATE *(Quickly pulling her away from Parker)*: That's my Clicker.

(*Clio walks away from them both.*)

DINAH: Well . . .

(Silence.)

And how's Patsy these days?

LEONARD: Yeah, how *is* Patsy?

CLIO: Patsy?

DINAH: His wife.

CLIO: Oh.

PARKER: Fine.

DINAH: I love Patsy.

PARKER: Everyone loves Patsy.

DINAH: Well, she's a great woman.

PARKER: Tell me about it.

(Silence.)

LEONARD: Come on, take off your coat and stay a while.

(Parker takes off his coat, revealing a large dried bloodstain on his shirt. Everyone screams.)

LEONARD:	DINAH:	CLIO: Blood!	TATE: Are you
Jesus Christ!	Parker . . . ?!		all right?!

LEONARD: You were telling the truth!

DINAH: A mobile home *did* run wild!

TATE: Holy shit!

CLIO *(Covers her eyes and sways)*: Oh God!

(Parker collapses in a chair, burying his face in his hands.)

DINAH *(Rushing over to him)*: Oh, Parker . . .

LEONARD: Son of a bitch . . .

DINAH: Baby, baby . . .

CLIO *(Sinking into the sofa)*: I'm going to faint.

LEONARD: I thought you made it up.

DINAH *(To Parker)*: Speak to me.

LEONARD: I'm stunned.

(Clio faints.)

TATE *(Rushing over to Clio)*: Darling . . .

DINAH *(To Parker)*: Say something!

LEONARD: He was telling the truth all along.

TATE: Can you hear me?

LEONARD: You could knock me over with a feather.

(Clio comes to and groans.)

TATE *(Grabbing her hands)*: My beauty, my sweet . . .

CLIO: Whoooooo . . .

TATE: What happened?

DINAH *(Unbuttoning Parker's shirt)*: Here, let's get you out of this.

(Dinah eases it off him. The blood has seeped through to his undershirt.)

| DINAH: | CLIO: More | LEONARD: | TATE: Oh |
| Uughhh! | blood! | Jesus Christ! | no . . . ! |

(Clio passes out again as Dinah helps Parker off with his undershirt. Traces of blood linger on his chest. More horrified gasps.)

DINAH: Baby, baby, does it hurt?

PARKER: It's not my blood.

(Dinah recoils from him with a groan.)

LEONARD: Whose *is* it?

TATE *(To Clio)*: Speak to me!

PARKER: It's from the ten-year-old boy who died in my arms.

LEONARD: Oh God!

CLIO *(Coming to)*: Where am I?

TATE *(To Clio)*: Right here, safe and sound with me.

PARKER: His car was sliced in half by the thing.

DINAH: Awful, awful . . .

PARKER: It was the strangest sight . . . seeing this *house* plowing down the highway.

LEONARD: He's cold, Dine, get him something to put on.

DINAH: Right, right . . . *(She exits)*

PARKER: It was a split-level ranch with redwood siding.

TATE: He's in shock.

PARKER: I saw a woman through the window. She was doing the dishes in the kitchen sink, washing this huge enamel pot. You know, one of those black and white speckled things you cook corn or lobsters in . . . She was scrubbing it with this yellow brush . . . I've never seen such a color. It was that neon yellow students underline textbooks with—only brighter. But how could that be? People don't live in those giant mobile homes when they're being transported, and they certainly don't do the dishes while they're moving. Yet I saw her as clear as day . . . There was no sign of her after the crash, though . . . Strange . . . It's a miracle more people weren't killed when you stop to think about it. A fifty-ton split-level ranch ricocheting across a four-lane highway . . . It's a wonder any of us escaped.

DINAH (*Returning with an assortment of kingly robes and doublets*): Here, I brought you some things from my collection.

PARKER: Eeny, meeny, miney, moe.

LEONARD: Dinah, this isn't a play.

(Silence.)

CLIO (*To Dinah*): Didn't you do the costumes for that wonderful *Hedda Gabler* we saw at the New York City Festival a few years ago?

TATE: I remember that, lots of starched linen and high-button shoes.

DINAH: You saw it?

CLIO: We see everything at the Festival.

LEONARD: She also works at Baltimore Rep, the Boston Theatre Company, Altered Stages . . .

CLIO: You're a busy woman.

DINAH: A frantic woman!

PARKER: Ohhh, I'm freezing. (*Reaching for a robe*) Let me have one of those, would you?

DINAH (*Handing him one*): God, what *was* that from?

CLIO: Ohh, it looks great.

PARKER: Yeah?

DINAH: *Pericles? Coriolanus? (Adjusting the shoulders)* It fits perfectly.

CLIO: Well, the woman's a brilliant designer.

PARKER: Hear, hear.

DINAH: Uuugh!

LEONARD: *Richard the Second.*

DINAH: *Richard the Second!*

CLIO: I love that play.

PARKER: It's the best, the best.

LEONARD:
> For God's sake let us sit upon the ground,
> And tell sad stories of the death of kings . . .

DINAH: Talk about ancient history . . .

PARKER: Sold out every night.

LEONARD:
> How some have been deposed, some slain in war,
> Some haunted by the ghosts they have deposed,
> Some poisoned by their wives, some sleeping killed . . .

DINAH: You should have seen Leonard.

LEONARD:
> All murdered . . .

DINAH: He was so handsome, he looked like a god.

CLIO: He still does.

DINAH *(To Leonard)*: You hear that?

CLIO: You've got great bones.

PARKER: Why do you think I call you "Handsome," Handsome?

DINAH: Ahhh, the lure of beauty.

TATE: The lure of beauty . . .

DINAH: It's a killer, a killer.

LEONARD *(Grabbing a robe and putting it on)*:
> For within the hollow crown
> That rounds the mortal temples of a king
> Keeps Death his court; and there the antic sits,
> Scoffing his state and grinning at his pomp . . .

PARKER *(Unsheathes an imaginary sword and starts doing* Henry V*)*:
> Once more unto the breach, dear friends, once more,
> Or close the wall up with our English dead . . .

LEONARD: *Henry the Fifth!*
CLIO: Go for it!

LEONARD *(Entering into the spirit)*:
> But when the blast of war blows in our ears,
> Then imitate the action of the tiger.
> Stiffen the sinews, conjure up the blood . . . *(He pauses, unsure of the words)*

DINAH: Disguise . . .

LEONARD:
> Disguise fair nature with hard-favored rage . . .

PARKER:
> Cry havoc and let slip the dogs of war!

(Parker links arms with Leonard and starts marching around the room with him.)

Hut, two, three, four; hut, two, three, four . . .
DINAH: And they're off: The March of the Kings!
PARKER AND LEONARD: Hut, two, three, four; hut, two, three, four . . .

(Parker toots an imaginary trumpet and Leonard mimes playing a xylophone.)

DINAH: Don't mind them, this is something they do.
CLIO: Hey, wait for me! *(She dashes in front of them and mimes being a baton-twirling drum majorette)*

(They march around the room with rising gusto.)

PARKER: About . . . face!

(The band switches direction and function. Parker plays a trombone, Clio bangs a drum and Leonard becomes the baton-twirling drum majorette.)

Fall out! *(Sweeping Clio into his arms)* Well, you're quite an accomplished little musician.

(Leonard continues to march, tossing an imaginary baton.)

CLIO: I played trumpet in my high school band.

(Parker keeps Clio in his embrace; they lock gazes.)

TATE *(Taking Clio's arm)*: Clio's a woman of many talons.
PARKER: So I see.
DINAH *(Linking arms with Parker)*: Still the same old Parker.
TATE: She acts, she marches, she plays musical elephants . . .
CLIO: Come on, Toto, let up.

(Dinah and Tate separate Parker and Clio. Leonard keeps marching around the room tossing his baton.)

DINAH: Leonard . . . ?
PARKER: Go, Handsome!
DINAH: Don't encourage him.
LEONARD: Hut, two, three, four; hut, two, three, four . . .
PARKER *(To Dinah)*: So, you're here year-round now?
DINAH: This is it. Just me, Leonard and the bees.
PARKER *(To Clio and Tate)*: They used to have the most magnificent apartment on Central Park West.
CLIO: No kidding.
DINAH: Leonard inherited it from an aunt.
PARKER: Ceilings up to here, and forget the view.
TATE: We have a place there, too.
DINAH: But then things got tough and we had to sell.
LEONARD *(Whirling in the opposite direction)*: About face!
TATE: In the Beresford.
DINAH: I don't want to hear.
CLIO: What a coincidence!
TATE: The top two floors.

DINAH *(Places hands over her ears)*: Don't!

LEONARD: Double time! *(He marches and tosses in double time)*

DINAH: Oh well, easy come, easy go.

CLIO: We've just bought a summer place here.

PARKER: Ahhh—

TATE: We're renovating the Van Alstyne mansion next door. Fourteen rooms and six fireplaces.

CLIO: It's a nightmare.

DINAH: Leonard, you're making me dizzy!

(Leonard comes to a stop.)

PARKER: Renovations always are. *(Pause)* So, what do you do, Todd?

CLIO *(Correcting him)*: Tate.

TATE: I'm a scream writer.

DINAH: Wait, I thought you said . . .

TATE: I write screams.

CLIO: Don't listen to him, he's pulling your leg.

(Tate suddenly screams very loud. Everyone freezes.)

He's an editor.

PARKER: Well, well . . .

CLIO: Editor-in-chief, as a matter of fact.

(Tate screams again.)

He's head of Raven Books.

PARKER: Whoa, that's one of the classiest publishing houses in the country!

TATE: So I'm told.

LEONARD: Well . . .

(Silence.)

(To Dinah) Sweetheart, haven't you forgotten something?

DINAH: Who, me?

LEONARD: It starts with *D.*

DINAH: Let me think. Um, *drinks,* hors *d'*oeuvres . . .

LEONARD *(In a whisper)*: Dinner.

DINAH *(In a panicked little voice)*: Dinner?

LEONARD: It's almost eleven o'clock.

DINAH: Oh my God . . .

PARKER: Thanksgiving with all the trimmings?

LEONARD: Thanksgiving with all the trimmings!

DINAH: *Dinner!*

TATE: You need any help?

PARKER *(To Clio and Tate)*: It's the only meal she ever makes. Birthdays, Easter, Fourth of July, out comes the Butterball.

CLIO: Tate does Thanksgiving at our house.

DINAH: DINNER! . . . *(She hikes up her skirts and dashes into the kitchen. She starts hurling pots and pans every which way)* Start the beans, fix the cranberry sauce, finish the sweet potatoes . . .

CLIO: He's a great cook.

PARKER: Lucky you. *(Drifting over to her again)* And lucky Tate.

CLIO *(Gazing into Parker's eyes)*: Why, thank you.

TATE: Lucky Tate, that's me all right. Yes siree Bob, I've got it all.

> Old King Cole
> Was a merry old soul
> And a merry old soul was he,
> He called for his pipe
> And he called for his bowl,
> And he called for his fiddlers three . . .

(There's a series of loud crashes from the kitchen.)

DINAH: Whoops . . . easy does it, easy does it.

LEONARD *(Yelling to Dinah)*: ARE YOU OKAY IN THERE?

DINAH: FINE, FINE, NOT TO WORRY . . . Open the cranberry juice, dump it into a bowl, add a little orange juice, cut up some celery . . .

TATE:

> Every fiddler, he had a fiddle,
> *And a very fine* fiddle had he . . .

CLIO: Don't mind him, it's stress.

PARKER: Ah, stress.

LEONARD: Good old stress.

CLIO: He works too hard.

(Silence.)

DINAH *(Rushing back into the room, wearing an apron)*: Talk, talk—everything's under control. It will just be a couple of minutes. *(She dashes back to the kitchen)*

(Silence.)

TATE: I've always liked Old King Cole, he knew how to enjoy life. He had his pipe, his bowl, his fiddlers three . . . I've often wondered if he was married. If there was an old *Queen* Cole in the picture. What do you think, Clee?

CLIO: I have no idea.

TATE: Maybe it was the *absence* of a wife that made him so merry. He didn't have to worry what she was up to all the time. What do you think?

CLIO *(Getting upset)*: I said, I don't know.

TATE: I say he was unencumbered.

CLIO: Totey, please . . .

(Silence.)

DINAH *(Reenters the room)*: Talk, *talk*! *(She waits)*

(The silence deepens.)

LEONARD *(To Parker)*: So . . .

(Dinah rushes back to the kitchen.)

. . . how come you never call?

PARKER: Never call?

LEONARD: It's been six years and not a word, a murmur, a sneeze. I thought we were friends.

PARKER: We are friends.

DINAH *(From the kitchen)*: OH NO, I DON'T BELIEVE IT!

LEONARD: I haven't worked since *Cyrano*. It's been eleven years, *eleven years*! You're a big director now . . . movies, TV specials every other week . . . Why won't you hire me?

PARKER: I was almost killed a couple of hours ago.

LEONARD: I was your favorite actor!

PARKER: A ten-year-old boy died in my arms.

LEONARD: I need a job.

PARKER: You know what he kept saying?

LEONARD: This is a tough business, I'm not getting any younger.

PARKER: "I've got a stitch in my side."

LEONARD: I need all the help I can get.

PARKER: *"I've got a stitch in my side!"*

LEONARD: I'm going crazy.

DINAH *(Staggers in, carrying an enormous raw turkey)*: LOOK, I FORGOT TO TURN THE OVEN ON!

TATE: Oh no!

DINAH: Snow white and cold as ice.

LEONARD: Dinah supports us now.

PARKER: His legs were severed at the knee.

LEONARD *(Indicating the turkey)*: There I am . . .

PARKER: They were lying on the hood of his car.

LEONARD: Dead meat!

PARKER: It could have been me, so kick up your heels while they're still attached.

DINAH: What am I going to do?

TATE *(Taking the turkey from her)*: Not to worry, I'll just fillet it into cutlets, dust them with a little rosemary and olive oil and stick them under the broiler. They'll be ready in no time. *(He exits to the kitchen)*

DINAH *(Near tears)*: I'm so ashamed.

PARKER: Drain the cup and dance the dance.

DINAH: Everything was going to be perfect.

LEONARD: So, it's dancing you want. I'm versatile, what are you looking for? A little soft shoe? *(Dances)* A little tap?

DINAH: My one foolproof meal . . .

CLIO *(Heading toward the kitchen)*: Well, I think I'll go see what Tate's up to.

(Leonard tap-dances in front of her, deliberately blocking her way.)

Excuse me, I was just . . . *(Trying to get past him)* Sorry,
sorry . . .

LEONARD: I may not be as young as I once was, but I still have
technique.

DINAH: This is getting scary.

(Clio finally manages to escape.)

LEONARD: No, wait! I know, you're looking for something a little more south of the border. You're just a stone's throw
away from Mexico these days. Why didn't you say something? *(He starts doing flamenco steps)*

DINAH: Everything's out of control.

PARKER: Easy, Handsome, easy . . .

LEONARD: I'm intuitive, but I'm not a mind reader. *(He dances
with rising gusto, adding yelps and hand clapping)*

DINAH: Parker's homecoming, and look at us. I'm a wreck, you're
dancing the flamenco, and our guests are making dinner!

Act Two

Scene 1

An hour later. Dinner is almost over and hilarity reigns. Leonard, Dinah and Parker have just taught Clio and Tate how to play the finger-snapping, hand-clapping game, Concentration. Plates pushed to one side, they're about to start a new round. Leonard's at the head of the table, with Tate on his left. Dinah's at the opposite end with Parker on her left and Clio on his left. They've changed into elegant nineteenth-century Chekhovian costumes. The encroaching trees and shrubs are starting to close in on them.

LEONARD *(Establishing the rhythm)*: Are you ready? . . . If so . . . here we go . . . starting with . . . names of boats. *(Pause)* The *Titanic*!

TATE: The *Andrea Doria*!

DINAH: Um, um . . . the *Lusitania!* Parker . . . ? *(Placing her hand on his)*

PARKER: The *Normandie*! *(He empties his wine glass and slams it down for emphasis)*

CLIO: *Kon-Tiki.*

LEONARD:	DINAH:	TATE: Nice!	*(Parker touches her*
Whoa!	Very good!		*shoulder, making a*
			hissing sound.)

LEONARD *(Picking up speed)*: Um . . . the *Nina*!
TATE: The *Pinta*!
DINAH *(With a Spanish flourish)*: And the *Santa Maria*! Olé!
PARKER: The *Mayflower*! *(Reaches across Clio and helps himself to more wine)*
CLIO: The *Arabella*, John Winthrop's boat.

LEONARD:	DINAH:	TATE: That's	*(Parker*
She's good.	My, my . . .	my girl!	*whistles.)*

CLIO *(Helping herself to more stuffing)*: Mmmm, I can't stop eating this stuffing!
LEONARD *(Picking up speed; in a French accent)*: The *Île de France*!
TATE *(Likewise)*: The *De Grasse*!
DINAH: Um, um . . . Help, I can't think!
THE OTHERS *(To Dinah)*: You're out, you're out.
LEONARD: Go on, Park, it's your turn.
PARKER: The *Constitution*. *(He drains his glass)* Great wine!
DINAH: I've got it, I've got it, the *Intrepid*!
LEONARD *(To Parker)*: Glad you like it.
CLIO: The *Mauretania*! Ohhh, this stuffing! *(Helping herself to more)*
DINAH: The *Queen Mary*!
LEONARD: Dinah, you're out.
DINAH: The *Queen Elizabeth*!
LEONARD: The *Pequod*!
TATE: The *Pequod*?
DINAH: The *Q.E. II*!!
LEONARD: From *Moby Dick*.
TATE *(To Leonard, breaking the rhythm)*: I know where the *Pequod* comes from, I thought we were only naming real boats.
LEONARD *(To Tate)*: All boats, the more literary the better.
DINAH: The H.M.S. *Pinafore*!
TATE: Then why didn't you say so at the outset?
LEONARD: My apologies.
TATE: It is helpful to know the rules, you know.

LEONARD: You're right, you're right, I wasn't thinking.

TATE: Who knows what I might have come up with, I am an editor, after all.

CLIO *(Piling more stuffing on her plate)*: Ohhhh, what is it about this stuffing?

TATE: The *Antelope* from *Gulliver's Travels*, the *Patna* from *Lord Jim*, the *Nellie* from *Heart of Darkness* . . .

DINAH *(Starts singing)*:

> I am the monarch of the sea,
> The ruler of the Queen's Navee,
> Whose praise Great Britain loudly chants.
> And we are his sisters and his cousins and his aunts . . .

Come on, Parker, help me.

TATE *(To Leonard)*: So the sky's the limit? You're including boats from films and lyrics as well?

LEONARD: Everything, the works.

CLIO *(Joining Dinah)*:

> And so do his sisters and his cousins and his aunts!
> His sisters and his cousins,
> Whom he reckons up by the dozens,
> And his aunts!

PARKER *(Applauding Clio)*: Bravo, bravo! More wine?

CLIO *(Starting to get tipsy)*: Let 'er rip!

PARKER *(Filling Clio's glass and then his)*: I've got to hand it to you, Handsome, this is terrific wine.

CLIO: And forget the stuffing!

LEONARD: Glad you like it, glad you like it.

PARKER: I haven't had this much fun in a dog's age.

(Tate hands his glass to Parker to refill.)

TATE: Party, party!

CLIO *(Running her hands down her bodice)*: And it's so great getting to wear these costumes!

PARKER *(To Dinah)*: *God, I've missed you!*

DINAH: Oh, Parker . . .

CLIO: I feel like we're all in *The Cherry Orchard* or something.

PARKER: Remember the old days?

CLIO: I've played Varya three times.

DINAH: We used to dress up every night.

LEONARD: It's true.

PARKER: Every night. *(Returning Tate's filled glass)* Here you go.

CLIO: It's one of my favorite roles.

DINAH: Monday, Greek tragedy; Tuesday, Restoration comedy; Wednesday, Theater of the Absurd . . . God, what happened?

PARKER: Good question.

LEONARD: Life.

PARKER: Shit.

TATE: Same difference.

PARKER: Hear, hear.

(Silence.)

CLIO *(Reciting as Varya)*: "I don't think anything will come of it for us. He is very busy, he hasn't any time for me—and doesn't notice me. God knows, it's painful for me to see him—"

DINAH *(To Parker)*: You went into movies, Leonard went crazy and I . . . who knows.

PARKER: Leonard's always been crazy.

LEONARD: I *have* always been crazy. I wonder why.

PARKER: Because you're an actor.

DINAH: Because he lost touch.

PARKER: All actors are crazy.

CLIO: Thanks a lot.

DINAH: He can't cope, he lives in his own world.

TATE:

Hey diddle diddle! The cat and the fiddle,
The cow jumped over the moon . . .

LEONARD:

The little dog laughed
To see such sport
And the dish ran away with the spoon.

(To Tate) You're right, these little babies say it all.

(Silence.)

CLIO *(Reciting as Varya again)*: "Everybody talks about our marriage, everybody congratulates us, and the truth is, there's nothing to it—it's all like a dream—" *(Pause)* "You have a brooch looks like a bee."
PARKER *(Applauding Clio)*: Nicely done.

TATE:

> Hickety, pickety, my black hen,
> She lays eggs for gentlemen.

(Silence.)

LEONARD *(To Parker, with sudden rage)*: *You abandoned me, you ingrate!*
DINAH: Leonard?
LEONARD: Once you left the theater, I never worked again.
PARKER: Hey, hey, you can't pin that on me.
LEONARD: No one wanted me. I was too old, too young, too tall, too short, too real, too . . .
DINAH: That's not true, you were offered all kinds of roles.
LEONARD: Yeah, lousy ones.
PARKER: Work is work.
LEONARD: Bad plays, incompetent directors . . .
PARKER: You do what you have to do.
LEONARD: I have standards . . . unlike some people I know.
DINAH: Now, now . . .
LEONARD: Not all of us sell out.
PARKER: Opportunities present themselves, things change.
LEONARD: I don't change.
PARKER: Everything changes.

TATE:

> Little Boy Blue,
> Come blow your horn,
> The sheep's in the meadow,
> The cow's in the . . .

PARKER, LEONARD AND DINAH: *Will you shut up!*

TATE: Sorry, sorry . . .

(Silence.)

DINAH: Me, I'm designing six shows this season. It's insanity, but, hey, it puts food on the table.

TATE: And it was delicious.

DINAH: Thanks to you.

LEONARD *(To Parker)*: Why won't you cast me in a movie?

TATE *(To Dinah)*: Please.

LEONARD: Huh? *Huh?!*

PARKER: It's a different medium.

LEONARD: You mean, you only cast stars.

DINAH *(Suddenly clamps her hand down on her head)*: Ohhh, I just had the most massive déjà vu. Whoooooo . . .

CLIO: What causes those anyway?

DINAH: Ahhhhhhh . . .

TATE: They're small cerebral strokes, gentle prods to remind us that lunacy's just a heartbeat away.

LEONARD: Let's hear it for the crazy people! *(He rubs his finger up and down his lips)*

DINAH: Easy, honey, easy.

LEONARD *(Reaches a crescendo and stops)*: Ahhh, I needed that.

DINAH: The great thing about Leonard is he lets everything out. There's no holding back with him. Lucky dog.

LEONARD: It's one of my many gifts.

DINAH: It *is* a gift.

TATE: Indeed.

DINAH: I wish I had it.

LEONARD *(Bowing)*: Why, thank you.

(Silence.)

PARKER: Well, where were we?

(Silence.)

CLIO *(To Leonard)*: You just said the *Pequod*.

LEONARD: Right, right . . .

TATE *(Resumes the rhythm)*: The *African Queen*!

DINAH: The *Love Boat*!

LEONARD:	TATE:	PARKER:	CLIO: No fair,
Honey, you're	I thought she	What's going	no fair.
out!	was out.	on?	

PARKER *(Picking up speed)*: The *Caine Mutiny*!
CLIO: *Mutiny on the Bounty*!
LEONARD: The *Dixie Queen*!
DINAH: The Good Ship Lollipop!
THE OTHERS *(To Dinah)*: YOU'RE OUT OF THE GAME!
DINAH: Ohhh, Noah's ark on you all!
LEONARD: Let's add marine figures of speech.
TATE: Um . . . *(Picking up speed)* Ship of state!
DINAH: Ship of Fools!
PARKER *(Eying Clio meaningfully)*: Shipshape!
CLIO *(Returning his gaze)*: Dreamboat.
PARKER *(Dropping the rhythm)*: Thar she blows!
CLIO *(With rising ardor)*: Batten down the hatches!
TATE *(To Clio)*: That's not a figure of speech.
DINAH: And it's not your turn.
PARKER *(Moving closer to Clio)*: Man overboard!
CLIO: SOS, SOS . . .
PARKER: Coming about!
DINAH: Hey, hey . . .
CLIO: Shiver my timbers!
TATE: What's going on?
PARKER: Yo ho ho and a bottle of rum!
CLIO: Heigh ho, heigh ho, it's off to work we go.
PARKER: I'll huff and I'll puff and I'll blow your house down!
CLIO: Not by the hair of my chinny-chin-chin!
DINAH: Guys . . . ?!
TATE *(To Parker)*: It's not your turn!
PARKER *(To Clio)*: Rapunzel, Rapunzel, let down your hair!
CLIO: My, what big teeth you have!
PARKER *(Licking his chops)*: All the better to eat you with!
TATE AND DINAH: STOP THE GAME, STOP THE GAME!

(Silence.)

CLIO (*Collapsing against Parker*): Ohhh, that was fun . . .
PARKER: You're really good.
CLIO: Well, you're not so bad yourself.

(*Dinah and Tate eye her angrily; she quickly straightens up.*)

DINAH: So . . . anyone want seconds on anything?

(*Silence.*)

(*She rises and starts to clear the table*) Then on to the salad!
TATE: There's more?
CLIO: I'm going to burst.
PARKER: What are you trying to do? . . .
LEONARD: Hold on to your hats, you ain't seen nothing yet!
PARKER: Kill us?

(*Dinah exits to the kitchen.*)

PARKER (*To Clio*): So . . . how often do you come up here? Just weekends or . . . oh sorry . . . sorry . . .

CLIO (*To Parker*): I can't believe I finally met you! (*Hand over her heart*) Parker Bliss . . . !

(*Silence.*)

LEONARD (*To Tate*): So . . . how's the renovation coming? I see you're stripping the paint right down to the . . . sorry . . .

TATE (*To Leonard*): Tell me, when was this house built? I figure it was more or less the same time as . . . whoops . . .

(*Silence.*)

PARKER (*To Clio*): I was just wondering how often you . . .

CLIO (*To Parker, her hand over heart*): Boom boom, boom boom, boom boom . . .

(*Silence.*)

LEONARD *(To Tate)*: That's got to cost serious money. I also notice you're repointing all the . . .

TATE *(To Leonard)*: I've checked the records at the County Clerk, but they don't have anything before 1850 because of the . . .

(Silence.)

PARKER: . . . come here?
LEONARD: . . . chimneys!
TATE: . . . fire!
CLIO *(Placing Parker's hand over her heart)*: Feel it.
PARKER *(Feeling it)*: Whoa!
CLIO: Boom boom, boom boom, boom boom!

(Parker keeps his hand on her heart as Tate shoots them murderous looks.)

(Putting her hand over Parker's) Scary, huh?

(Dinah staggers in carrying a salad inside an insanely large bowl fashioned from a skylight. She pauses at the sight of Parker and Clio so intimately involved and drops the salad in front of them with a resounding thud.)

DINAH: UUUUGH!
PARKER *(Pulling back in his chair)*: JESUS CHRIST . . .
CLIO: Look at the size of that bowl!
DINAH: I picked it fresh this morning.
CLIO: A person could take a bath in it.
DINAH: From inside the coat closet. It's like a greenhouse gone mad—mushrooms nesting in the mittens, avocados blooming in the galoshes, broccoli sprouting out the umbrellas . . .
LEONARD: She's exaggerating.
DINAH: A wave of vegetable lust is surging through the house, it keeps us awake at night. The pollinating and fertilizing, the germinating and foliating—you've never heard such a din . . . Green beans quickening, okra stiffening, zucchini swelling . . .
LEONARD: Dinah!
DINAH: Oh, the burgeoning and urgency of it all! *(Picks up a bottle of Wish-Bone Italian salad dressing and reads the ingre-*

dients in a booming voice) "Water, soybean oil, vinegar, salt, garlic, onion, sugar, red bell peppers, lemon juice . . ."

(Dinah shakes the bottle so violently that everyone cowers in their seats.)

LEONARD: Easy, easy!

DINAH *(Still shaking the bottle)*: And then there's the roiling of the leafy things that wait! Swiss chard shuddering, spinach seething . . .

LEONARD: Don't mind her.

DINAH: Arugula unfurling on the chairs. Cabbage writhing, endive panting, hearts of palm ululating under the bed. *(She pours the dressing over the salad, splashing everyone in the process)*

| LEONARD: Watch it! | CLIO: Help! | TATE: Hey what's . . . | PARKER: Look out! |

DINAH: And don't forget the clamor of the ripening fruit. *(She starts tossing the salad)* The crooning of the cauliflower, the pleading of the chili peppers . . .

LEONARD: Dinah, Dinah . . .

DINAH: *(Taking on their voices)*: "Yoo hoo, here I am, behind the curtains." "Pssst, over here, under the sink . . ."

PARKER *(Pushing away from the table)*: Hey, hey . . .

DINAH: The entreaties of the tomatoes, the yodeling of the yams . . . "Look up, I'm inside the light fixture." "Open your eyes, you fool, I'm right under your nose!" *(She starts heaving spoonfuls of salad onto Parker)*

LEONARD *(Head in his hands)*: Jesus God . . .

DINAH *(Burying Parker with rising abandon)*: The gasping and groaning, the clasping and moaning, you've never heard such carryings on. Cucumbers thrusting, carrots plunging . . .

PARKER *(Trying to ward her off)*: What do you think you're doing?

DINAH: Eggplants crying out for more . . .

LEONARD *(Grabbing her arms)*: Stop it, Dinah. Stop it!

DINAH: Tendrils snapping, seeds spattering, ruby red juices seeping through the floor . . .

LEONARD: *I'm begging you!*

PARKER *(Rises, pushing Dinah to the floor)*: GET A GRIP ON YOURSELF!

(Dinah lands with a scream. There's an awful silence as everyone stares at her.)

TATE:

> Mary, Mary, quite contrary,
> How does your garden grow?
> With silver bells and cockleshells
> And pretty maids fornicating in a row.

(Silence.)

LEONARD *(Overcome)*: God, oh God, oh God . . .
TATE: Well, that was quite a . . .

(Silence.)

CLIO *(Rising)*: Excuse me, which way to the little girls' room?
LEONARD *(Pointing)*: Down the hall.
PARKER *(Rises, pulling back his chair)*: Madame . . .
CLIO *(To Parker)*: Don't get up.

(Dinah gets up with a groan as Parker doffs an imaginary hat toward Clio.)

DINAH *(To Parker, dusting herself off)*: Ever the perfect gentleman.

(Clio sashays down the hall. She throws Parker a backward glance and disappears. Silence.)

LEONARD: Well . . .
DINAH: I'm sorry, I don't know what came over me.
LEONARD *(Softly)*: Po-Po, Po-Po, I want Po-Po!
DINAH *(An echo)*: Po-Po.
TATE: The stick of the blind man invents a new darkness.
PARKER *(To Tate)*: What was that again?
TATE: The stick of the blind man invents a new darkness.
PARKER: Nice, very nice.

TATE: I read it on a placard in a bus the other day.

LEONARD: My pope, my pip, my little pup . . .

DINAH: My dope, my dip, my little dup.

LEONARD: My yes, my own!

DINAH: My bless, my throne!

TATE *(Sotto voce to Parker)*: Who's Po-Po?

PARKER: Their married daughter who lives in Tacoma. They're very close.

TATE: Ohh, I thought it was a pet.

PARKER: They like to shout out her name.

TATE: "Po-Po"?

PARKER: It's short for Phoebe.

LEONARD *(Mournful)*: Po-Po, Po-Po, I want Po-Po!

PARKER: It's something they do. It's a way of staying in touch.

LEONARD *(Waving to Dinah)*: Hi, Dine.

DINAH *(Waving back weakly)*: Hi, Leonard.

LEONARD: How's it going?

DINAH: I don't like this anymore.

LEONARD: Me either.

DINAH: *No, I really don't like it!*

(An awful silence.)

TATE: Well, this has been quite an evening.

PARKER: I'll say.

TATE *(To Parker)*: You narrowly escaped death, we met our new neighbors, had a few laughs, got through the blight. I mean, *night*. That's the hard part.

DINAH: Tell me about it.

PARKER *(Raising his wine glass)*: To getting through the night.

(Parker drinks. Tate joins him.)

DINAH *(Starts clearing the table)*: So how about a little dessert?

PARKER: There's more?

TATE: I couldn't eat another bite.

PARKER: Me either.

LEONARD: When you come to our house for dinner, you dine, right Dine?

(Parker groans at the play on words.)

DINAH: You got it! And now for dessert—the pearl in the oyster, the ruby in the crown . . . *(She plunges into the kitchen)* Pumpkin pie, homegrown, if you please!

PARKER: Dinah, Dinah . . . !

TATE: Holy shit!

LEONARD: My favorite!

DINAH: And . . . *(Returning, bearing pies aloft)* Honey nougat meringue, compliments of Leonard's bees.

LEONARD: Let's hear it for the bees!

TATE: When it rains, it pours!

DINAH *(Setting them down with a thud)*: Gentlemen, go to it!

(Clio emerges from the bathroom and slowly makes her way back to the dining room. Parker turns and sees her.)

LEONARD *(Beaming at Dinah)*: Look at her! Have you ever seen anyone more beautiful? *(Pause)* Well, have you?

DINAH *(To Leonard, embarrassed)*: Honey . . . ?!

PARKER *(Quickly turning back to look at Dinah)*: Never!

TATE *(Reaching for the meringue)*: Well, maybe just a spoonful.

DINAH *(Handing each one a server)*: Dig in, dig in.

PARKER *(Rising from his seat)*: Excuse me, I'm afraid I'm going to have to use the facilities first . . .

(Leonard attacks the pumpkin pie and Tate samples the meringue as Clio and Parker collide in the darkened hallway.)

CLIO: Oh, hi.

PARKER: Hi.

CLIO *(Brushing against him)*: Sorry, I was just . . .

PARKER *(Suddenly grabs her in his arms)*: Ohhh, you wonder, you marvel, you shining girl . . . *(He pushes her against the wall)* You destroy me! I can't see, I can't walk, I'm in flames. *(He starts kissing her)*

CLIO: No, no don't, they'll see us.

PARKER *(All over her, barely audible)*: I wanted you the moment I saw you . . .

CLIO *(Starting to melt)*: Ohhhh . . . ohhhhhhh . . .

PARKER: Your face, your eyes, your skin, your voice . . . Sweet Christ, I've never seen anything like you . . .

CLIO (*Returning his kisses*): Ohhh . . . ohhhhhhh . . .

(*Even though they can't see them, Dinah and Tate hear every word and freeze in horror.*)

Parker Bliss . . .

PARKER: Clio Hands . . .

TATE (*Rising from his seat*): You son of a bitch . . .

LEONARD (*Wolfing down more pie*): Ohhhh, this is great pie, Dine, *great* pie!

Scene 2

Seconds later, Clio and Parker enter the room, shamefaced. No one moves.

DINAH (*To Parker*): How could you . . . ?

TATE (*On his feet*): I'm going to kill you!

LEONARD (*In ecstasies over the pie*): Ohhhh, ohhhhh . . .

(*A ghastly silence as everyone looks at Leonard.*)

DINAH (*Embarrassed*): Leonard . . . ?

TATE (*To Parker*): That's my *wife*, you asshole!

LEONARD: It's so *moist*! (*He groans with pleasure*)

PARKER (*Returning to the table*): Well, it's getting late.

CLIO (*Looking at her watch*): It *is* getting late.

LEONARD: It's her specialty.

TATE (*Advancing toward Parker*): Just who the hell do you think you are?

LEONARD (*Gobbling down more*): Her *pièce de résistance* . . .

PARKER (*Backing away*): Hey, hey . . .

CLIO (*Threading her arm through Tate's*): Come on, we've got to get up early tomorrow.

TATE (*Shaking Clio off*): I don't like guys manhandling my knife. (*He pushes Parker backward*)

CLIO AND DINAH (*Correcting him*): Wife.

PARKER: Take it easy.

TATE *(Pushing him harder)*: Make me!

LEONARD: Hey, what's going on?

DINAH *(To Leonard)*: Later, later . . .

PARKER: Are you threatening me?

TATE *(Pushing him harder)*: What does it look like?

CLIO *(Trying to pull Tate away)*: Toto!

TATE *(Violently pushing Clio away)*: Get your hands off me!

CLIO *(Massaging her wrist)*: Ow!

LEONARD *(Looking up from his pie)*: What happened?

PARKER *(To Tate)*: Don't push her.

TATE *(To Parker)*: What did you say?

LEONARD *(Louder, to Parker)*: What happened?

PARKER *(To Tate)*: I said: Don't. Push. Her.

DINAH *(To Leonard)*: Later, honey, later.

PARKER *(To Tate)*: What's the matter, do you have a hearing problem?

TATE: No, I have an asshole problem and it's you! *(He takes a swipe at Parker)*

CLIO: Tater, *please*!

DINAH *(Rushing between them)*: My costumes, my costumes!

CLIO: Oh God, the costumes! Careful, careful . . .

(Tate and Parker quickly shed their costumes.)

LEONARD: Will someone please tell me what's going on?

DINAH: Forget it Leonard, just crawl back in your hole.

CLIO: They're so beautiful, it would be terrible if they got damaged.

DINAH: It's like living with a dead person. You've gone, checked out, flown the coop . . .

PARKER *(Putting up his dukes)*: Okay, come to Papa . . .

LEONARD: "Flown the coop" . . . ?

TATE *(Dancing around him)*: You lowlife, you scum . . .

LEONARD *(To Dinah)*: What are you talking about?

DINAH: It's every man for himself.

PARKER *(Moving in on Tate)*: Pretentious wimp . . .

DINAH *(Rushing to shield Parker)*: Don't touch him!

CLIO *(Pulling at Tate)*: Stop it!

TATE *(Pushing Clio)*: Get away from me, bitch!

PARKER *(To Tate)*: Come on, hit me, hit me.

CLIO *(To Tate)*: Fuck you!

DINAH *(To Tate)*: I'm warning you. *(She bares her teeth and snarls)*

CLIO *(To Tate)*: Just, *fuck you*!

DINAH *(To Tate)*: Ass-wipe!

CLIO *(To Tate)*: Dickhead!

LEONARD *(To Tate)*: Scumbag!

TATE *(To Leonard)*: Just a minute here, he made a play for *my wife*!

DINAH: Butt-wad!

CLIO: Shit-face.

LEONARD: Jerk-off!

TATE: Not that it's any great surprise, given her track record.

CLIO: What's that supposed to mean, "given her track record"?

TATE:

> Jack be nimble,
> Jack be quick,
> Jack jump over
> The blind man's stick.

> You'd better have quick reflexes, it's dark out there and very dangerous, in case you haven't noticed. There's a randomness at large, something wayward and unnatural.

LEONARD: One false move and you're done for. Kaput, finis . . . exit the king.

TATE: Mother Goose was no fool, she knew what was going on. Her rhymes are charms against disaster. Shout them out loud and often enough and you'll be safe. You should hear Clicks and I when the going gets rough . . . She's very good. She makes up her own.

(Silence.)

PARKER: Well, I don't know about the rest of you, but I've got to get up early tomorrow. Patsy's got an opening at the Modern.

DINAH: Oh, don't go!

TATE *(To Parker)*: At the Modern?

PARKER: My wife's a sculptor.

CLIO *(To Tate)*: Come on, Pooks, time to go.

(Tate doesn't move.)

Pookie?!

TATE: Right, right! *(To Parker)* You wouldn't be talking about Patsy Cincinnati, would you?

PARKER: You got it.   DINAH: That's her.   LEONARD: The one and only.

CLIO AND TATE *(Stopping in their tracks)*: You're married to Patsy Cincinnati?

PARKER: Whoops, I'd better put on some clothes here. *(He grabs his shirt and starts putting it on)*

CLIO: Wow, Patsy Cincinnati!

TATE: She's major, her work's shown all over the world.

PARKER *(Thrusts out his arms and bows, revealing the blood-stain again)*: Meet Mr. Patsy Cincinnati.

(They all scream with horror.)

DINAH: You can't wear that. Put the Chekhov shirt back on.

(Dinah helps Parker into the shirt. Clio and Tate look down at themselves and realize they're still in costume. They hastily start to change.)

CLIO: What's she like?

TATE: At the Tate, the Jeu de Paume, the Reina Sofia . . .

LEONARD: Tiny.

DINAH: And very feminine. You'd never know she was a sculptor to look at her.

LEONARD: You can practically pick her up with one hand.

CLIO: You're kidding!

PARKER: I wouldn't try it, though.

TATE: The Castello di Rivoli, the Hara Museum, the Moderna Museet . . .

PARKER *(To Tate)*: Well, well, don't we know the art scene.

(Silence.)

DINAH: She has wonderful hair.

PARKER: She does have wonderful hair.

DINAH: *(Indicating on herself)*: Corkscrew curls out to here.

CLIO: Patsy Cincinnati . . . Wow.

PARKER: I could drop off the face of the earth and she wouldn't even notice.

DINAH AND LEONARD: *Parker?!*

PARKER: You know what she calls me these days? Maestro! She's forgotten my name. She leaves these messages on my answering machine—"Hi, maestro, it's me. How's Hollywood?" But hey, I can't complain, she's got a great eye. Look, she picked out this parka for me . . . *(Putting it on)* "I wanted to get you something warm," she said. "I don't want my maestro shivering on the set." Well, you know Patsy and her circulation, the woman's got a perennial chill . . . *(Pause)* Let's just hope I don't run into any more runaway mobile homes on my way back.

DINAH: Oh, don't leave.

LEONARD: Mobile homes, sinking homes, no one's safe.

TATE: You can say that again. Well, we ought to be heading along too. *(Hands Clio her coat)* Here you go, Clee.

CLIO *(Putting it on)*: Thanks, Pooks. Luckily, we're right next door.

LEONARD: Well, you never know, crazed Enid Brill could always pop out of the bushes and mow you down.

DINAH *(Clinging to Parker's arm)*: Oh, stay a few minutes more.

TATE: Stop by the next time you pass the house, we could use a break.

CLIO *(Hugging Dinah)*: Yes, do, I feel so drawn to you. You're so there.

TATE *(Pulling Clio toward the door)*: Come on, Clue . . .

CLIO *(To Dinah)*: If I don't call you, you call me, okay? It can get pretty lonely around here, in case you haven't noticed. I've been abandonéd.

LEONARD *(Impressed with her accenting)*: My, my!

CLIO: Stranded in the middle of nowhere.

TATE *(Putting his arm around her)*: But with me.

CLIO: I'm never with you. You're either working or locked up with the painters and carpenters. When I walk in a room you don't even see me. I wave and it's like no one is there. Well, some day you'll take me in and when that happens . . .

(Getting weepy) Oh my . . . *(Recovering)* Once we get the place fixed up we'll just be here weekends and during the summer, but Tate insists we live here while the work's being done. You know, *to keep an eye on things.* He's temporarily moved his office up here. I've never renovated a house before, so I'm not that much help. I look at wallpaper, pick out paint and talk to the contractor—that is, when he shows up. Which is hardly ever.

TATE *(Places hands over his ears)*: Don't . . .

CLIO: He's impossible. He's also the fattest man I've ever seen. And the hairiest. He has a full beard and is covered with fur, thick brown fur. He looks like a woolly mammoth.

LEONARD AND DINAH: Frank Flood.

CLIO AND TATE: Frank Flood.

DINAH: She's right, he *does* look like a woolly mammoth!

PARKER: Woolly mammoths . . . I love woolly mammoths!

LEONARD: He's the best, the best.

TATE: But try getting him to make an appearance.

CLIO: I'm quite fond of him, actually. He's one of the few people I see. I have fantasies of leaping on his shoulders and galloping back to the dawn of time. Just him and me and the saber-tooth tigers. *(Pause)* Thank God I've got a film this spring.

(Clio reaches into her bag, pulls out a scrap of paper and quickly scribbles down her phone number.)

TATE *(Shaking hands with Dinah and Leonard)*: We had a great time. Good food, lively conversation . . .

CLIO *(To Dinah)*: Now call me.

DINAH: I will.

CLIO: Don't forget.

DINAH: Wait a minute, let me give you some of Leonard's honey. *(She starts rummaging through a drawer)*

PARKER *(Shaking hands with Clio)*: It was a pleasure.

CLIO: Likewise. *(She slips Parker the piece of paper with her phone number on it)*

DINAH *(Handing Tate several jars of honey)*: Here you go.

PARKER *(Glancing at the piece of paper)*: Why, thank you.

TATE: Much obliged. *(Pulling her toward the door)* Okay, Coco, time to go home.

LEONARD: I'll get the door. *(He opens it)*

(The wind howls louder than ever.)

Fucking wind!

TATE: Thanks again. Next time you must come to our house. *(He pulls Clio out after him)*

CLIO *(Waving)*: Good night, good night . . .

DINAH: Quick, shut the door.

LEONARD *(Slams the door behind them)*: Son of a bitch!

DINAH: Well, that was quite a . . .

(Silence.)

LEONARD *(To Parker)*: Come on, take off your coat and stay a while.

PARKER *(Zipping up his parka)*: I've really got to go.

DINAH *(Hanging on him)*: Stay, stay!

PARKER: I can't.

LEONARD: We haven't begun to catch up.

DINAH: Spend the night.

PARKER: I *can't*!

LEONARD: Please?

DINAH: Pretty please?

PARKER *(Opening his arms to Leonard)*: Come here, you lunatic.

(Leonard rushes into Parker's arms.)

(Lifting him off the ground) Ughhh!

LEONARD: Come on, stay! You can sleep in Po-Po's room.

PARKER *(Lets him go and opens his arms to Dinah)*: Hey, Threads . . .

DINAH *(Rushing into Parker's arms)*: Oh Parker, Parker . . . !

PARKER: That's my girl.

DINAH *(Clinging to him)*: Don't go!

PARKER *(Pulling away)*: I've got to, Patsy's waiting.

DINAH: Stay, I'm begging you!

PARKER *(Putting an arm around each of them)*: Guys, it was great, just like the old days. I forgot how much fun you were. I don't have friends like you anymore. Funny how things change.

LEONARD: Hilarious.

PARKER: Here I am this big movie director and I don't have any real friends.

LEONARD: My heart is breaking.

PARKER: And then there's the work, which is a whole other kettle of fish. Or is it worms? It sure ain't Shakespeare. Oh well, we do our best. Right?

LEONARD: Do we?

PARKER *(Heading out the door)*: Okay, I've got to go.

DINAH *(Reaching for him)*: Come back!

PARKER: I'll call you in a couple of days, I promise. *(And he's gone)*

DINAH *(Running out the door after him)*: Don't leave me . . .

LEONARD: Easy, Dine, easy . . .

DINAH: Don't leave me!

LEONARD *(Pulling her back inside)*: Where are you going?

DINAH: Come back!

LEONARD *(Slamming the door shut)*: It's cold out there.

DINAH: *(Getting weepy)*: He left, he left . . .

LEONARD: Well, that's Parker for you. Selfish son of a bitch.

DINAH *(Throwing herself facedown on the sofa)*: Oh, Leonard . . .

(Silence.)

LEONARD: So, what did you think of the evening?

DINAH: It was a disaster.

LEONARD: It *was* a disaster, wasn't it?

DINAH: Total.

LEONARD: What did you think of our new neighbors?

DINAH: I couldn't stand them.

LEONARD: She was very taken with you.

DINAH: I'd say Parker was the one she was taken with.

LEONARD *(With disgust)*: Parker!

(Dinah sighs. Silence.)

You know, you looked really beautiful tonight.

DINAH: Please!

LEONARD: No, you did.

DINAH: Not next to her.

LEONARD: I'd take you over her any day, no contest.

DINAH: Well, Parker seemed to like her.

LEONARD: Parker . . .

(Silence.)

Well, that was quite some performance with the salad.

DINAH: Salad . . . ?

LEONARD: Talk about throwing yourself at someone.

DINAH: I don't know what came over me.

LEONARD: How do you think it made me feel?

DINAH: I couldn't stop myself.

LEONARD *(Covering his ears)*: I don't want to hear.

DINAH: Once I started, I just . . .

LEONARD: I said, *I don't want to hear!*

DINAH: Sorry, sorry . . .

LEONARD: Give a guy a break.

(Silence.)

DINAH *(Rising)*: God, look at the place. It looks as if a bomb went off. *(She starts putting the costumes away)*

LEONARD: Something did happen between you. It was during the production of *Cyrano*. There was a real charge between you. Hello . . . ? You there in the Chekhov outfit. I'm right, aren't I? You can tell me, it was almost ten years ago.

DINAH: Twelve.

LEONARD: Whatever.

DINAH: Twelve and a half, to be exact.

LEONARD: Parker's a very charismatic guy, look what happened to Whoosis tonight.

DINAH: *Clio Clio! Think Cleopatra, for Christ's sake! It's not that hard a name!*

LEONARD: You don't have to yell.

DINAH *(Starts clearing the table)*: I mean, after a while . . .

LEONARD: She succumbed while her husband was in the room, at least you were more discreet. Come on, tell me, I can take it.

DINAH *(Sings, carrying the dishes into the kitchen)*:
Someone's in the kitchen with Dinah
Someone's in the kitchen I know-ow-ow-ow . . .

Someone's in the kitchen with Dinah,
Strumming on the old banjo . . .

LEONARD: What happened?

DINAH *(Returning)*:
They're strumming fee, fie, fiddly-i-o;
Fee, fie fiddly-i-o;
Fee, fie, fiddly-i-ooooo . . .
Strumming on the old banjo.

LEONARD: Well . . . ?
DINAH: Give it up, Dinah, just *give it up*.
LEONARD: I'm waiting.
DINAH: Okay . . . We were in your dressing room going over some costume changes after the show one night. The theater was empty, it was just Parker and me in a sea of plumes and doublets, and suddenly he's all over me, his hands, his mouth, his tongue, anything that protrudes . . . And he's murmuring, "Ohhhh, you wonder, you marvel, you shining girl. You destroy me! I can't see, I can't walk, I'm in flames . . . Your face, your eyes, your skin, your voice . . ."
LEONARD: Why does that sound so familiar?
DINAH: Because he just said it to Clio five minutes ago. The only difference is she gave in and I didn't.
LEONARD: What did you say?
DINAH: I said, *she gave in and I didn't*! What's the matter, are you deaf now too?
LEONARD: Nothing happened?
DINAH: I guess I showed them. Oh yes, I showed them good!
LEONARD: *Nothing happened?*
DINAH: That's right, rub it in.
LEONARD: Nothing happened.
DINAH: And one more time. *(Moving her arms like a conductor, she mouths, "Nothing happened")* It's a shocker, but there you are.
LEONARD: I don't know what to say.
DINAH: The joke's on me. Everyone assumed it was a fait accompli, so it wouldn't have made any difference. Good old Dinah, ever the dutiful wife. *(Imitating herself)* "It's not

right, Leonard would never get over it, he's bound to find out, I know him. He'll see it in my eyes, he'll smell it in my hair, nothing gets past him when it comes to me."

LEONARD: You were faithful.

DINAH: If you can call it that. I wanted him, I just couldn't go through with it. Don't ask me why, I've been trying to figure it out for the past eighty years. No, ask, ask . . . on second thought, you'd better not, it's too humiliating.

LEONARD: You didn't do it, you didn't do it!

DINAH: I lacked courage, I wasn't up to it. It's pathetic.

LEONARD: And all this time I thought . . . *(Folding her in his arms)* Oh, baby, baby . . .

DINAH: I wanted him.

LEONARD: You didn't do it.

DINAH: I wanted him.

LEONARD: It's all right.

DINAH: Oh, Leonard . . .

LEONARD: Let it out . . .

DINAH: You're not listening to me. *(She starts to cry)* I said, "I wanted him, I wanted him, I wanted him, I wanted him . . ."

LEONARD: I know, I've always known. I've just been lying low. But you . . . how you held your ground all these years . . . It takes my breath away. You don't lack courage, you can't contain it! You're like the cauliflower under our bed, fierce and tenacious . . .

DINAH: Oh, Leonard . . .

(They look at each other and slowly embrace. The wind starts to howl.)

LEONARD: Fucking wind!

DINAH: I can't take it anymore! *(She rushes to the front door and flings it open, facing the wind)* HEY, YOU OUT THERE, LET UP ALREADY! SHOW A LITTLE RESPECT FOR ONCE. WE'VE GOT SOME SERIOUS CATASTROPHES ON OUR HANDS!

(The wind howls louder.)

A BREAKDOWN HERE, A LOSS OF NERVE THERE, A
MAJOR IMBALANCE IN THE ORDER OF THINGS . . .
(Pause) SAVINGS GONE . . .

LEONARD *(Joining her)*: A BACKED-UP SEPTIC TANK . . .

DINAH: TWENTY DOLLARS IN THE CHECKING ACCOUNT . . .

LEONARD: CORRODING WATER PIPES . . .

DINAH: TEN MORE YEARS ON THE MORTGAGE . . .

LEONARD: A LEAKING ROOF . . .

DINAH: WE'D APPRECIATE SOME PEACE AND QUIET, IF
YOU DON'T MIND.

(Dinah retreats a few steps.)

LEONARD: Bats in the attic . . .

DINAH: Mice in the basement . . .

LEONARD: Swallows in the kitchen . . .

DINAH: Eagles in the pantry . . .

LEONARD: *(To Dinah)*: *Eagles* in the pantry?

DINAH *(Heading back into the wind, yelling with new fury)*: I'M
NOT ASKING, I'M TELLING YOU. IT'S TIME FOR A
CHANGE!

*(Leonard joins her, pulling her close. They hold their ground
against the gale which finally starts to subside.)*

END OF PLAY

Rembrandt's
Gift

Production History

Rembrandt's Gift received its world premiere in March 2002 by the 26th Annual Humana Festival of New American Plays, Actors Theatre of Louisville. It was directed by John Rando. The set design was by Paul Owen, costume design was by Jane Greenwood, lighting design was by Tim Saternow and sound design was by Kurt B. Kellenberger. The stage manager was Alyssa Hoggatt. The cast was as follows:

POLLY SHAW	Penny Fuller
WALTER PARADISE	Josef Sommer
REMBRANDT VAN RIJN	Fred Major

Rembrandt's Gift was revised and produced in September 2005 at the Madison Repertory Theatre in Madison, Wisconsin. It was directed by Rick Corley. The set design was by Jack Magaw, costume design was by Janice Pytel, lighting design was by Jacqueline Reid, composition/sound design was by Joe Cerqua and fight choreography was by Tony Simotes. The stage manager was Jessica Connelly. The cast was as follows:

POLLY SHAW	Wendy Robie
WALTER PARADISE	Douglas Rees
REMBRANDT VAN RIJN	Larry Neumann, Jr.

Characters

POLLY SHAW, a photographer, sixties

WALTER PARADISE, her husband, an actor and hoarder, beset with Obsessive-Compulsive Disorder, sixties

REMBRANDT VAN RIJN, the great Dutch painter, fifty-seven

Act One

The day after tomorrow.

Walter and Polly's top-floor loft in downtown Manhattan. Towers of folded theatrical costumes, including hats, boots, kingly robes, swords and parasols rise to the ceiling, obscuring the windows and blocking out the light. The costumes are slowly advancing into the room, pushing the sleeping, eating and living areas closer and closer together. Narrow footpaths wind through this maze, disappearing into other rooms that have already been swallowed up. Only one small corner has resisted this onslaught— Polly's studio. It contains a standing mirror, a field camera and a few samples of her photographs, which transform minute areas of her naked body into brutal landscapes. This bizarre sanctuary is protected by a blizzard of locks, both ancient and state-of-the-art, that adorn the front door. A poster of Rembrandt's Kensington self-portrait, advertising his latest retrospective at the Metropolitan Museum of Art, hangs on the wall. It glows eerily, thanks to one of Polly's ingenious lighting effects. It's early spring and still quite dark. The sun slowly starts to rise. Polly and Walter are in bed. Walter is snoring.

POLLY: Walter? Walter?

(Walter snores louder.)   215

Are you awake?

(And louder.)

Sweetheart?

(And louder still.)

I can't sleep! *(In a singsong)* Walllllter? Oh Walllllter? WALTER?
WALTER *(Waking with a start)*: Ugh! Ugh!
POLLY: I've been tossing and turning all night! Sweetheart?
WALTER: Uuuuugh . . .
POLLY *(In a loud whisper)*: Are you awake? Darling?
WALTER *(Groggy)*: I am now.
POLLY: *This is it!*
WALTER: Do you have any idea how many times I've been up
    tonight?
POLLY: The landlord's coming to evict us. Thanks to you and
    your damned hoarding!
WALTER: Try, seven.
POLLY: With the New York Fire Department!
WALTER: No, make that eight.
POLLY: *Finita la commedia!*
WALTER: Fucking prostate!
POLLY: What are we going to do?
WALTER: I'd like to see you try and urinate with a prostate the
    size of an Idaho potato!
POLLY: Where are we going to go?
WALTER: I finally fall asleep after peeing my guts out half the
    night and what do you do?
POLLY: It's starting to get scary . . .
WALTER: Wake me up because you can't sleep!
POLLY: Very scary!
WALTER: You don't give two shits about my prostate!
POLLY: That's not true. I adore your prostate!
WALTER: Bullshit!
POLLY: I worship the ground it walks on.
WALTER: Prostates don't have legs!
POLLY: All right, I worship the ground it . . . dangles over.
WALTER *(Angrily getting out of bed)*: Yeah, yeah . . .
POLLY: Hey, where are you going?

WALTER: Where do you think I'm going? To pee. For the ninth time tonight, in case you're interested. *(Spotting Rembrandt's self-portrait)* Not him again!

POLLY: Yes, him again, he comforts me! He was our age and he kept going.

WALTER: He's like one of those creepy Jesus pictures with the 3-D eyes! It's enough you have him staring at me all day, but then you have to rig up special lights so he hounds me all night as well!

POLLY: It's a great painting!

WALTER: It's a depressing painting!

POLLY: Look at the outlines of those mysterious hemispheres . . . They're so abstract! It's like he suddenly started dabbling in Cubism. I mean, here's this seventeenth-century artist gazing out at us, and he's painted these totally modern circles in the background. What is he trying to say?

WALTER: How should I know? Ask him!

POLLY: And they're so perfectly drawn! Yet the hands that wrought them are a blur. As if too exhausted . . . or disgusted to complete themselves.

WALTER *(Heads into the bathroom)*: I'm getting out of here.

POLLY: If you squint, they look like maps of the world, but there's no trace of continents or oceans. They're just outlines . . . and incomplete ones at that. So why did he put them there? And what are they supposed to mean? You've got to admit, it's pretty tantalizing! *(Pause)* HELLO? CAN YOU HEAR ME? Walllllter? Oh WALLLLLLTER? *(Listening)* What are you doing in there? You're not washing your hands again, are you? You already spent two hours at the sink this evening! Your skin will fall off if you keep this up! Walter? SWEET-HEART . . . ? *(Pause)* Yoo-hoo, are you still alive?

(Silence. Walter flushes and returns.)

So, how did it go?

WALTER: I came, I saw, I conquered.

POLLY: Good boy.

(Silence.)

WALTER *(Getting back into bed)*: Excuse me, but do I know you?

POLLY: I'm your wife.

WALTER: Ah.

POLLY: Polly.

WALTER: Ah . . .

POLLY: Polly Shaw.

WALTER: Ah . . .

POLLY: The photographer who did all those self-portraits a hundred years ago.

WALTER: Right . . .

POLLY: The photographer whose studio gradually disappeared under all your crap.

WALTER: Right, right . . .

POLLY: The photographer who's going to be evicted later this evening.

WALTER: That's enough, dear.

POLLY: And who are you, if you don't mind me asking?

WALTER: Man of a thousand faces—tyrant, madman, lover and fool.

POLLY: I mean, what the hell have you become?

WALTER: Your wish is my command—Oedipus, Iago, the Tin Woodman . . .

POLLY: I give up. *(Pause)* Sing to me.

WALTER: Sing to you?

POLLY: It calms me down.

(Walter sings "The Sidewalk Is Laid Out in Concrete Squares" like a Baroque round. Polly joins him in sweet harmony. Then silence.)

Thanks, I needed that.

WALTER: Anytime, anytime. *(Snuggling up to her)* Mmmm, you're so warm . . . My little heating pad, my toaster oven, my sizzling hot plate . . .

POLLY: Hey, what are you doing?

WALTER: Adoring you. Mmmmmm, you smell like nutmeg . . . Have you been rolling in the spices again?

POLLY *(Pulling away)*: I don't like this anymore!

WALTER: Like what?

POLLY: Your craziness!

WALTER: Could you be more specific?

POLLY *(Leaping out of bed)*: You're burying us alive!

WALTER: Hey, where are you going?

POLLY: TO HELL IN A HANDBASKET!!

WALTER *(Grabbing her in his arms)*: There, there, something will come up, it always does.

POLLY: But I can't move.

WALTER: An act of God, a bureaucratic glitch, a man bearing gifts. *(Suddenly cocking his head)* Shhh! Listen! I hear someone breathing. *(Running over to the door)* I've got to check the locks!

POLLY: Honey, no! We haven't even had breakfast yet!

WALTER *(Throwing a kingly robe over his pajamas, he kneels by the door and starts checking the many locks, incanting in a breathy altered voice)*: One, two, buckle my shoe; three, four, lock the door; five, six, pick up sticks; seven, eight, lay them straight; nine, ten a big fat hen . . . Objects in the mirror are closer than they appear. By far, by far, by far, by far . . . Yet oh so near, so near, so near, so near . . .

POLLY *(Over him)*: Walter, please!

WALTER: Boy oh boy oh boy oh boyo, we don't want any accidents here. No siree Bob! No dead bodies piled up on this side of the road, thank you very much! And that means you, Eddie, Franz, Wilhelm and Pepe! *(Suddenly stopping)* Wrong! Wrong! Alphabetically, you asshole! You know the rules!

POLLY: Not this morning! Not today!

WALTER: Now you'll have to start all over again! *(Pummeling his head with each word)* STUPID! STUPID! STUPID! STUPID! *(Resuming his incantation, picking up speed)* One, two, buckle my shoe; three, four, lock the door . . .

POLLY *(Trying to pull him away from the door)*: We've got to start cleaning up . . .

WALTER: Five six, pick up sticks; seven eight, lay them straight . . .

(Polly knocks him off balance, he falls.)

(Anguished) Now I'll have to start all over again. Once I start, I have to finish. You know that!

POLLY *(Going to the closet)*: You are not checking those locks again!

WALTER: If I'm interrupted, it doesn't count!

POLLY *(Returning with several large black plastic garbage bags and heading toward a stack of costumes)*: Come on, sailor, let's get this show on the road.

WALTER *(In an awful voice)*: DON'T TOUCH MY THINGS!

(Polly starts singing "There's No Business Like Show Business" as she stuffs costumes into the bag.)

(Grabbing her wrists) I said, don't touch!

POLLY: But you never wear them!

WALTER *(Posing in his kingly robe)*: Excuse me.

POLLY: You haven't been onstage in over twenty years!

WALTER: I want to be ready when the call comes.

POLLY: The "call"? What "call"?

WALTER: The call to return.

POLLY: First of all, you're not going to get any call.

WALTER: A bird in the hand is worth two in the bush!

POLLY: And second of all, since when do actors have to provide their own costumes?

WALTER: I happen to have one of the definitive costume collections in the country.

POLLY: This isn't a collection, it's a catastrophe!

WALTER: Who else had the foresight to acquire Olympic Rep's entire costume shop when the theater went belly up?

POLLY: ONE PERSON CAN'T POSSIBLY WEAR ALL THIS CRAP!

WALTER: It's not to wear, it's to *have*! I'm an actor, Polly. These are the tools of my trade.

POLLY: But what about me and the tools of *my* trade?

WALTER: Tools? What tools?

POLLY: Some light would be nice . . . And a little room to move around in.

WALTER: What are you talking about? We have plenty of light.

POLLY: For growing mushrooms! I can't see my hand in front of my face! Which is something of a drawback if you're a photographer.

WALTER *(Kidding around)*: You're a photographer?

POLLY: I was, a hundred years ago. It's how I caught your eye, in case you've forgotten. *(Lowering her voice)* Remember my . . . breastscapes?

(Walter presses his hands to his heart.)

I miss it, Walter. I really do.

WALTER: Miss what?

POLLY: Plying my veils.

WALTER: What about your latest ear series?

POLLY: I'd like room to photograph more than my ears, thank you very much!

WALTER: It's some of your best work—the tiny winding canals, the fleshy lobes . . .

POLLY: Forgive me for being crass, but do you see anyone buying it?

WALTER: What do dealers know?

POLLY: What sells!

WALTER: Polly, Polly . . .

POLLY: Plus . . .

WALTER: Calm down . . .

POLLY: Plus, if there were a fire in here, the place would go up like a tinderbox!

WALTER: If there were a fire? What fire?

POLLY: Any fire!

WALTER: I'm a custodian, a curator . . .

POLLY: You're a hoarder and you need help! *(She resumes stuffing costumes into a plastic bag)*

WALTER *(Overlapping, trying to drown her out)*: Peas and carrots, peas and carrots, peas and carrots, peas and carrots, peas and carrots . . .

POLLY *(Stuffing more frantically)*: This is it, Walter! The decisive moment! Either we save ourselves or we're out on our asses!

WALTER *(Rushing at her)*: Stop it! Stop it! Put those back! I said put them back!

(They struggle. Suddenly there's an intergalactic explosion followed by anguished howls and the sound of breaking glass. Rembrandt van Rijn bursts through the mirror in a shower of blinding light, which becomes a spotlight that follows him everywhere. He's dressed like his Kensington self-portrait, clutching his palette, brushes and maulstick. Polly and Walter draw back in terror. His howls turn to desperate prayers recited in Dutch.)

REMBRANDT *(In Dutch)*: Lighten my darkness, I beseech thee, O Lord. I am an agèd man who hath lost his way. Give me light that I may see again . . . *(In a loop)*

POLLY *(Overlapping)*: Oh. My. God . . .

WALTER: Now just one minute . . .

REMBRANDT *(In Dutch)*: Lighten my darkness, I beseech thee, O Lord.

POLLY: My God, my God, my God, my God . . .

WALTER: Who the hell is he?

REMBRANDT *(In Dutch)*: I am an agèd man who hath lost his way.

POLLY: Sweetheart, do you see who that is?

WALTER: And how the hell did he get in here?

REMBRANDT *(In Dutch)*: Give me light that I may see again.

POLLY: I don't believe it!

WALTER: I just checked the locks!

REMBRANDT *(Raising his hands, suddenly speaking in English)*: Lighten my darkness, I beseech thee, O Lord.

POLLY: Look at his clothes . . .

REMBRANDT: I am an agèd man who hath lost his way.

WALTER: Answer me, how did he get through that door?

REMBRANDT: Give me light that I may see again!

POLLY: The white hat, the lace dickey, the fur-trimmed coat . . .

WALTER: Of course! How stupid could I be?

POLLY: The palette and paintbrushes . . .

REMBRANDT: Darkness o'erwhelms me! I have lost everything— family, home and good name.

WALTER: You came through the mirror!

POLLY: It's Rembrandt!

REMBRANDT: Mercy! Mercy!

WALTER *(To Polly)*: He's a fucked-up second-story man!

POLLY: Walter, it's Rembrandt van Rijn!

WALTER *(Twirling him around)*: Nice threads! Right out of a Restoration comedy . . . I like a man with style, even if he is a thief. Nice, very nice. *(He pauses and bows)*

(Rembrandt stares at him, confused. Walter bows again. Rembrandt mimics him. Walter does a more florid bow, Rembrandt imitates that as well.)

Clever, very clever. *(To Polly)* He's quite a mimic.

POLLY: I can't breathe!

(Walter does a little soft-shoe number. Rembrandt copies it to perfection. Walter pauses to think and then launches into a spirited tap routine.)

(Sotto voce to Walter) Honey, what do you think you're doing?

(Rembrandt executes the tap routine flawlessly.)

(In a stage whisper) It's Rembrandt! He came!

WALTER *(Fast, trying to trip him up)*: "Peter Piper picked a peck of pickled peppers; a peck of pickled peppers Peter Piper picked"?

REMBRANDT *(Even faster)*: "If Peter Piper picked a peck of pickled peppers, where's the peck of pickled peppers Peter Piper picked?"

POLLY: I have just one question: How on earth can Rembrandt speak English so well?

WALTER *(In a grand voice, testing him further)*: "Now is the winter of our discontent made glorious summer by this sun of York . . ."

REMBRANDT: "And all the clouds that lour'd upon our house in the deep bosom of the ocean buried."

POLLY: And Shakespeare, for God's sake! Well, why not? There were probably Shakespearean traveling companies all over Europe. One just never imagines Rembrandt reciting *Richard the Third*.

WALTER: You're telling me this is Rembrandt?!

POLLY: It's a miracle! My prayers have been answered!

WALTER: And I'm supposed to be the crazy one around here!

POLLY: You said something would come along and save us. *(Nudging Walter, eyeing Rembrandt's brush and palette)*

WALTER: It was a figure of speech.

POLLY: Well, here he is! *In the flesh!* I'm going to die!

WALTER: The resemblance is striking, I admit.

POLLY *(With a flourish)*: Welcome to our humble home!

WALTER: The face, the hat, the palette and brushes . . .

POLLY: The pool of light . . .

WALTER: Pool of light?

(Rembrandt notices that he's standing in a spotlight. He takes several steps to escape it. It follows him.)

POLLY *(In a stage whisper)*: See, it follows him wherever he goes.

(Rembrandt starts rushing around the room trying to shake it, but can't.)

Forgive our manners, we should introduce ourselves. I'm Polly Shaw and this is my husband, Walter Paradise.

WALTER: She's the famous one.

POLLY: Now, now . . .

WALTER: One-woman shows all over the world . . .

POLLY: Please!

WALTER: Feted by the greats and near greats . . .

POLLY: A thousand years ago.

WALTER: This woman redefined the limits of nude self-portraiture.

(Rembrandt is now doing vaudeville moves trying to escape the spot. He has a sudden coughing fit and starts to stagger. Polly catches him and guides him to a chair.)

POLLY: Sit, sit . . . The poor thing's exhausted. *(Crouching down beside him)* What is it? What's wrong?

(His coughing intensifies.)

WALTER *(Backing away from him)*: Jesus Christ, he's probably got the plague! It wiped out half the population of Amsterdam during his lifetime.

POLLY *(Terrified)*: The plague?!

WALTER: The guy's a carrier and now we've been exposed!

(They cover their faces as the spotlight around Rembrandt slowly fades.)

Thanks, pal, thanks a lot!

REMBRANDT *(Weakly)*: Prithee, calm thyselves, thou hast no cause for alarm. I suffer not from the plague, though those closest to me have succumbed to its deadly grip. My beloved wife, Saskia, and our first three children, while still in their infancy. *(He suppresses a sob)* Only Titus remains . . . My family is gone. Funeral bells toll night and day. Ne'er an inch of ground remains to bury the dead. Those who are interred are exhumed to make room for those freshly ta'en. 'Tis an irony most cruel that this old body has 'scaped its wrath—the eldest and most pitiful. I am at the nether end of my years—bankrupt and ruined. I survive on scraps of bread and herring and have few students and fewer commissions. A large painting of mine was recently returned by the elders of the Town Hall, rejected for its bold chiaroscuro. Eager to gain favor, I cut it down and reworked it, only to have it returned. I have become the laughingstock of Amsterdam, carving up my canvases like blocks of cheese. 'Tis the classical style that's in favor now. Vermeer and his pristine interiors which appear to have been exhaled onto the canvas, not painted. Verily, the artist's hand hath been severed, so I no longer enjoy my former reputation. Gone are the anatomy lessons, the militia portraits and silk merchants with their plump wives . . . All that remains is this sagging visage, so I pass my days amusing myself in the guise of prophets, saints and fools . . . Moments ago I was seized with such despair, I hurled myself into the very glass that mocked me, but rather than shatter, it melted like ice on a summer day and I found myself here—dancing and speaking a language I know not, with nary a drop o' blood on my hands. I ha' been visited by a host of wondrous dreams in my fifty-seven years, but this one now with thee—'tis the strangest of them all.

(A long silence as Polly and Walter gaze at him.)

WALTER: Jesus H. Christ . . .

POLLY: He thinks it's a dream.

REMBRANDT: Could you spare a scrap of bread? I swoon with hunger.

POLLY: Quick, get him something to eat.

WALTER *(Exiting to the kitchen)*: Aye, milady.

POLLY *(Yelling after him)*: What would a Dutchman like?

WALTER: Something with a little . . . *hollandaise* sauce, get it? *(He roars with laughter)*

REMBRANDT: 'Tis not merely the body that dances to hunger's tune, but the mind as well.

POLLY: How about a nice piece of Gouda cheese?

WALTER *(With an edge)*: *I'm looking!*

REMBRANDT: I am like a specimen in an anatomy lesson whose brain hath been removèd.

POLLY *(Yelling to Walter)*: How about some of that macaroni and cheese from last night?

WALTER *(Yelling back)*: Nope! We polished it off!

REMBRANDT *(Holding them up)*: Behold these hands . . . I know them not!

POLLY: Just bring whatever's there.

WALTER: It's pretty slim pickings.

REMBRANDT: My eyesight fails. 'Tis so dark I cannot see.

POLLY: Yeah well, we don't get much light these days.

REMBRANDT: Your windows appear to be covered. Prithee, art thou in mourning?

POLLY: In a manner of speaking.

WALTER *(Returning with the contents of the refrigerator)*: Half a bottle of seltzer, a head of wilted lettuce and a box of suppositories!

POLLY: That's it?

WALTER: We're down to two meals a day, if that. Groceries are sky high. It would be cheaper to just eat the money. Toss a couple of bills into a frying pan, sauté 'em with a little garlic and olive oil, add a couple of IRS refunds . . . My mouth is watering just thinking about it.

POLLY *(Handing Rembrandt the head of lettuce)*: Eat, eat!

(Rembrandt tears into it like a starving animal. Polly and Walter watch him, appalled.)

WALTER *(To Polly under his breath)*: I remember reading that he died in poverty, but I had no idea it was that bad.

POLLY: Fame is fleeting. It's the fate of every artist. Look what happened to my so-called "career" . . . Sweetheart, why don't you get him some cereal?

WALTER: Great idea! I should have thought of it in the first place. *(He heads back to the kitchen)*

POLLY *(To Rembrandt)*: I was a trailblazer when I started, but then Walter went crazy and I kind of . . . you know . . . left the premises. It was so gradual I hardly noticed. When I saw friends on the street, they walked right through me. There's no indentation on my side of the bed anymore. It looks as if Walter sleeps alone. Pretty soon I won't even cast a shadow . . . Now you see me, now you don't.

WALTER *(Yelling from the kitchen)*: Here's something that will stick to his ribs: Life—the easy way to get your essential vitamins and minerals.

REMBRANDT *(Confused)*: Life?

POLLY: The cereal! You know, like Just Right or Total.

WALTER: Plus . . . it's chock full of bran which helps with regularity—so they say. *(Returning with a spoon and a bowl filled to the brim, handing them to Rembrandt)* Dig in, dig in.

(Rembrandt lowers his face into the bowl and starts gobbling it up.)

WALTER AND POLLY: The spoon, use the spoon!

(Rembrandt switches to the spoon, greedily shoveling the cereal into his mouth.)

WALTER: It's our favorite brand.

POLLY: We usually add a bit of fruit. You know, some berries or bananas, but they're sky high these days.

(Silence as they watch him eat. When he finishes, he dries his mouth on his sleeve.)

REMBRANDT: If my stomach could speak t'would thank thee with words to melt thy heart. Day and night I pray for deliverance.

POLLY: Join the group.

REMBRANDT: From hunger, penury and above all—neglect.

POLLY: We're about to be evicted.

REMBRANDT: I am an agèd man in an unjust world.

POLLY: Tell us about it!

WALTER: Sons of bitches!

REMBRANDT: "Vanity, vanity, all is vanity."

POLLY: What can you do?

WALTER: Bastards!

REMBRANDT: "One generation passes away, and another generation comes; but the earth abides forever."

POLLY: We get our fifteen minutes of fame, and that's it!

WALTER: Jerk-offs!

REMBRANDT: "The sun also rises, and the sun goes down."

POLLY: Goombye please!

WALTER: Assholes!

REMBRANDT: Naught but the grave awaits!

POLLY: It's not fair!

WALTER: Cocksuckers!

(Silence.)

POLLY *(To Rembrandt)*: Poor baby, you don't know where you are, do you? You're at 103 Mercer Street. In Soho . . . *(Pause)* South. Of. Houston . . . *(Pause)* In New York City, cultural capital of the Western world.

WALTER: YOU'RE IN THE UNITED STATES, BABY!

POLLY: The good old U.S. of A., in the year two thousand and _____ *(Whatever the year is)*

(Rembrandt starts to scream.)

There, there, no one's going to hurt you.

WALTER: Easy, buddy, you'll wake the dead. Wait a minute, if you're Rembrandt, you're already dead!

REMBRANDT *(Sinking to his knees in prayer)*: Almighty and most merciful Father, forgive me my sins that I may dwell with thee in . . .

WALTER: Sorry, sorry, I wasn't thinking.

POLLY: The greatest painter who ever lived . . . in our home! Your self-portraits kill me! Walter said something would come along and save us—an act of God, a bureaucratic glitch, a man bearing gifts and here you are—Rembrandt van Rijn . . . sitting in *our* chair, eating *our* cereal and—

WALTER: For Christ's sake, Polly, let him speak!

POLLY: Well, pardon me for living!

REMBRANDT: How do you know I am Rembrandt when I ne'er introduced myself?

POLLY: Easy. *(She points at his self-portrait)*

(He sees it and screams in horror.)

WALTER: It's her favorite.

REMBRANDT: God ha' mercy on my soul!

WALTER: Not that the others aren't great.

REMBRANDT: 'Tis the very portrait I was working on!

WALTER: If you ask me, it's a toss-up between this and your self-portrait as the Apostle Paul.

POLLY: No, no, this is better, hands down.

REMBRANDT: But 'twas not finished!

POLLY: Those strange hemispheres in the background . . .

REMBRANDT *(Rushing to examine it)*: Verily, it hath completed itself, yet there's no trace o' paint!

POLLY: It's a poster . . . You know, a photograph!

WALTER: How could he possibly know what a photograph is, they hadn't been invented in his lifetime.

REMBRANDT: Prithee, how did this come into your possession?

POLLY: I got it at the Met.

REMBRANDT: IgotitattheMet?

POLLY *(Slowly)*: The Metropolitan Museum of Art . . . On Fifth Avenue and Eighty-second Street . . .

WALTER: The premier art museum in the country, if not the world.

REMBRANDT: 'Tis a dealer I am not acquainted with.

POLLY: A museum isn't a person, it's a place!

WALTER: A fancy building where you go to see art—paintings, sculptures, armor, mummies . . .

REMBRANDT: Thou speak'st of the Stadtholder's gallery in the palace, I know it well. My *Passion of Christ* panels hang on its very walls.

POLLY: You've been having one of those blockbuster retrospectives . . . You know, when a large body of an artist's work is assembled from all over the world. *(Reading it)* "Rembrandt: Saints and Sinners; September 30 through May 19." Forget the crowds!

WALTER: The pushing and wheelchairs . . .

POLLY: The crush at the gift shop . . .

WALTER: The children in strollers . . .

POLLY: The lines at the coat check . . .

WALTER: The lines at the restrooms!

POLLY: The babbling acousta-guides . . .

WALTER: The monkeys and hyenas . . .

POLLY: No, no darling, that's the zoo!

WALTER: You couldn't drag me back there for all the tea in China!

POLLY: We probably know more about you than you do! The Leiden years, the history paintings, the landscapes, etchings, engravings, portraits and self-portraits . . . It's all there. The whole kit and caboodle.

REMBRANDT: Thewholekitandcaboodle?

WALTER: The whole nine yards.

POLLY: The whole ball of wax.

REMBRANDT: Thewholeballofwax?

POLLY: Almost every painting, drawing, etching and drypoint you ever made!

REMBRANDT: They are in favor? They are seen?

WALTER: They're not only seen, you've become a fucking household word, my man!

POLLY *(Sotto voce)*: Language, Walter, language!

REMBRANDT *(Grabbing Polly's hands)*: I must go, forthwith!

POLLY *(Gasping at his touch)*: Ohhh . . .

WALTER: But you don't have a ticket!

POLLY: You're so . . . strong!

REMBRANDT: If a hint of compassion stirs within thy breast, take me, that I may witness this miracle with mine own eyes. *(Glancing at Walter's costumes)* I will shed this tattered cloak for something more suitable. *(He whips it off and pulls down a brocade doublet)*

WALTER: Hey, what do you think you're doing?

REMBRANDT *(Struggling to get into it)*: Uuugh . . . uughhh . . . I fear 'tis too small. *(He tosses it on the floor)*

WALTER *(Picking it up and putting it on over his kingly robe)*: Watch it, buddy, I wore that in *Cyrano*. *(From the balcony scene)* "Your name swings like a bell in the belfry of my heart . . . Roxanne, Roxanne, Roxanne . . ."

POLLY: Walter was an actor, in case you were wondering.

REMBRANDT *(Grabs a voluminous purple cape and puts it on, striking a heroic pose)*: I fear I resemble a large purple-throated thrush.

WALTER *(Taking it from him and putting it on over the others)*: Oedipus the King . . . God, when was that? Twenty years ago? Twenty-five? *(As Oedipus)* "Alas, alas, wretched that I am! Whither, whither am I borne in my misery?"

POLLY: He was the leading man at the Olympic Repertory Company for years.

(Rembrandt takes another robe and looks at himself in the mirror.)

You should have seen him . . . He was a god! A god!

REMBRANDT *(Putting on a feathered hat, then taking Polly's arm and leading her toward the door)*: And so, like Agamemnon bound for Troy, let us set forth! Lead the way, O Queen.

WALTER *(Blocking his way)*: Not so fast! Those are my costumes, from my personal collection! They do not leave this house!

POLLY: They're part of his stockpile. Also, we don't dress like that anymore.

REMBRANDT *(Looking at Walter)*: But look, you, madame, he . . .

POLLY: Is crazy.

WALTER: Thanks, Pol.

POLLY: He's a sick man.

WALTER: All right, Polly, that's enough.

POLLY *(Lowering her voice)*: He's got OCD.

REMBRANDT: OCD?

WALTER: And she's off.

POLLY: You know, Obsessive-Compulsive Disorder . . .

WALTER *(Trying to drown her out)*: Peas and carrots, peas and carrots, peas and carrots . . . *(Overlapping the following)*

POLLY: When you're in the grip of a ritual and can't stop. Like washing your hands or checking the locks.

WALTER: Why not get a bullhorn and announce it to the entire neighborhood!

POLLY: He's also a hoarder. He can't throw things out.

WALTER: A little louder please, we can't quite hear you!

REMBRANDT: Prithee, no more . . . 'Tis an affliction I know well.

POLLY: He tried medication and behavior therapy, but couldn't stick with it.

WALTER: You try those serotonin reuptake inhibitors and see how much you like them! Crippling sweats, dry mouth, ringing in my ears . . . I couldn't remember my lines.

POLLY: Walter records books on tape now. That is, when he's offered one.

REMBRANDT: There was a time when I too was a collector.

POLLY: How long has it been? Ten years? Twelve? Fifteen?

REMBRANDT: 'Tis oft said that my fondness for art and curiosities was the cause of my ruin. Seven years ago my creditors seized my worldly goods and put them up for auction.

WALTER: No!

POLLY: I don't believe it!

REMBRANDT: I swear it on my mother's grave. Everything seized and scattered to the seven winds. Verily, every treasure I bought to add luster to my work. Everything, everything . . .

WALTER: Fucking bastards!

REMBRANDT: Forty-seven specimens of land and sea creatures— hides, antlers, minerals and shells . . . Antique weapons, helmets, swords and pistols . . . A large number of heads and hands cast from life . . . Harps, stringed instruments, a Turkish bow . . . Globes, chairs, mirrors and frames . . . Textiles, costumes, jewels and fans . . . And then my art collection, the envy of the Stadtholder himself. Works by van Eyck, Brueghel, Raphael and more. And my books. My books!

WALTER: Stop, stop!

POLLY: How could they?

REMBRANDT: 'Twas the heirs of my beloved first wife that accused me of squandering her dowry. Jackals! They know naught of a painter's needs!

(A long silence.)

POLLY: I don't know about you, but I could use a change of mood.

(Polly goes to their CD player and plays Bach's joyful bass-soprano duet, "Mit unsrer Macht ist nichts getan" from his chorale, Ein Feste Burg, *BWV 80.)*

Ah, that's more like it!

REMBRANDT *(Looking around the room, astonished)*: Prithee, lady, where are the musicians?

POLLY: It's a CD.

REMBRANDT: OCD?

POLLY: No, CD.

REMBRANDT *(Parroting her)*: "No, CD"?

POLLY: Just two letters . . . CD. For compact disc.

REMBRANDT *(Understanding)*: Oh, CD!

POLLY: You got it!

REMBRANDT *(Turning it into a little song and dance)*: OCD; no, CD; OCD; no CD . . .

WALTER: We have the technology to record music and play it back whenever we want to hear it.

POLLY: At home, in the car, at the beach, in the gym . . .

WALTER: Classical, jazz, rock and roll—you name it.

POLLY: I like Baroque music, but Walter prefers Aaron Copland.

WALTER: Did someone say "Aaron Copland"? *Stand back!*

(Walter switches on "Hoe-down" from Copland's Rodeo *and launches into an Agnes de Mille–type ballet, adding his own crazy Western touches.)*

POLLY: It reminds him of his glory days.

(Walter's dancing becomes wilder and wilder.)

That's enough, dear, he gets the point.

(Walter winds down and collapses in a chair. Rembrandt applauds as Polly turns off the CD player. Rembrandt rises. Silence.)

| REMBRANDT: Forgive my impatience, but I am most eager to visit this mausoleum wherein my work is . . . | WALTER: So, how would you like to see some of Polly's . . . | POLLY: Maybe you could help us clear out some of this . . . |

(Silence.)

ALL THREE: Sorry, sorry!

(Silence.)

| REMBRANDT: If you could draw me a map, I will venture forth on my own and . . . | WALTER: She's been documenting her body ever since she was . . . | POLLY: Walter said something would come along and . . . |

ALL THREE: Sorry, sorry!

REMBRANDT: I MUST SEE THIS PLACE, I MUST! *(He rushes to the door and tries to open it, but is stopped by all the locks. He tries to open them, grunting)* Ugh! Ugh! Ugh!

WALTER: Hey, hey! What do you think you're doing?

POLLY: It looks like he's trying to open the door.

WALTER *(Grabbing him from behind)*: Hands off! Those are my locks! No one touches them! I don't care if you're Jesus Christ himself!

REMBRANDT: I am most anxious to visit this mausoleum.

WALTER AND POLLY: Museum, museum!

REMBRANDT: To see that my work endures . . . 'Tis past imagining!

WALTER: Boy, is he in for a surprise!

POLLY: If we go, you'll have to change your clothes.

REMBRANDT: But these are my only vestments.

WALTER: Now just one minute, no one's going anywhere.

POLLY: Don't worry, Walter will lend you something.

WALTER: I will?

POLLY *(Sotto voce, kicking him in the shins)*: Damn right! He's Rembrandt for Christ's sake!

WALTER: But . . .

REMBRANDT: Pray you, sirrah, allow me to pay for them. *(Fishing around in his pockets)* Fortune smiles on me, for in my pockets are several guilders.

WALTER: Guilders? That's funny! *(He starts laughing)* Like the Pakistani at the newsstand is going to sell me a newspaper for a handful of . . . *guilders*! *(He laughs harder and harder)*

POLLY *(Embarrassed)*: Darling?

WALTER *(As if talking to the Pakistani)*: "Yes, I'll take a copy of the *Times*, that bottle of Poland Spring water and this pack of mints. Here you go . . ." *(Handing over invisible coins)* "Here's five thousand *guilders*!"

(Walter weeps with laughter. Rembrandt eyes him nervously.)

POLLY: Don't mind him, he has a tendency to get carried away. *(Pause)* Walter! Walter?! PULL YOURSELF TOGETHER!

WALTER: Sorry, sorry . . .

POLLY *(To Rembrandt)*: Sit tight. I'll look in his closet and see what I can find.

REMBRANDT: Do not leave me alone with him!

POLLY: I'll just be a sec. *(She exits)*

REMBRANDT *(Reaching for her)*: Come back, dear lady. Come back!

WALTER: Forgive me, I don't know what came over me.

REMBRANDT: 'Tis passing strange that a handful of coins could provoke such mirth!

WALTER: Could I have a look at some of those . . . *(Trying not to laugh and failing) guilders*! I used to collect coins as a boy.

REMBRANDT *(Handing him several)*: Good, my lord, consider them yours.

WALTER: Holy shit, these are beautiful!

REMBRANDT: But worth precious little, alas.

WALTER: To you perhaps, but they'd fetch a pretty penny on the antique coin market. Maybe Polly's right. Maybe you really are Rembrandt, after all!

(Polly enters with a T-shirt, worn jacket and a pair of Walter's trousers.)

POLLY: Ta-da!

WALTER: Look at these coins, Pol, they're worth a fortune.

REMBRANDT *(Fishing around in his pocket)*: But, stay, I have another of greater worth. *(Pulling it out)* Aye, here 'tis. *(Rubbing it on his sleeve)* 'Twas a gift from Rubens upon his return from Florence. 'Tis not a guilder, but a florin, bestowed on him by Ferdinand de Medici as payment for his *Baptism of Christ*. 'Tis exceeding rare, cast by the great Benvenuto Cellini himself. Marry, 'tis of solid gold, and the detail, most wondrous fine. I have kept it these many years, as 'twas Rubens who op't mine eyes to the splendor of the Italians, above all Caravaggio, the greatest of them all. Rubens gave me this coin as a sort of—dare I say it?—challenge! "Perhaps, one day you may stand alongside Caravaggio. Perchance e'en above him!" *(Placing it in Polly's hand)* Prithee, accept it from me now.

POLLY: I couldn't possibly.

REMBRANDT *(Closing his hand over hers)*: With my humblest thanks for thy many kindnesses.

POLLY *(In a swoon)*: I don't know what to say.

WALTER: You might start with, "Thank you." *(Cuffing Rembrandt)* It's very generous of you.

REMBRANDT *(Moving close to Polly, lowering his voice, seductively)*: On this side, Salome doth remove her seven veils for John the Baptist . . .

(Polly emits a little cry.)

(Moving closer) And on this, Bathsheba bathes in preparation for her wedding night . . .

(She emits another.)

(Increasingly seductive) Biblical scenes were much favored by the Italians, particularly those involving . . . *women.*

(And another.)

Provocateurs of treachery and desire.

(Rembrandt looks into her eyes. She becomes increasingly smitten as they gaze at each other.)

WALTER *(Feeling left out)*: Polly? *(Pause)* Poll? *(Pause)* Yooo-hooo . . . *(In a whisper)* The clothes.
POLLY *(A million miles away)*: Clothes? What clothes?
WALTER: My clothes you were going to lend his nibs.
POLLY *(Waking up)*: Right, right. *(Handing them to Rembrandt)* Here you snow . . . I mean, go.
REMBRANDT *(Bowing slightly)*: I humbly thank thee, madame.

(Rembrandt removes his hat and coat and is about to take off his trousers, but stops.)

POLLY: Oh, don't mind lust. I mean us!
WALTER: He might like a little privacy, Polly.
POLLY *(Laughing breathlessly)*: Right, right . . . Since this is a loft, everything's exposed . . . I mean, out in the open.
WALTER *(Grabbing Rembrandt's arm)*: Here, I'll take you to the bathroom. You can change there. *(They exit)*
POLLY *(Yelling to Walter)*: Now don't start washing your hands or we'll never get out of here!

(The moment she's left alone, Polly picks up Rembrandt's coat and buries her head in it. As she inhales its scent, we hear Walter showing Rembrandt around the bathroom.)

REMBRANDT: Marry, what is this?
WALTER: Indoor plumbing! Shower, sink and toilet. You bathe here, brush your teeth here and piss here. Go on, give it a whirl!

REMBRANDT *(Flushing the toilet)*: I push this lever and, lo, a whirl-pool rises up! *(He flushes again)* I push it again and it reappears! 'Tis wondrous strange! *(He starts to laugh, flushing away)*

WALTER: I'll get out of your way so you can have some privacy.

(Walter leaves Rembrandt, returning to Polly. Polly quickly drops Rembrandt's coat.)

You ought to see him in here! He's like a kid on Christmas morning. *(Picking up Rembrandt's coat)* Look at this . . .

POLLY *(Dreamily)*: Rembrandt's coat . . .

WALTER: It's threadbare! Well, the poor guy died a pauper, you heard him.

POLLY: Shhh! Not so loud.

(Walter puts it on and starts striking poses.)

(In a whisper) Sweetheart, what do you think you're doing? Take it off . . .

(He grabs Rembrandt's brushes and palette as well.)

What if he comes out and sees you?

(Gone, he reaches into the coat pocket and pulls out a pre-tend button.)

WALTER *(Imitating Rembrandt)*: I wouldst like to present thee with this button. It looks like an ordinary button, but, in truth, it fell off Michelangelo's trousers as he was working on the Sistine Chapel . . . As he reached from his scaffold to fill in God's index finger, it popped, of a sudden, off his fly and did'st spin most marvelously through the air. As fate would have it, I happ't to be strolling by when it landed at my feet with a tinkling, "Hey nonny, nonny!" Whereupon I picked it up and placed it in my pocket. Marry, 'twas the only button that kept the poor man's modesty intact! God knows how he got through the rest of the day. Methinks with a rope tied 'round his waist. But such are the vicissitudes of the artist's life . . . Prithee, allow me to present it to thee now,

dear lady . . . Or as we say in my country: "For you, my little Delft teacup!" *(He mimes giving it to her)*

POLLY: Funny, very funny . . . but if we're going to the museum
we ought to get going!

WALTER: You were serious?

POLLY: How else did you expect him to get there?

WALTER: We're taking Rembrandt to the Met?

POLLY: How many artists get an opportunity like this?

WALTER: But we'll be trampled to death!

POLLY: No one will recognize him. He'll be wearing your clothes.

WALTER: I don't believe I'm having this conversation!

POLLY: Then stay home.

WALTER: What are you trying to do, kill me?

POLLY: Nobody said you had to come.

WALTER: You know what happens when I'm around crowds.

POLLY: I'm perfectly capable of taking him myself. In fact, it
would make more sense if you didn't come. That way you
could start cleaning up for the landlord.

POLLY *(Disgusted)*: Comstock . . .

WALTER: Now just a minute . . .

POLLY: You can get a head start.

WALTER: First of all, no one's "cleaning up for Comstock"! And,
second, you're not going alone with him to any goddamn
museum!

POLLY: We'll only be gone a couple of hours.

WALTER: I don't trust that man around the corner!

POLLY: We'll be back before you know it.

WALTER: I had my doubts about him when he first showed up, but
the guy's revealed himself. He's a rank opportunist. He's not
bearing any gifts, Polly—just weeping and the gnashing of teeth!

POLLY: I'm taking him and that's that!

*(Rembrandt suddenly appears in Walter's clothes, trans-
formed into a modern man.)*

REMBRANDT *(Striking a pose)*: Behold the man! *(He notices that
Walter's wearing his coat. He smiles)* S'blood, thou art more
Rembrandt than I myself!

*(The three gaze at each other in amazement, trying to figure
out who's who.)*

Act Two

There's a lighting change to suggest several hours have passed in which the three of them have gone to the museum and returned. A bright midday sun vainly tries to seep through the blockaded windows. Nothing happens for several moments. Then we hear Walter struggling with his keys at the door as Polly and Rembrandt wait for him to open it.

WALTER: Damned keys!
POLLY: Easy, sweetheart, easy . . .
WALTER: NONE OF THEM WORK!
POLLY: Losing your temper won't help.

(Walter tries another key and shakes the door, roaring with frustration.)

REMBRANDT: Prithee, allow me.
WALTER: SON OF A BITCH!
REMBRANDT: My cousin Nicolaes Uylenburgh was a locksmith, so I am familiar with the physics involved.

(Walter tries another key and pounds on the door.)

POLLY: Come on, let him do it!

REMBRANDT: There was a time I considered being a professional thief.

POLLY: Give him the keys, Walter!

WALTER *(Throwing the keys at him)*: Okay, Okay . . . Since you're the big genius around here, you try!

REMBRANDT *(Opening lock after lock)*: I used to fashion mechanical toys for my children—singing birds, juggling clowns and, for Titus, an elephant that played a tune . . . When. You. Pulled. Its. Tail!

(He opens the door and they enter. Rembrandt's in the lead with Polly on his arm. He's a changed man, radiating confidence and carrying several bulging shopping bags from the museum. Polly has changed into an attractive outfit. Walter brings up the rear.)

(Suggestively to Polly) As with all procedures of a delicate nature, one must rely on observation—matching the configuration of the object one wishes to insert . . . into the cavity that awaits.

(Polly emits a little cry.)

WALTER: The guy can do anything! Paint, recite Shakespeare, open locks! Why don't we just ask him to move in with us? He could share our food, our toilet and our bed!

POLLY: Walter?!

REMBRANDT *(Grabbing Polly's hands)*: Verily, lady, I am a new man. To see such a multitude of my works displayed . . . I am o'ercome with gratitude.

POLLY: How could I resist, given how upset you were when you arrived?

REMBRANDT: 'Twas as if I were the prodigal son, returned to sudden grace. My works once so maligned are now embraced, e'en revered. Though I was sorely distressed by the number of my pupils' works that were confused with mine—*The Polish Rider, The Toilet of Bathsheba, Christ and the Woman of Samaria.* E'en a child could see the difference!

POLLY: I kept wishing I could tell everyone who you were. Think of the pandemonium that would have broken out if they'd known Rembrandt was actually *there*—standing in the room!

WALTER: Well, the way you were falling all over him, it was clear you thought he was pretty special.

POLLY: "Falling all over him"?

WALTER: It was downright embarrassing!

REMBRANDT *(Bowing his head in prayer)*: "I returned, and saw under the sun that the race is not to the swift, nor the battle to the strong . . . neither yet bread to the wise, nor yet riches to men of understanding, nor yet favor to men of skill; but time and chance happeneth to them all." Amen.

POLLY: Boy, you really know your Bible.

REMBRANDT: I was raised within the tenets of the Reformed Church, but my mother, God rest her soul, was Roman Catholic. Amsterdam is the envy of the world, for we practice religious tolerance. Calvinist and Catholic wed, Christian and Jew live side by side.

POLLY: Walter's Jewish, but I'm nothing.

REMBRANDT: In faith, to be nothing is impossible. In Spinoza's words, "Nature abhors a vacuum." *(Taking off his jacket to show off the Rembrandt T-shirt he got at the museum)*

WALTER: Yeah, yeah . . . you have your picture on a T-shirt, big deal! *(Pause)* Son of a bitch, I forgot to double-lock the door in all the excitement! STUPID, STUPID, STUPID, STUPID!

(Walter slaps the side of his head. He rushes to the door and starts incanting over the locks in his altered voice. Polly and Rembrandt's conversation overlaps.)

One, two, buckle my shoe; three, four, lock the door; five, six, pick up sticks; seven, eight, lay them straight; nine, ten, a big fat hen . . . Objects in the mirror are closer than they appear.

POLLY: Darling, please!

REMBRANDT: Prithee, madame, what is he doing?

POLLY: It's just one of his rituals . . .

REMBRANDT: He appears to be sorely distressed.

POLLY: You know, repeating nonsense phrases to ward off disaster. If he keeps saying them, it makes him feel safe.

WALTER: By far, by far, by far, by far . . . Yet oh so near, so near, so near, so near . . . Boy oh boy oh boy oh boyo, we don't want any accidents here. No siree Bob! No dead bodies piled up on this side of the road, thank you very much! And that means you, Eddie, Franz, Pepe and Wilhelm . . .

REMBRANDT: Madame, I know only too well. When we remove our clothes at day's end to search for signs of plague, we sing nursery rhymes as we check groin and armpits for the fatal purple blooms. *(Singing a Dutch nursery rhyme as he launches into a dizzy checking ritual)*

> Een twee drie vier
> Hoedje van, hoedje van
> Een twee drie vier
> Hoedje van papier
> Als het hoedje dan niet past
> Zet het in de glazen kast
> Eeen twee drie vier
> Hoedje van papier . . .

(The two men get louder and louder.)

POLLY *(Suddenly screaming)*: STOP! STOP! FELLAS, PLEASE! I CAN'T TAKE IT ANYMORE!

(They stop. Dead silence.)

Thank you.

REMBRANDT: Forgive me, madame, I fear I forgot myself. *(Picking up his shopping bags)* Permit me to express my gratitude for bestowing these gifts on me. They are wondrous strange indeed. *(He pulls out an assortment of Rembrandt date books, calendars, coffee mugs, place mats and scarves)* And each with this poor face affixed thereon.

POLLY: In your face, we see all our faces.

REMBRANDT: 'Tis the only one available to me, alas, for I no longer receive the commissions I once enjoyed.

POLLY: Join the group. I haven't sold anything in ages.

WALTER: Thirty years ago, she was it! One-woman shows . . . fancy awards . . . you couldn't open a magazine without seeing her face. Or tits.

REMBRANDT: Tits?

WALTER: You know . . . *(Indicating on himself) boobs . . . knock-ers . . . jugs . . . ! (Handing him a lavish book of her pho-tographs)* Feast your eyes on this! It's a collection of her pho-tographs, published by the Museum of Modern Art.

POLLY: Back in the Stone Age.

(Rembrandt starts looking through the book, becoming increasingly aroused.)

It wasn't out of vanity, I assure you. Oh, I was attractive enough, but hardly a beauty.

WALTER: Don't listen to her, she was a knockout, a *knockout*!

POLLY: I just got really curious as I started maturing into a . . . you know . . . *woman*! I'd always been this scrawny tomboy when suddenly these . . . breasts started to bloom . . . *(Caress-ing them)* It was astonishing! I mean, what were the chances? It was inevitable of course, but to get two of them! That *matched*! . . . I was beside myself! When I got in the shower, I couldn't keep my hands off them! They were so soft, yet firm . . . So I took to striking dramatic poses to show them off. *(Doing it)* Raising my arms over my head, clasping my hands behind my neck, arching over the back of a chair, get-ting down on all fours . . .

(Walter and Rembrandt groan appreciatively.)

I was staggered! I couldn't believe they were part of me, that they were *mine*! So I got a camera and taught myself the rudi-ments of photography. Looking back on it, I was incredibly resourceful, managing to turn my closet into a makeshift darkroom. I was barely fifteen, but desperate to document this . . . *metamorphosis*! Isn't that why we pick up a camera or paintbrush in the first place? To fathom a mystery! The artistry and control come later. There were plenty of guys doing female nudes—Stieglitz, Brandt and Weston—but who better than a woman to celebrate her coming of age? And by the same token—her inevitable disintegration. I never had children, you see. And you know what they say about childless women—that if you've never borne life, you age twice as fast. It's a hormone thing.

REMBRANDT: "Hormone thing"?

POLLY: When your female organs begin to shrivel up.

WALTER: *Polly?!*

POLLY: When I began, my entire body filled the frame, but as I matured, I started to narrow the focus. The sum of the parts no longer interested me. I wanted to isolate them, and, in so doing, startling new landscapes were revealed—knees became mountain ranges; thighs, riverbeds; and breasts, ancient burial mounds . . .

REMBRANDT: These images ravish mine eyes, massing and dissolving, suspended twixt light and dark. They are naught of this world, but have the lightness and transparency of dreams. *(Pause)* Instruct me!

POLLY: I beg your pardon?

REMBRANDT: Prithee, teach me this bewitching art.

POLLY: How to take pictures?

REMBRANDT: Thou hast pierced the skin, revealing our very thoughts and desires. Prithee, give me instruction forthwith!

POLLY: But I was hoping to clean up before the landlord comes.

WALTER: There will be no, what you so blithely call . . . "cleaning up" around here! *(Exiting)* I'm going to the bathroom to scrub the filth of that museum off my hands.

POLLY: Try to finish before next month!

REMBRANDT *(Grabbing her hands and falling to his knees)*: Teach me now, I implore thee!

POLLY: Well . . . if you insist.

REMBRANDT: And so I live again! *(He lifts her hand to his lips and lovingly kisses her palm)*

(Polly gasps, electrified by his touch. They look at each for a long moment, then she heads over to her studio area. Rembrandt follows her, moving closer and closer.)

POLLY *(Becoming increasingly giddy)*: Well, the first order of business is to show you my camera. This baby's called a field camera, and, like all cameras, is made up of your five basic components: *(Showing him)* body, lens, shutter, viewfinder and focusing mechanism. It's more cumbersome than a thirty-five millimeter, more primitive than a digital, but can't be beat for portraits. *(Picking up speed)* This is the front lens, the aperture ring, the shutter-speed dial, the cocking lever, the cable release, the lens board, the focusing knobs, the bellows . . .

REMBRANDT: Prithee, stay a moment, my poor brain cannot keep pace with the speed of thy discourse. I am not accustomed to women who . . . who . . . who . . .

POLLY: Know cameras like me.

REMBRANDT: Who possess such lively powers of . . . expression.

POLLY: Why, thank you.

REMBRANDT: As well as being as . . . as well as being as comely as thou art.

POLLY *(Emitting a little cry)*: Comely . . .

(Silence as they gaze at each other.)

(Trying to be businesslike) Before we start, it's a good idea to get some preliminary readings with a Polaroid. Now hold still and look at me.

(Rembrandt strikes a commanding pose. Polly backs up and snaps his picture, setting off the flash.)

REMBRANDT *(Staggering around the room)*: S'blood! I am blinded, blinded!

POLLY: It was just a flash.

REMBRANDT: Darkness envelops me!

POLLY *(Laughing)*: I'm sorry, I should have warned you first.

REMBRANDT: Verily, I am like sightless Tobit in my etchings. *(Staggering around the room with his arms outstretched)*

POLLY *(Grabbing his hand)*: Gotcha! *(Holding up three fingers)* All right, how many fingers?

REMBRANDT: A curtain of lace floats before mine eyes. Would'st there be three?

POLLY: You got it! *(Pulling the picture out of the camera)* Ah, here it comes . . . *(Showing it to him)* Take a look.

REMBRANDT: Sweet Christ who died for our sins!

POLLY: This is nothing. You should see what they're doing with digital cameras! Polaroids are passé, but they work for me. *(Handing the camera to him)* Just look through here and push this button.

REMBRANDT: Merciful God, the image is so clear!

POLLY: What did I tell you?

REMBRANDT *(Gesturing)*: Prithee, stand there.

POLLY: You want me to pose for you? For *Rembrandt*?!

REMBRANDT: 'Tis my most ardent wish.

POLLY: But what should I wear? I mean, would you like me in some sort of costume, like one of Walter's robes? *(She grabs one, striking a heroic pose)* or something more "Dutch," with a ruff at the neck . . . *(She pulls some paper towel off a roll and crinkles it around her throat, like a severe Dutch matron)* I'll wear anything you like. Your wish is my . . . Oh God, you don't want me to pose um . . . *nude,* do you? *(A shower of nervous laughter)* Not that I'm self-conscious in front of a codpiece . . . I mean camera . . . It's just that I'm always the one holding it . . . the camera, that is . . . not the codpiece! God, what's wrong with me? *(Laughter)* I have no trouble photographing myself nude, but the idea of posing for someone else . . . for you . . . to be terrific . . . I mean, specific . . . For Rembrandt! *(More laughter)* Of course once the pictures are hung, everyone sees me naked anyway. I can't tell you how many openings I've been to where all the men are gaping at close-ups of my hoo-ha while trying to carry on a normal . . .

REMBRANDT: "Hoo-ha"?

POLLY: Oh God, did I say that?

REMBRANDT: 'Tis a word I know not.

POLLY: You know, "whimwham," "doodlesack," "holy of holies," "honeypot" . . . "snatch" . . . "pooter" . . . "pussy" . . . "penny box" . . . "Lady Jane" *(Indicating on herself)* "glory hole" . . .

REMBRANDT: The speed o' thy discourse o'erwhelms me. Thy tongue is wondrous nimble.

POLLY: So they say . . .

REMBRANDT: Now look into mine eyes.

POLLY *(In a little voice)*: Into thine eyes? *(Struggling to meet his gaze)* You make me blush.

REMBRANDT *(Getting her in focus)*: And soft, what charming blushes they are . . . Polly.

POLLY: You said my name!

REMBRANDT *(With feeling)*: Polly Shaw.

POLLY *(Likewise)*: Rembrandt van Rijn.

(Silence as they gaze at each other.)

(In an offhand way) I've been meaning to ask, what do your friends call you?

REMBRANDT: Why, Rembrandt, of course.

POLLY: But it sounds so . . . I don't know . . . formal! Didn't you ever have nicknames? Like . . . I don't know . . . Remmie or Remster?

REMBRANDT *(Looking at her through the camera)*: Verily, the sun doth pale beside thee. Thou art like a starry night, a burning bush. I am blinded, Polly Shaw.

(He takes her picture, the flash goes off.)

POLLY *(Covering her eyes, crying out in surprise)*: Oh God!

(The following should be like a dance in slow motion. Rembrandt approaches her. She pulls back. He gently peels her hands off her eyes. She looks at the floor. He raises her chin. She takes a deep breath and they gaze into each other's eyes. Rembrandt lowers his head and tries to walk away, but Polly puts her hand on his arm, stopping him. They look at each other again. Polly smiles, takes his hand and places it on her breast, then covers it with her hand as in his Jewish Bride *portrait. They gaze at each other again. Rembrandt pulls her into his arms. They kiss and kiss.)*

WALTER *(Entering the room, freezing in his tracks)*: Polly?! What the hell is going on?

(Polly and Rembrandt spring apart. Dead silence.)

SAY SOMETHING, GODDAMNIT! SPEAK TO ME, WOMAN!

(Silence.)

I'm waiting.

REMBRANDT: Prithee, sirrah, if thou would'st allow me to interject . . .

WALTER: Excuse me, but I believe I was addressing my wife!

(Silence.)

REMBRANDT: I'm loath to surmise what black thoughts must be coursing through thy brain. I . . .
WALTER: Did you hear what I said?
POLLY *(To Rembrandt)*: Let me . . .

(Silence.)

WALTER *(Circling Polly like a wild animal)*: Yes?

(The silence deepens.)

POLLY: He said he wanted to try my camera, so I was showing him how it works and then, and then . . .

(Silence.)

WALTER: Yes?
POLLY: He said he wanted me to pose for him. That I was like a starry night, a burning bush.

(Rembrandt groans.)

WALTER: And . . .
POLLY *(The words just pop out)*: I love him.
WALTER: I beg your pardon?
POLLY: I said, I love him!
WALTER: But he's not real!
REMBRANDT: Sirrah, one moment, I pray . . .
WALTER: The name is *Walter!* Polly, the man's an apparition, a figment of your imagination.
POLLY: I don't care what he is, I love him just the same!
WALTER *(To Rembrandt)*: I can just imagine all the crap you were feeding her. *(To Polly)* Do you know how many women this guy bedded and then fleeced?
REMBRANDT: Sirrah, you offend me!
WALTER: Unlike most people, I read all the crap that accompanies these goddamn shows. Your friend here was very bad

news! His first wife, who happened to come with a considerable dowry, wasn't even dead a year when he took up with his son's nurse, Geertje Dircks . . .

(Rembrandt groans.)

Next came eighteen-year-old Hendrickje Stoffels, his delectable new housekeeper. She didn't have money, but, oh, what she could do with a feather duster, if you get my drift . . .

(Rembrandt buries his head in his hands.)

But how would he dispose of his loyal Geertje, who had gotten used to the comfort of his bed? Why get her sent off to a house of detention. Which is exactly what he did.

REMBRANDT *(Sputtering with rage)*: 'Tis slander most vile! Slander, I say!

WALTER: The art world was scandalized . . . The great Rembrandt bedding one serving girl after another.

REMBRANDT *(Lunging at Walter)*: Enough! I will still thy poisoned tongue!

WALTER *(Grabbing a stage foil and slicing it through the air)*: Avaunt, knave, and fight me like a man! *(He tosses a foil to Rembrandt)*

REMBRANDT *(Catching it and slicing the air just as impressively)*: Knave, you say? Thou call'st me knave?!

POLLY *(Under her breath)*: He fences too!

WALTER *(Lunging at him)*: Shithead!

REMBRANDT: Hedgehog!!

WALTER: Ass-wipe!

(They launch into dazzling swordplay.)

REMBRANDT: Spotted snake!!!

WALTER: Fuck face!

REMBRANDT: Dung beetle!!!

POLLY *(Enjoying every minute of it)*: Boys, boys . . .

WALTER: Who do you think you are barging in here like some common thief?

REMBRANDT: But, sirrah, thou welcomes't me like the prodigal son.

WALTER: How many times do I have to tell you? The name's *Walter*! And you're no more the prodigal son than I am! You're a two-bit hustler and I won't take it anymore!

(He lunges at him, setting off a new flurry of swordplay.)

POLLY: They're fighting over me . . .

WALTER: You're trying to run off with my wife!

POLLY: *Me!*

REMBRANDT: But 'twas she who placed my hand upon her breast, in the pose of *The Jewish Bride*. She who cast her net, I swear it!

WALTER: And what a net it is! Snagging all manner of prey in its shining folds. Don't think you're the first to be caught in its web, Rembrandt van Rijn . . . She waves it like a bright flag. And who can blame her? Living like this? Dying like this . . . Once her prince, I've become her jailer. Only habit keeps her by my side. But to leave me for you—a scoundrel and a rake . . . You call yourself an artist and indeed you are, sirrah! A *con* artist!

(He drops his sword and lunges for Rembrandt's throat. They fall into a comical wrestling match, biting and kneeing each other in the groin.)

POLLY: STOP IT, STOP IT! SOMEONE'S GOING TO GET HURT!

WALTER: That's the point, my dear, to knock his fucking teeth out!

(They eventually lose steam and collapse on the bed, suddenly two old men, gasping for breath.)

POLLY *(Rushing to Rembrandt's side)*: Are you all right?

WALTER: Is *he* all right? What about *me?* I'm your husband, for Christ's sake!

POLLY: If you so much as scratched his hands you're in big trouble!

WALTER: Not if he's making out with *my* wife!

(Walter lunges at Rembrandt again and starts choking him.)

POLLY: That's it! I'm leaving!

(The two struggle again. Rembrandt finally pries Walter's hands off his throat and retreats to a corner.)

(Heading for the door) Did you hear me? I said I'm leaving. I can't take it anymore!

WALTER: Take what?

POLLY: Your craziness!

WALTER: What craziness?

POLLY: *What craziness?* You mean I have to tell you? *(Pointing to his stacks of costumes)* That! That! And that! Your incantations and exhortations, your phobias and rituals, your rages and bellowing, your snoring and peeing . . .

WALTER: Now just one minute, I happen to have an enlarged prostate. And I bet your fancy admirer over there has one, too! He just doesn't know it because the prostate gland wasn't discovered until 1803 . . . by, by . . . Peter Prostate! Court physician to William the Beside Himself.

POLLY: Plus . . . plus Comstock's coming to evict us any minute, and I'd just as soon not be here when he shows up.

WALTER: But I love you.

POLLY: Sure, you care about me in the abstract, but your obsessions take precedence.

WALTER: I have a disorder.

POLLY: Do tell.

WALTER: I can't help myself.

POLLY: Well, I can help myself and I'm getting out of here before it's too late!

WALTER: Where are you going?

(A pause as she considers.)

POLLY *(Rushing to Rembrandt's side)*: With him!

WALTER: And where exactly might that be? Where he's going, that is? Back to seventeenth-century Holland in the midst of a plague? That sounds like fun. Running sores and bleeding at the mouth together. Of course, there's always staying put in the good old U.S. of A. Perhaps in this very neighborhood, except real-estate prices have gone through the roof, which is why Comstock wants to evict us so badly . . . But with a little luck you could probably find something . . . Not in

Manhattan, mind you, but maybe in the Bronx or Queens . . . And then there's always Hoboken! Hell, you might even find a place with a nice little backyard. You could have Sunday barbecues with Vermeer and the whole swinging crowd from Delft . . . S'blood! This is sounding better and better.

POLLY *(Getting teary)*: I just want to be with him.

WALTER *(To Rembrandt)*: But do you want to be with her? *(Lowering his voice)* A woman of her age.

POLLY: Walter?!

WALTER: He's smitten now because you're his green card, so to speak. But just wait till someone younger and more succulent comes along. Not that you don't have your succulent moments . . .

POLLY: I don't have to listen to this. *(Trying to pull Rembrandt toward the door)* Come on, let's go.

WALTER *(Blocking her way)*: I have just one question.

POLLY: Good-bye, Walter.

WALTER: Is this about wanting to go off with him or wanting to get out of here?

POLLY: What's the difference?

WALTER: All the difference, my love. Because if it's a change of scene you're after, I can do something about that.

POLLY: What? Get rid of all your crap? I've heard that before! Come on Rembrandt, it's getting late. *(Taking his arm)*

REMBRANDT *(Grabbing her book of photographs)*: Verily, I will follow thee to the twenty-seven corners of the earth. Thou art my muse, Polly Shaw. I see again! I love again! I am a man again! *(He roars)*

WALTER *(Putting on a magnificent robe)*: And so the time has come to don my kingly robe and play my final scene.

(He pulls both sheets off the bed, spreads them on the floor, and starts tearing down his stacks of costumes, piling them onto the sheets. Rembrandt and Polly cower in a corner. Walter recites as Iago from Othello*:)*

O, beware, my lord, of jealousy;
It is the green-eyed monster, which doth mock
The meat it feeds on . . .

(To Polly) You cannot leave, you are my wife!

> . . . that cuckold lives in bliss
> Who, certain of his fate, loves not his wronger . . .

(To Polly) We've been together over thirty years. Thirty years!

> But, O, what damned minutes tells he o'er
> Who dotes, yet doubts, suspects, yet strongly loves!

(To Polly) Your heart beats in my chest and your gaze flows through my eyes.

> Poor and content is rich, and rich enough;
> But riches fineless is as poor as winter
> To him that ever fears he shall be poor:
> Good Heaven, the souls of all my tribe defend
> From jealousy!

(To Polly) You're my heart and greatest joy.

(Silence.)

POLLY: Holy shit . . .

WALTER *(Taking Polly's hand)*: Help me, woman, Comstock will be here within the hour!

POLLY: You're doing it! You're actually doing it! It's a miracle!

WALTER: No, *you're* the miracle, Polly! My shining girl!

POLLY: Hoarders are incapable of instantaneous cleanups! I've read the studies. They can only get rid of their stuff in stages. If then . . .

WALTER: Well, obviously they never consulted me.

POLLY: But to do it all at once . . .

WALTER: For you . . . anything! Including the impossible . . . which has always been my strong suit. *(He drags the sheets laden with costumes out of the room. From offstage)* Don't just stand there! Get us more sheets and tablecloths!

POLLY: It's as if you've suddenly sprouted wings or something. But then you've never quite been of this world.

(She flies into gear, opening cabinets, pulling out sheets and tablecloths.)

REMBRANDT *(Waving at her)*: Polly . . . ? Polly?!

POLLY: Look what I found! A drop cloth from when the painters were here a hundred years ago. *(She holds it up)*

REMBRANDT: Time's a wasting!

WALTER *(Grabbing her in his arms, giving her a hearty kiss)*: You're a genius, Poll! A fucking genius!

(The two of them spread the drop cloth over the floor.)

REMBRANDT: We must make haste!

POLLY: This is fun!

WALTER: This *is* fun! But we've got to get a wiggle on. Comstock will be here before you know it.

REMBRANDT: Lady, my impatience turns to anger. I fear I ha' been deceived!

WALTER *(Attacking another tower of clothes)*: "Once more unto the breach, dear friends, once more; Or close up the wall with our English dead!"

(Polly roars with gusto.)

REMBRANDT *(Reaching for her)*: Pray, give me thy hand, forthwith.

POLLY *(Joining Walter, starts to sing)*: "London bridge is falling down, falling down, falling down, London bridge is falling down, my fair lady!"

(Hurling the costumes down to the drop cloth. Walter and Polly continue to sing:)

WALTER AND POLLY: "How then shall we build it up? . . . Build it up with silver and gold . . ."

(As the windows are suddenly revealed, the light of the setting sun floods the room. Rembrandt looks on with a mixture of terror and panic. Midway in their giddy labors, he starts to speak, overlapping them:)

REMBRANDT: And so the dreamer wakes from his slumber, pitiful fool! In faith, I am the most wretched of men! To be granted a glimpse of paradise, then have it snatched away . . . 'tis past enduring. Once again I am alone, cast off, sans family, friend or home, adrift in a roiling sea . . . I pitch and toss, my teeth rattling like coins in a beggar's cup. *(In another voice)* "Alms for the poor! Alms for the poor . . ." Darkness engulfs me. A map! A map! Give me a map that I may find my way. *(Noticing Polly's book in the light, he opens it, scanning several pages)* But stay . . . these images glow as brightly as the sun. Verily, their brilliance o'erwhelms me . . . *(Suddenly noticing Polly in the golden light)* Nay, tis *thy* brilliance, lady . . . *thy* spirit which ignites this sweet dawn. So rise up poor pilgrim, gather thy paints and brushes and get thee hence to greet it.

(He looks for something to paint on, spies his poster and hastily pulls it down.)

POLLY: Hey, what do you think you're doing?
REMBRANDT: I would prefer working on a canvas, but as the wise man said, "A rabbit in the pot, is worth two on the roof."

(He sets up a makeshift easel by the mirror, which is miraculously whole again.)

POLLY: That baby cost me thirty-five dollars!
REMBRANDT *(Catching his reflection)*: Fie! I do not know myself in these strange vestments. Pray, where might I find my cloak and hat?
POLLY *(Pointing to a chair)*: Over there, right where you left them.
WALTER: Come on, Pol, give me a hand.

(Rembrandt puts on his coat and hat as Polly and Walter drag out the costumes on the drop cloth.)

REMBRANDT *(Gazing in the mirror)*: "For now we see through a glass, darkly, but then face to face . . ." What bliss to wield these brushes again. Look you, how they dance!
POLLY: Oh my God! He's painting over his self-portrait! Walter, come quick!

WALTER *(Joining her)*: Son of a bitch!

REMBRANDT: 'Tis wondrous strange to complete a painting that's finished for me.

POLLY: Hey, wait a minute, now I can ask him my question! Excuse me, but what is the meaning of those hemispheres in the background? They're so . . . *abstract.*

REMBRANDT: "Abstract"?

POLLY: Reduced to their essence.

REMBRANDT: Ahh, my circles.

WALTER: She loves those crazy things!

REMBRANDT: In faith, they are a mystery to me, as well . . . Verily, 'tis all a mystery. The whole kitandcaboodle!?

WALTER: Hey, wait a minute . . . Shouldn't you be documenting this? I mean, how often does Rembrandt show up in your living room and start painting a self-portrait?

POLLY: You're right, you're right.

WALTER: So grab a camera, and get to work!

(Polly dashes off to find a thirty-five millimeter camera.)

(Keeps tidying up the room) Don't mind us, but the landlord's going to be here any minute.

POLLY *(Returning)*: I got it! I got it!

WALTER: Go, Poll!

POLLY *(Dancing around Rembrandt, snapping away)*: Beautiful! Beautiful!

WALTER: That's my girl!

POLLY *(In raptures)*: Look at me, Walter! I'm working again! I'm taking pictures again!

(The three of them throw themselves into their separate labors.)

WALTER: Just think of the bundle we'll make once you get these babies published—*Rembrandt at Work on Mercer Street* . . . Good, my woman, we'll finally be able to put in a new bathroom!

POLLY *(Shooting Rembrandt at different angles)*: Yes! Yes!

REMBRANDT: Visions marvelous strange crowd mine eyes! *(Pointing)* There: *The Return of the Prodigal Son*—and there:

Simeon in the Temple with the Christ Child—and there: mad
Lucretia with her dagger . . . They cry out to me in wild
despair . . . *(One voice)* "Look on our suffering and weep!"
(Another voice) "Illumine our agony for all to see." But soft,
who is that grinning fool and why does he look so familiar
to me? 'Tis another self-portrait, I warrant thee . . . Pray,
from whence do these apparitions rise?

WALTER: Holy shit, he's seeing the paintings he hasn't started yet.
It's not déjà vu, but "future vu"!

REMBRANDT: Avaunt! 'Tis time to return to my labors. They are
my cross and my salvation! I thank thee with all my heart for
ministering to me in mine hour of need. *(With a quick salute)*
And so farewell.

*(Polly impulsively hands him her book of photographs.
Palette and brushes in hand, he plunges through the mirror
with the same intergalactic sound effect that accompanied
his arrival; then silence.)*

POLLY *(Dazed)*: He left.

WALTER: Hey, he got what he came for. A little touch of Polly in
the night.

POLLY: He left.

WALTER: Easy come, easy go.

POLLY: I was just getting up a head of steam.

WALTER: Excuse me, but he's not the only guy on the block.
(Striking a series of poses) Who better than an actor to pose
for you?

POLLY: Hey, he forgot his lace dickey! *(Picking it up and placing
it over her crotch)* Rembrandt's dickey . . .

WALTER *(Laughing)*: Polly . . . you're being obscene!

POLLY *(Tossing the dickey on the floor)*: So, it's just you and me
again, sailor!

WALTER: As it was in the beginning, is now and . . .

(There's a sudden knock on the door.)

POLLY: IF YOU'VE COME BACK FOR YOUR FANCY DICK-
EY, YOU CAN FORGET ABOUT IT!

COMSTOCK *(From off)*: Open up! It's Comstock!

WALTER AND POLLY *(Frightened)*: Comstock?

COMSTOCK: With the New York Fire Department!

WALTER *(In a falsetto voice as Blanche DuBois)*: Just a minute
    . . . I just stepped off the streetcar, Mr. Comstock, and haven't
    had a chance to freshen up.

COMSTOCK *(Banging on the door)*: WHAT'S GOING ON IN
    THERE?

WALTER: Art, Mr. Comstock! Art is being made!

*(He turns on Copland's dreamy "Saturday Night Waltz"
from* Rodeo *and starts to dance.)*

COMSTOCK: OPEN THE FUCKING DOOR!

WALTER: Go, Polly! Do your stuff! I will be your muse!

POLLY *(She starts photographing him)*: Yes! Yes! Yes! Yes!

COMSTOCK: DID YOU HEAR WHAT I SAID?

POLLY *(Snapping away)*: Beautiful, beautiful! You should see
    yourself!

ANOTHER VOICE *(From off)*: OPEN THE DOOR OR WE'RE
    BREAKING IT DOWN ON THE COUNT OF THREE.

POLLY *(To Walter)*: Go on, get it. This light is incredible!

*(It suffuses the room, getting brighter and brighter. Polly
dashes around, taking pictures of everything.)*

WALTER: You want me to open the door . . . Just like that?

POLLY: I want you to open the door . . . Just like that.

WALTER *(Heading toward the door, then freezing)*: But the locks?

POLLY *(Clicking away)*: Everything's dappled with gold.

WALTER: They make this weird sound whenever I go near them.

COMSTOCK: ONE!

POLLY: I don't believe it! I can see again, I'm taking pictures
    again! You cleared the decks! You finally cleared the decks!

(Walter stares at the door, unable to move.)

WALTER: Help me, Polly. *(Pointing at the poster)* You helped him!

COMSTOCK: TWO!

WALTER: Get your ass over here and open the goddamned door!

POLLY: Hold your horses, Comstock, I'm coming! *(She puts down her camera and heads toward the door. She starts undoing the locks)* "One, two, buckle my shoe; three, four, open the door." *(Flinging it open)* We did it, Walter! We finally did it!

(A blinding white light accompanied with swirls of smoke pours through the door. Polly pulls Walter to her side. They approach it, hand in hand, like two brave children.)

END OF PLAY

TINA HOWE's most important plays include *Birth and After Birth*, *Museum*, *The Art of Dining*, *Painting Churches*, *Coastal Disturbances*, *Approaching Zanzibar*, *Pride's Crossing*, *Chasing Manet* and translations of Eugène Ionesco's *The Bald Soprano* and *The Lesson*. These works premiered at The Public Theater, the Kennedy Center, Second Stage Theatre, The Old Globe, Lincoln Center Theater, Actors Theatre of Louisville, Atlantic Theater Company and Primary Stages. She has received numerous awards, including an OBIE for Distinguished Playwriting, a Tony nomination for Best Play, an Outer Circle Critics Award, a Rockefeller grant, two NEA fellowships, a Guggenheim fellowship, an American Academy of Arts and Letters Award in Literature, the Sidney Kingsley Award, the New York Drama Critics' Circle Award, two honorary degrees and the William Inge Award for Distinguished Achievement in the American Theatre. A two time finalist for the Pulitzer Prize, Ms. Howe has been a Visiting Professor at Hunter College since 1990 and is about to head their new MFA Program in Playwriting. Her works can be read in numerous anthologies as well as in *Coastal Disturbances: Four Plays by Tina Howe*, published by Theatre Communications Group; her translations of Ionesco's *The Bald Soprano* and *The Lesson*, published by Grove Press and *Shrinking Violets and Towering Tiger Liles: Seven Brief Plays about Women in Distress*, published by Samuel French. Ms. Howe is proud to have served on the council of the Dramatists Guild since 1990.